FOM-Edition Research

Series Editor

FOM Hochschule, FOM Hochschule, Feucht, Bayern, Germany

FOM University of Applied Sciences, in close cooperation with recognized European universities, offers extra-occupational doctoral programs to very good master's graduates. This series of publications provides the framework for making excellent dissertations from these doctoral programs accessible to the interested professional public. Thus, the series makes it possible for the empirical results, innovative concepts and well-founded analyses from the field of economics to be widely recognized and to enrich the scientific discourse.

Apart from this series, FOM University of Applied Sciences founded a scientific publication series, the FOM-Edition, which is specifically dedicated to the publication projects of its lecturers. The FOM-Edition is divided into the following sections: textbooks, case study books, specialist books, and an international subseries.

More information about this series at http://www.springer.com/series/16193

Ulrich G. Strunz

The Impact of Individual Expertise and Public Information on Group Decision-Making

Ulrich G. Strunz
Nürnberg, Germany

Dissertation, Universidad Católica San Antonio, 2020.

ISSN 2524-7026   ISSN 2524-7034   (electronic)
FOM-Edition Research
ISBN 978-3-658-33138-2   ISBN 978-3-658-33139-9   (eBook)
https://doi.org/10.1007/978-3-658-33139-9

Responsible Editor: Anna Pietras
This Springer Gabler imprint is published by the registered company Springer Fachmedien
Wiesbaden GmbH part of Springer Nature.
The registered company address is: Abraham-Lincoln-Str. 46, 65189 Wiesbaden, Germany

Acknowledgments

This is the result of your actions, and my stubbornness.
A very warm thank you, to
My parents
Hannah
Kristina Jacoby
Bela, Boris, Christian, Marian, Michael, Mischa, Wiktor
Jürgen Rippel
Jochem Müller
Georg Müller-Christ
Alfonso Rosa García
Germán López Buenache
Barnim Jeschke
Familie Schmid, Gasthaus Klostermaier Icking
NeoBird Nuremberg
Christian Chlupsa
Gabi, Ute, Julia, Ariane, Rita, Petra, Holle, Anja, Norbert Samhammer
My immune system.

Contents

Acronyms and Abbreviations

AI	Artificial intelligence
AMT	Amazon Mechanical Turk
CH	Cognitive hierarchy
C-IC	Combined information condition
CPS	Complex problem-solving
Curiosity IO	Curiosity Information Online
D-IC	Disillusioning information condition
EI-I	Environmental influence interpretation
EWA	Experience-weighted attraction learning
F-L	Framed-logic
fMRI	Functional magnetic resonance imaging
GDM	Group decision-making
G-IC	Group information condition
GUI	Graphical user interface
HIT	Human intelligence task
ID	Identifier
IPCC	Intergovernmental Panel on Climate Change
MIDDI	Multiplicity, Interdependency, Diversity, Dynamics, Imponderability
MTurk	Amazon Mechanical Turk worker
NB-L	No-border logic
N-IC	No-information condition
NPS	Non-routine problem-solving
PPF	Predictive processing-framework
QRE	Quantal response equilibrium
R-IC	Routine information condition

SI-I	Social influence interpretation
ToE	Tower of Europe
ToH	Tower of Hanoi
UNO	United Nations Organization
VOTAT	Vary one thing at a time
VUCA	Volatility, uncertainty, complexity, and ambiguity
WMC	Working memory capacity
WTO	World Trade Organization

List of Figures

List of Tables

Introduction

According to the 2019 World Trade Report, service trades are likely to increase their share of global trade by 50 percent until 2040. Services will benefit most likely from increasing the automatization and digitalization of former face-to-face processes, and from an increasing demand of online services due to demographic change. The WTO states that global cooperation has to be increased such that all economies can collectively benefit from increasing service trade.

With the globalization of services comes a globalization of knowledge. According to the Research Perspectives of the Max Planck Society, globalization is a nonlinear process, which can lead not only to homogeneity and the standardization of culture, but also to an increase in complexity, as tools and ideas tend to outpace cultural progress. As face-to-face problem-solving will be replaced more and more by digital services, global problems that require global cooperation will have to gain competence in global and complex problem-solving (CPS).

A prominent example of such a complex, global problem is anthropogenic climate change. The Intergovernmental Panel on Climate Change (IPCC) challenges the high imponderability of climate change and its impact on decision-making and policies with their "Integrated Risk and Uncertainty Assessment of Climate Change Response Policies". In their report, the IPCC states the understanding that decision-makers tend to rather base their decisions on intuitive thinking processes than on thorough analysis and that the perception of risk has to be included in climate change risk management (Kunreuther et al., 2014).

Human decision makers are led not only by rational decision-making, but insights derived from behavioral economics show that people are guided by intrinsic motives, bias, and myopic interpretations of feedback—casting doubt on whether humanity is capable of effectively solving complex problems of global proportions.

© The Author(s) 2021   1
U. G. Strunz, *The Impact of Individual Expertise and Public
Information on Group Decision-Making*, FOM-Edition Research,
https://doi.org/10.1007/978-3-658-33139-9_1

With growing successes in the area of artificial intelligence (AI), the United Nations Economic and Social Council has stated concerns that AI may not only offer advantages, but also

"disrupt societies in fundamental ways",

with people being replaced by automated decision-making devices (United Nations Economic and Social Council, 2019, p. 5). For this reason, talent search is of crucial importance to support domains threatened to be replaced by artificial systems. The UNO High-level Committee on Management places a focus on the identification of talent by automated processes in the area of assessment and testing (United Nations Economic and Social Council, 2019). The hybrid approach of embedding expert knowledge into neural networks, commonly used for AI systems, has been suggested and implemented through the combined effort of various institutes (Barca, Porcu, Bruno, & Passarella, 2017; Chattha et al., 2012; Silva & Gombolay, 2019), raising questions regarding the accountability and regulation of such AI-guided decisions (Doshi-velez & Kortz, 2017). Since the global-employment-changing economic crisis in 2008, the creation of sustainable employment has become a core goal for European institutions, such as the European Foundation for the Improvement of Living and Working Conditions. For systems to act sustainably, they must be flexible and resilient, while knowledge about a system's state is key (Jeschke & Mahnke, 2013). The European Commission further increased flexibility of the European "Stability and Growth Pact" in 2015, to "build up fiscal buffers" for its member states; these buffers were indeed implemented successfully, according to a 2018 report by the European Commission (European Commission, 2018).

The search for expert knowledge is guided not only by ethics. In trying to gain knowledge of a system as large and complex as the European market, obtaining sufficient amounts of empirical data can be a challenge. Expert knowledge can be used to replace missing data in order to support sound predictions. With highly complex problems comes uncertainty, especially when empirical data is limited. Psychological observations have shown that expert knowledge tends to be biased, when expert knowledge faces uncertainty unguided (European Food and Safety Authority, 2014). Expert identification and management have been suggested by the European Food Safety Authority to be organized in a structural manner, and should result in a database of experts. The "Division for Sustainable Development" of the United Nations Department of Economic and Social Affairs builds upon multi-agent action networks, consisting of resources, knowledge and experts in order to achieve their global sustainability goals. In their 2016 report, the top three challenges listed as related to such networks are limited financial resources, followed secondly by changing mindsets and change management, and thirdly, by human resources, as depicted in figure 1.1 (Division for Sustainable Development. United Nations Department of Economic and Social Affairs, 2016, p. 13).

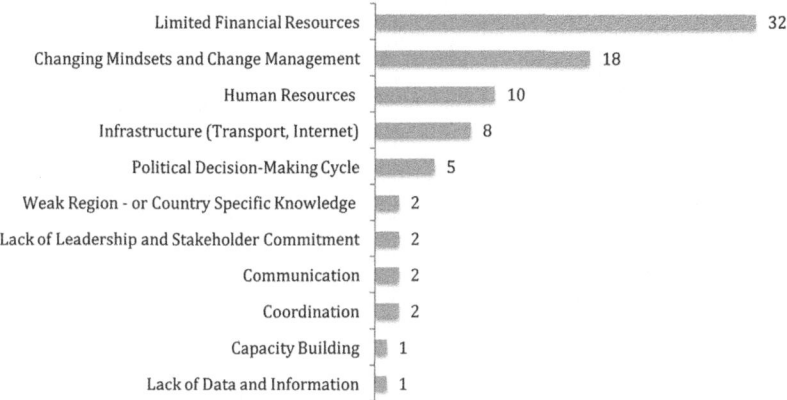

Figure 1.1 Top challenges of modern decision-making networks. *Source* Division for Sustainable Development. United Nations Department of Economic and Social Affairs, 2016, p. 13

Future economies will inevitably face global problems, due to the ever-growing connectivity and service-oriented trade. Novel ideas and technological breakthroughs will outpace slow cultural development leading to increasing complexity. Global asymmetries in knowledge and information will further fuel change, making routine problem-solving unreliable and making its outcomes volatile, thus endangering those who cannot maintain modern workspace requirements.

CPS and non-routine decision-making experts need to be identified and placed in an environment, where their actions are the most fruitful, such that others can imitate and learn from their success. This scenario could be enabled by a cheap and effective online assessment tool, as financial resources are limited by default. As expert knowledge is especially biased when addressing problems under uncertainty, this thesis focuses on two major goals: i) development of a non-routine problem-solving (NPS) assessment in the form of a highly efficient, online, web browser-based software tool; and ii) obtaining empirical results related to the human individual and group decision-making (GDM), faced with uncertainty, change, different system states, and various forms of environmental public information.

Data and according information on human decision-making behavior was acquired by a randomized experiment, which is considered to be the "gold standard" in scientific research (Rubin, 2008). As in any experimental design, participants were randomly assigned to different public information conditions, where circumstances were actively manipulated. The experiment was both run off- and online, however, the online experiment granted many advantages over its offline counterpart, mostly being more cost-efficient, and enabling the possibility to model all participants' perspectives via strategy- or logic-categories. Experiments are considered to increase innovation (Kohavi, Longbotham, Sommerfield, & Henne, 2009) and cost-efficient online assessments may support institutions and companies alike in finding experts, assigning them to their most skill-effective working domain, measuring and controlling the impact of information and ultimately supporting management in coping with complex problems successfully.

Theoretical Background

2

Imagine being born and raised on the Hawaiian island Kaua'i, close to the shield volcano Wai'ale'ale. On this island, yearly rainfall reaches 15 meters and more (Kido, Ha, & Kinzie, 1993, p. 44). You were stuck in this small region on this remote island your entire life, without any information ever having reached you to indicate that this extreme amount of rainfall was extra ordinary. To you, heavy rain is the daily norm. Your day-to-day decision-making has been thus influenced by this routine and led you to form the belief that constant rain is entirely normal. Even small periods of "rain dropouts" will not change your belief that rain is the regular "status quo" of life. You develop some strategy to survive on the island making use of the rain, by building water mills, collecting rain water to drink and recover energy in warm baths. Your tribe members too develop survival strategies based on the stream of rain, however, while all of them do not question there being lots of annual rain, some have noted that the small periods of "rain dropouts" were influenced by godly external factors, which cannot be influenced and were entirely random. Others question this worldview, suggesting that they had observed some regularities in the occurrences of "rain dropouts", which, to their understanding, could be used to maximize the water mills effectiveness. Some tribe members even assure you that "rain dropouts" could not only be anticipated, but were influenced by tribal sacrifices.

While worldviews of each tribe member might differ, all of them are true experts when it comes to making use of rain. Despite this, all individual worldviews of the tribe are wrong, since they lack global information about the true nature of rainfall. However, chance of collective survival was enhanced by actions and believes based on some mental model surrounding local experience with rain. So even though worldviews were at best a true representation of reality locally, in other words a homeomorphic mental model, these mental models did produce

U. G. Strunz, *The Impact of Individual Expertise and Public Information on Group Decision-Making*, FOM-Edition Research, https://doi.org/10.1007/978-3-658-33139-9_2

good performance measured in days of survival. These mental models had even proven to be effective in a group. Individual expert knowledge led to collective strategies following some focal point being "dealing with heavy rainfalls". This focal point enabled the tribe to include heterogeneous decisions into a "direction" or path towards a common goal, even though each individual's decision is also influenced by other tribe members' decisions. It might also be that some individual decisions were bad decisions, based on a locally wrong mental model, but ultimately led to a good group outcome, vice versa.

These outcomes might lead to falsely confirming a certain mental model. A tribe member who believes in having found some pattern regarding "rain dropouts", might invest less working time on "water mills" shortly before he anticipates lack of rain, focusing more on bathing in warm rain water. This lack of work discipline might alter decision-making of those who belief that bathing enraged the gods, which, to their understanding, led to less rain. As they see more and more "pattern-belief members" bathing, the "sacrifice-belief group" begins to collect more rain water, working in nightshifts, as a sacrifice to soothe the gods. Assuming that a short "rain dropout" actually occurred, which was no surprise to the "chaos-belief-group", who regard short dropouts to happen randomly all the time, the sacrifice-, the pattern-, and the chaos-belief groups are all locally confirmed in their believe. However, group performance was still upholding well, since one group gathered strength by relaxing, others collected more resources for drier times, while the rest maintained their working routine. The collective group performance equilibrium was proven to be stable.

A change in environmental conditions, such as "rain dropouts" only impede performance when individual strategies are touched, meaning, as long as there is enough rainfall reliability, individual decisions will not change too much. With a growing duration of "rain dropouts", chances are that individual decisions will adapt to these changes, even influencing group performance, "perturbing" the collective group decision network. These perturbations can themselves lead to a change in individual decision making, when tribe members' decision output, such as production, depend on each other. Causally linked decisions might break or be formed anew, re-arranging the "rules" of the network. In any case, "change in rules" of this network, whether it stemmed from environmental changes, mental models, third-party decisions or group-dynamics has to be first identified by an individual decision maker, building a new mental model based on this novel knowledge, before a new strategy was applied based on this new knowledge to reach a certain goal.

From this small island economy "Gedankenexperiment" several important aspects can be derived that play a role in modern scientific approaches to decision-making.

As mentioned at the beginning of the story, all tribe members (agents) only had access to local information: represented metaphorically by the small island, which can be regarded as a market, where decision-making takes place. Even though each individual had full access to necessary market information, decision-making differed and was not optimal, as the delay of rainfall was interpreted differently. Feedback was interpreted myopically to confirm the own belief. Agents do not even act optimally when provided perfect information and knowledge of the system structure, due to the "misperception of feedback", which is part of day-to-day economic reality (Sterman, 1989). The tribe had three different theories regarding the "data" stemming from rainfall observations: the first group believed in being able to anticipate rainfall-dropouts by observing "patterns", the second group thought it to be possible to control "rain-dropouts" and the third group saw "rain-dropouts" as an entirely random environmental condition, which cannot be controlled at all. The discrepancy between the tribe's data and their theories lead to "errors", which will influence outcomes of decision-making. From an empirical perspective, defining "error" is a complex task, which has a long history of development, and marks a corner stone in economic statistics (Louçã, 2007). Error can occur by an improper choice of some model, lacking precision in measurement or can even stem from cultural chaos (Louçã, 2007). The nature of an error may also vary. They can be seen as being part of nature, being an unobservable disturbance or as unpredictable random behavior. Some mathematical descriptions define error as residual and observable, some see them as corrigible, and some not. Disturbances can get "their own life" and are more than nonconformity of some anticipated value and in any event, an unobserved "disturbance vector" and an observed "residual vector" should be distinguished (Louçã, 2007, p. 151).

In other words, even a small and simple economy can develop complex and unpredictable self-organizing behavior. Durlauf (1998) defines "economic complexity" as a system where choices depend directly on the decisions of others. Such systems are evolving, and cannot by be fully understood or described by "steady states", when there is limited information about the intentions and goals of third party agents (Durlauf, 1998). Such "steady states" are unchanging regularities or "atoms" of a system. The author further explains that "complex systems" inhibit nonlinear attributes because of the interdependence in decisions of its acting agents, and that a very important aspect of complex systems is its past history of events or its order of information by which its future outcomes are dependent on. This complex history can possibly result in "path dependence"

(Durlauf, 1998). "Path dependence" roughly describes "ugly habits" of a system, which are persistent and can lead to recessions.

To understand a complex system's behavior by applying models, several problems have to be coped with, being that simply looking at unchanging consistencies does not suffice, high volatility of predictions may arise from nonlinear dynamics, and "bad system behavior" can only be explained with large amounts of data. The human brain does not perform well at storing such large amounts of data, and are better suited in pattern recognition by visual inputs (Simoes & Hidalgo, 2011), as the human brain is in constant search of known patterns, acting as an "association machine" (Chlupsa, 2017). For this reason, clear visual representations are used in models, coping with "economic complexity", such as the "Atlas Of Economic Complexity" (Hausmann et al., 2014). When no visual clues are provided to understand economic complexity, decision-makers might be overwhelmed by complexity, and even expert knowledge might not suffice. It was shown for example that antitrust analysis has become too complex for judges to evaluate accurately, when expertise knowledge is missing, and while basic economic training helps in simple cases, this training failed to show significant positive influence in complex cases, leading to the conclusion that there exist antitrust cases, which are in fact too complex for generalist judges (Baye & Wright, 2011).

Expert knowledge seems to be a necessity to successfully cope with problems concerning economic complexity. However, real world problems commonly are not well defined, can hardly be distinguished from their irrelevant environmental conditions and modelling such fuzzy problems in a way that makes them solvable often proves to be the true challenge (Davidson & Sternberg, 2003). This also relates to problems stemming from economic complexity, as the individual goals and interpretations of others are unknown and constantly changing, while this information or lack thereof is ultimately able to influence the outcome of one's decision. Just like economic complexity, individual agents or decision-makers can also be described as constantly evolving systems, called "cognitive systems", which are constantly modeling their environment, focusing on "local aspects" representing barriers to the effective solution of a problem (Holland, Holyoak, Nisbett, Thagard, & Smoliar, 2008).

It is then not a far-reaching assumption to define an economy in psychological terms. A market can be understood as a network of subjective instances serving as an input for strategies and volition in decision-making (Arthur, 1995). Agents or cognitive systems make choices based on their currently valid beliefs, which are subjective and often unknown to others. These beliefs are constantly tested by the system, which itself is built from all agents' subjective beliefs (Arthur, 1995).

So, while the small island economy from the Gedankenexperiment does fulfill all mentioned attributes of "economic complexity", which economic systems are considered as "complex" in reality? The complexity of an economic system also represents national production capabilities as non-tradable inputs (Hausmann & Hidalgo, 2010; Hidalgo & Hausmann, 2009), which influence the country's productivity, where an increase of complexity in a country's production structure is positively related to its capabilities (Zhu & Li, 2017). According to Felipe et al. (2012) Japan, Germany, the U.S.A, France and other wealthy countries are considered countries with high complexity, while countries with relative low income per capita such as Cambodia, Papua New Guinea and Nigeria are considered to hold low complexity (Zhu & Li, 2017).

While real life economies do not have to cope with changes in "rain frequencies" such as the small island economy, a country does have to cope with climate, technological, socio-economic and political change, also holding uncertain future scenarios; a "best-guess" what might happen, as performed by the three different belief-groups from the Gedankenexperiment, fails to be a good way to cope with such uncertainty, as in such decision-making domains, multiple possible paths lead to different future scenarios, whose occurrence probabilities are not associated and probability ranking cannot be applied (Maier et al., 2016). It is then better to create some strategy, which performs well during multiple scenarios.

However, the development of such a "stable" strategy isn't easily constructed in complex economies, as belief alters decision-making. Whether or not a cognitive system considers some event being a random outcome or manmade, has an impact on the agent's decision-making. When an event is considered random, agents stick with simple rules to optimize their strategy—when an event is thought of being manmade, agents try to figure out patterns to optimize (Schul, Mayo, Burnstein, & Yahalom, 2007). Agents might stick to their personal belief even though new information indicated that a deviation from their strategy might be beneficial, which is linked to several decision anomalies, such as the confirmation bias, inertia bias, or weighting bias. It can also be linked to "routine". The three belief-groups from our Gedankenexperiment stick to their own routine, further strengthening their belief, possibly feeding their confirmation bias. It is known that strong routine enhances the preference of information that favors the routine, and makes information that contradicts one's routine less favorable (Betsch, Haberstroh, Glöckner, Haar, & Fiedler, 2001).

Altogether, the simple story about an island tribe, and respectful homage to the famous "Lucas islands model" by Nobel Prize winning economist Robert Lucas, Jr. (Lucas, 1972), shed light on many important aspects regarding decision-making and problem-solving. These aspects are to be explained in greater detail with their latest insights from scientific experiments in the following chapters.

2.1   Key Aspects for Real Economic Problem-Solving

Many models attempt to describe, how humans engage in problem-solving. By modelling problem-solving, multiple questions arise: which instances of reality are seen by humans as problems and how can problems be categorized? How do humans define the boundaries of some problem and how can such boundaries be modelled? How can humans naturally engage in searching for solutions and which scientific insights describe such problem-solving attempts? In order to implement problem-solving into domains of real, economic decision-making, several key aspects are to be explained in the following. Namely, two major categories describing problems in general, the definition and role of complexity regarding problem-solving, the definition and meaning of heuristics, and the definition and background of uncertainty.

2.1.1   Well-Defined Problems

In general, two types of categories describe problems that are to be solved: well- and ill-defined problems; this distinguishing generalization is effective, as all domains hold well- and ill-defined problems (Nye, Boyce, & Sottilare, 2016) and different cognitive areas are required for solving well- and ill-defined problems (Schraw, Dunkle, & Bendixen, 1995).

Problems that can be broken down to a series of sub-problems, and also provide enough information about their goals, solution-path and obstacles, are considered well-defined problems; these problems can usually be solved using recursive algorithms (Davidson & Sternberg, 2003).

The famous "Tower of Hanoi" problem is considered a "well-defined" problem (Davidson & Sternberg, 2003). It can either be solved perfectly using an iterative or recursive algorithm or by applying some strategy, consisting of several steps that will always solve the problem in the least number of steps.

Multiple classifications exist in order to distinguish between well- and ill-defined problems, as well- and ill-defined problems exist in a continuum (Le, Loll, & Pinkwart, 2013).

2.1.2   Ill-Defined Problems

Contrary to well-defined problems, recursive algorithms cannot be applied to solve such problems, as the problem cannot be modelled as some set of steps necessary to solve them; they lack information about some clear path to the solution or do not provide some statement about how the problem at hand can be solved (Davidson & Sternberg, 2003).

From the perspective of a rookie facing some problem, this problem might seem to be "ill-defined" due to lack of experience. However, in such a case the problem is merely "undefined" and not "ill-defined" (Nye et al., 2016; Strunz, 2019). A person who has never played the well-defined game of "Tower of Hanoi" before, will begin to develop some strategy and optimizing it further, until the most efficient strategy is found. At this point, "Tower of Hanoi" is regarded as a well-defined problem. This process is known as "learning", and for this reason, applying the domain "learning" to successfully distinguish between well- and ill-defined problems is useful.

When learning is applied to ill-defined problems, further categories are required. Ill-defined problems are regarded as "complex problems" and the attempt to solve them is regarded as "complex problem solving" (CPS) (Dörner & Funke, 2017).

As described before, most problems in real life are "fuzzy" problems or lack relevant information that make them fall in the category of complex problems. Any complex problem is always an "ill-structured problem" (Grünig & Kühn, 2013), which can be understood analogous to an ill-defined problem. Multiple domains are then necessary to consider when trying to define some theory of "problem-solving", since an agent most likely faces some unknown, ill-defined or complex problem in economic reality: first, information might be interpreted differently by each agent, leading to heterogeneous problem perceptions. Second, rookies might lack some definitive "recipe" of action required to solve a problem. Third, even when some action is considered to be suitable, it is not yet clear, which intrinsic processes led to the decision-making itself. Fourth, if this process was successfully analyzed, it is unclear how an agent considered the action as positive or negative, as in "bringing the agent closer to the goal". Last but not least, it is unclear how an agent would "find" a problem and "recognize" it as such; agents differ in their goal setting priorities and it is unclear why a certain path towards some goal is being chosen. As depicted in Figure 2.1 (Ohlsson, 2012, p. 122) all these five domains would have to be combined in order to picture "problem-solving" fully, described as "heuristic search". The cognitive psychologists Newell and Simon stated that humans were able to solve unfamiliar problems by tentatively choosing different actions, mentally projecting their outcomes of the chosen action, followed by some evaluation, which is then used as a new input for their decision-making process, such that they are able to alter their approach to solve a problem; Newell and Simon referred to this as "heuristic search" (Ohlsson, 2012).

Complex-Problem-Solving builds upon the understanding that ill-defined (ill-structured) problems lead to a lack of information, unattainable from the outset on first sight, where uncertainty follows up. Complex problems do not require complex solutions, however, a "bias bias" might lead to the underestimation of the performance of simplicity, which outperforms under conditions of high uncertainty (Brighton & Gigerenzer, 2015).

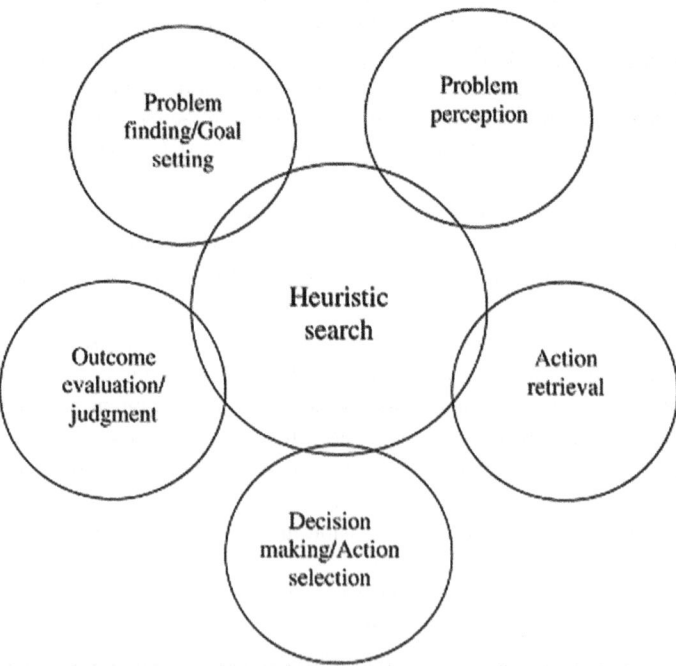

Figure 2.1 "The structure of a hypothetical theory of problem solving." *Source* Ohlsson, 2012, p. 122

2.1.3   Definitions of Complexity

"Complexity" in every-day language can describe problems that one regards as "difficult" to solve. In the economic domain task-difficulty and task-complexity are two different attributes: difficult problems are solved by incentivizing diverse problem-solving alternatives, while complexity is coped by institutions via selection criteria adjustment, different rates of variation and adjusting connectedness (Page, 2008). To make predictions about the future, economic models rely on assumptions about reality expressed by mathematical functions originating from theoretical physics, informatics or sociology.

Whenever complexity of some entity such as a market, country, global economy or project is to be measured, the modeler first has to define the "system" boundaries, its instances and their relations, which together equal the "system" itself that is separated from its environment. Before even defining "complexity" itself, it has to be noted that the modeler might run into the "frame problem" defining a system. By defining entities (states) and their relations, it makes sense to choose from a set of things that are meaningful to describe the system. For example, defining the system "engine" results in a meaningful list of cogs, metal rods and other things that when being changed in their structure or behavior, will also change the engine itself. However, by defining a list of things that are changed, everything else is ignored and assumed to not change at all, regarded as the "commonsense law of inertia" (Kameramans & Schmits, 2004). While this assumption solves the "frame problem" for more common models, more sophisticated solutions have to be applied to actually solve the frame problem when cognitive agents are to be modeled, such as the "Thielscher's Fluent Calculus", which is used, for example, when robots are required to face "non-determinism and uncertainty" (Kameramans & Schmits, 2004, p. 45).

In other words, when the modeler is interested in defining some "system" that is scanning its environment for change, in order to adapt its behavior to novel circumstances, just like a cognitive agent, its "states" or "entities" and their relations are to be modelled as "fluent" states. Fluent states' truth-values depend on the current context. Functions running on such fluent states are therefore adaptive. When a system is defined, its complexity can be measured.

Complexity enjoys many definitions that vary amongst the scientific domain it is used in. "Complexity" was first mentioned in an 1948 article titled "Science and Complexity", where it was stated that physical science was mostly interested in two-variable problems, and that life science regards such simplicity as not significant (Efatmaneshnik & Ryan, 2016). Today, the term "complexity" had been used in so many different variations and contexts that its meaning became unclear (Efatmaneshnik & Ryan, 2016). Efatmaneshnik and Ryan (2016) differentiate between objective and subjective complexity in their generic framework. They define objective complexity as the size of the minimum descriptions necessary to describe a system. Objective complexity is not dependent on any observer's perspective or viewpoint, but can be context and goal dependent. Subjective complexity on the other hand is dependent on the modeler's choice of reference model. As depicted in Figure 2.2 (Efatmaneshnik & Ryan, 2016, p. 4) objective complexity is defined by context and by the modeler's (observer's) definition of the system. So, while it is independent of the subjective viewpoint of some modeler, it still is dependent on the modeler's subjective definition of the observed "system".

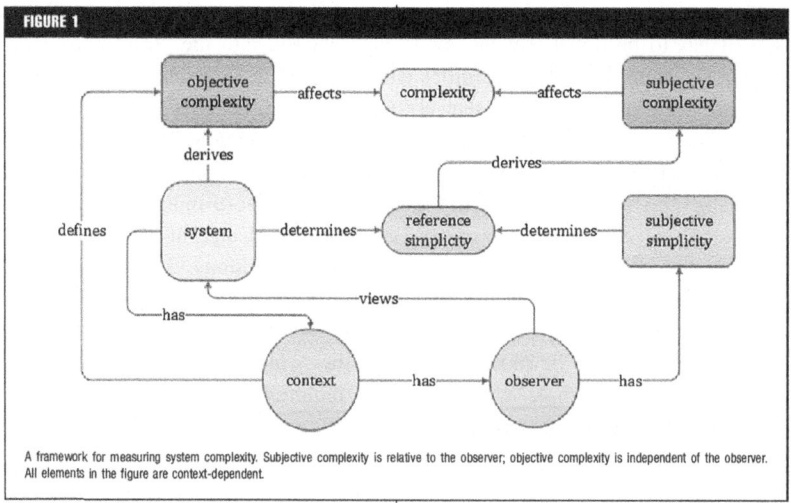

Figure 2.2 A generic framework for measuring complexity. *Source* Efatmaneshnik & Ryan, 2016, p. 4

The definition of the "system" and whatever the modeler subjectively regards as simple, both determine some "reference simplicity". Complexity is then the distance and size from this "reference simplicity". This generic framework by Efatmaneshnik and Ryan (2016) can be used for a variety of complexity measures, such as Statistical Complexity, Complexity in Engineered Systems, Complexity

Measures for Graphs, Complexity of Repeating Patterns and can be used for evolving, dynamic models, which include learning agents. Distinguishing between objective and subjective complexity enables the modeler to include multiple perspectives, whose reference simplicities naturally differ, leading to a "gap" between the agents' views. Every reference point comes with an objective complexity constant and various subjective complexity measures, which are dependent on the agent'.

As multiple cognitive agents will ultimately have different views on what defines (subjective) simplicity, they will inevitably have different viewpoints on the measure of complexity. This is where "complexity economics" sees reason to include these derivations into the conclusion of contracts. Complexity Economics states that multiple agents will disagree on the "reality" of a system after some written agreement or contract has been made. The agents then disagree on performance indicators, as indicated by figure 2.3 (Nota & Aiello, 2014, p. 88).

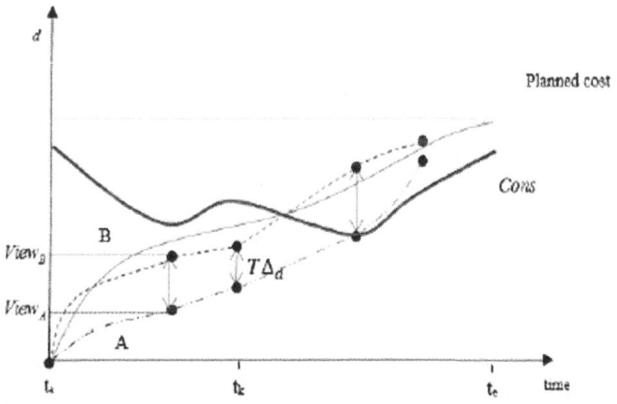

Figure 2.3   Deviation distance of two perspectives on the individually perceived reality of some project over time. *Source* Nota & Aiello, 2014, p. 88

This deviation of perspectives occurs when "system boundaries" are set by more than one modeler. For this reason "corporate decision-makers need to reflect the company as part of an open system" (Jeschke & Mahnke, 2016, p. 73), where system and its environment are defined by some meaningful boundary ("Sinngrenze"), which is open to a set of other meaningful entities coming from heterogeneous perspectives, definitions and viewpoints, as long as some internal selection rules are applied, where such entities can be approved or denied (Luhmann, 2012, p. 178).

In the domain of corporate decisions, such selection rules should be defined neither too broadly nor too narrowly, such that critical information is included and managerial focus is preserved (Jeschke & Mahnke, 2016). As depictured in figure 2.4, such system boundaries can be modelled by two dimensions: the range of the considered system constituents and the time horizon of system analysis (Jeschke & Mahnke, 2016, p. 74).

Figure 2.4 System boundaries defined by 2-dimensional selection rule. *Source* Jeschke & Mahnke, 2016, p. 74

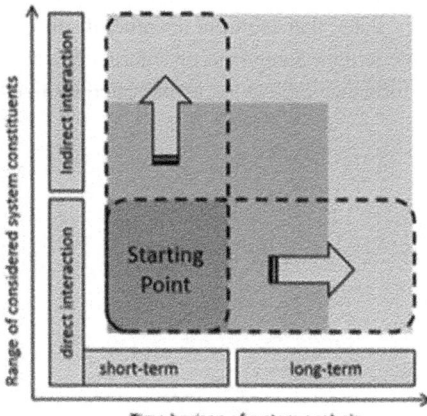

Based upon such a selection rule, the complexity of a system can be categorized, e.g. by multiple non-correlative dimensions such as multiplicity, interdependency, diversity, dynamics (Jeschke & Mahnke, 2016) and imponderability (Jeschke, 2017). By analyzing the system's complexity with this 5-dimensional model, 32 distinguishable types of complexity describe different scenarios of decision-making complexity. For each type, different approaches for CPS or operations to reduce uncertainty are suggested by Jeschke (2017), such as clustering-analysis to reduce uncertainty from high multiplicity, cross-impact-analysis to cope with interdependency, specialization to counter high diversity, sound Business-Process-Management in order to stay above high dynamics, and risk-management to handle high imponderability.

In the end, the reduction of uncertainty by heuristic processes can be assigned to all mentioned tasks in this sub-chapter. Heuristics are defined as conscious or unconscious processes that efficiently ignore information (Gigerenzer & Gaiss-maier, 2011). To define some system or in order to being able to talk about a system, it has to be instantiated by a meaningful boundary or Sinngrenze, which is performed by ignoring information, i.e. relying on selection rules. In order to measure system complexity, after the system was defined, the measurement of complexity is not only affected by objective complexity but also by subjective complexity, which—again—includes ignoring information, stemming from sub-jective simplicity, e.g. relying on expert knowledge. To categorize complexity, models such as the "MIDDI"-model (Jeschke, 2017) can be applied to produce multiple types of decision-making scenarios, so that suitable problem-solving ope-rations can be used to reduce uncertainty in a context-specific manner, relying on approved and proficient methods; ultimately ignoring alternative approaches, and therefore information, in order to be capable of acting efficiently and effectively.

The three tasks of defining a system, measuring the system's complexity and categorizing its complexity all frame reality by ignoring information to balance the amount of relevant information and associated costs to manipulate this infor-mation. Heuristic decision-making is not applied in all decision-making scenarios mentioned in this sub-chapter, but is applied when a suitable model is developed (e.g. defining some system), when a model is adapted to context (e.g. measuring system complexity) and when models are linked (e.g. categorizing complexity), to frame limitless information in order to make cost-efficient or cost-effective pre-dictions. Therefore, to make capital favorable decisions, it is necessary for some agent to possess as much information as possible in order to frame it in a pro-ductive way. A game-theoretical analysis showed that it was favorable to possess information rather than to have access to it (Ravid, Roesler, & Szentes, 2019), as agents must be incentivized to gather costly information, overlook information when its price is in equilibrium and because cheap information does not necessa-rily approximate full information. Ravid, Roesler and Szentes (2019) strengthen the need for the design of information channels by which agents in a certain decision-making systems, such as a market, can learn, as knowing that certain information can be obtained is not the same as actually knowing this information (Ravid et al., 2019).

2.1.4 Ignoring Information

While there exists debate on whether the concept of heuristic search was falsi-fied, can be falsified at all by the Popperian manner or if it even was an empirical hypothesis (Ohlsson, 2012), the concept of heuristic search is still brought into context with "planning" in more current studies (Baier, Bacchus, & McIlraith, 2007). Baier, Bacchus and McIlraith use a simplified "relaxed planning graph" that ignores information on negative effects. In other words, they compute a simplified model to reduce complexity to build a new model that processes costs to achieve a certain goal (Baier et al., 2007, p. 614).

Analogous to modern approaches to model planning-paths using heuristic search, the original idea of heuristic search was to also consider humans as information processing entities, who simplify reality by ignoring information due to their biological limitation (Simon & Newell, 1971). Just like mentioned algorithms, many papers from the 70's considered humans to conduct "heuristic processing", defined as an efficient problem-solving method, suitable for difficult problems by ignoring certain solutions in the set of possible solutions. This restriction is based on certain evaluations of the problem structure (Payne, 1976).

The most famous example on research regarding "heuristics" comes manifold from Kahneman and Tversky, who described three major heuristics, being "availability", "representativeness" and "anchoring and adjustment" (Tversky & Kahneman, 1974), which were used in human decision-making under uncertainty; "under uncertainty" refers to any decision-making process with the absence of known probabilities regarding events of the state-space. Decisions can also be made "under risk", where subjective or objective probabilities are provided. This basic differentiation dates back to 1921 and is still used to categorize decision-making scenarios (Knight, 1957). When a decision is made "under certainty", the consequence of each possible action is known (Mousavi & Gigerenzer, 2014).

In other words, human decision making was and still is theorized to be influenced by belief on the likelihood of events, where subjective or objective probabilities are not provided. Linked to this set of heuristics, a list of "biases" was given by Kahneman and Tversky, which represent deviations from the normative rational theory, caused by error in memory retrieval or violations of basic laws of probability (Gilovich, Griffin, & Kahneman, 2002).

Kahneman's and Tversky's heuristics-and-biases program had been challenged and criticized by the famous psychologist Gerd Gigerenzer (Gigerenzer, 1996). Gigerenzer (2011) states that heuristics are neither rational nor irrational. While heuristics can outperform statistical decision-making in complex environments, as rational models perform badly during uncertainty, caused by complexity (Mousavi & Gigerenzer, 2014), their accuracy depend on environmental circumstances. People are able to learn to choose adaptively from a collection of heuristics; he further states that it was necessary to develop simple decision-making guidelines for complex environments and to connect the simple heuristics framework with other theoretical frameworks (Gigerenzer & Gaissmaier, 2011).

Decision-making under uncertainty does not necessarily benefit from logic and statistics according to Artinger, et al. (2015). Their research showed that decisions made in complex and uncertainty environments actually benefit from simple heuristics, as they are less sensitive to chaotic environmental disturbances, such as variance in data, thus generating less error (Artinger, Petersen, Gigerenzer, & Weibler, 2015). An intuitive example, where a much simpler heuristic decision-making rule outperformed a more complex model under uncertainty, is the "Simple hiatus rule vs. Pareto/NBD" model. Here, the complex model inhibits more information than the heuristic approach, but the heuristic approach resulted in better predictions (Samson & Gigerenzer, 2016).

From these insights it can be derived that heuristic decision-making still plays an important role in modern approaches to cope with complexity. It not only seems to be natural for humans to use heuristics when making decisions under uncertainty—such an approach can also outperform statistical and logical models in anticipating development, when being computed by machines. Anyhow, uncertainty is an important factor to consider when predicting complex behavior. A case study had shown that failure to include stochastic effects derived from uncertainty in models analyzing traffic led to prediction biases up to 200% (Calvert, Taale, Snelder, & Hoogendoorn, 2018). Still, decision-making using heuristics is not a one-fits-all tool, outperforming statistical and logical computations in all circumstances. It rather presents itself as a skill that can be learned to overcome bias and reduce uncertainty to make predictions that can outperform chance when being surrounded by complexity.

2.1.5   Uncertainty

Living beings, such as cognitive systems or decision-making agents, can be considered as complex systems, where predicting their behavior might be of extreme challenge under uncertain or novel decision situations (Hernán et al., 2015). In day to day life the neural system reacts to different levels of uncertainty in a complex way, and subjective utility theory fails to correctly model human behavior. According to the reduction of uncertainty hypothesis, the human brain might be biased towards data which reduces uncertainty (Onnis, Christiansen, Chater, & Gómez, 2002).

In a purely formal, mathematical context required for simulation, uncertainty enjoys crisp definitions and even its own "Uncertainty Theory", which has become a branch of mathematics (Liu, 2018). This thesis relies on the explanation of uncertainty being *"any departure from the unachievable ideal of complete determinism"*

(Walker et al., 2003, p. 8). Risk and ambiguity are to be "limiting cases of a general system evaluating uncertainty", where decision makers differ in preference/aversion of risk and ambiguity (Hsu, Bhatt, Adolphs, Tranel, & Camerer, 2005).

The overall meaning of uncertainty varies and depends on the scientific field and domain it is used in. However, uncertainty is part of organizational day-to-day reality (Schilke, Wiedenfels, Brettel, & Zucker, 2017). In enterprises for example, uncertainty in decision-making is being dealt by Information Systems, such as Expert Systems, Enterprise Resource Planning and Supply Chain Management (Irani, Sharif, Kamal, & Love, 2014). Project management is dominated by models, which assume or build upon determinism (Padalkar & Gopinath, 2016), while it is known that real-world problems mostly have access to incomplete or approximate information, limiting the uncertainty reducing capabilities of even an idealized algorithm (Traub, Wasilkowski, Wozniakowski, Bartholdi, & Ford, 1985). With the rise of technological progress, partly stemming from quantum physics more than 60 years ago, it was already considered to be "unscientific" to assume infinite accuracy in any measurement, and that inevitable errors must be included in any theory, as they are considered being part of the sense-making of an environment, making strict determinism in scientific prediction an impossibility (Brillouin, 1959). This perspective also translates to economic predictions, as uncertainty prevails even with lots of information provided (Walker et al., 2003). In meteorological science inevitable uncertainties in initial conditions and model equations led to a shift of predicting the most likely outcome to a distribution of probabilities, as well as to the understanding of the need to include and represent "doubt" in forecasts (Palmer, 2017). This new process of modelling predictions is also influenced by external third parties. Scientists need to withstand the pressure to predict in a more deterministic way than is justified by the given data, stemming from media attention (Palmer, 2017).

The urge to avoid or work around the understanding of unavoidable uncertainty might stem from "intolerance of uncertainty", which had been described as the "most fundamental, underlying variable of anxiety disorders" (Gosselin et al., 2008, p. 1428). "Uncertainty avoidance", being intensely researched as a cultural factor to be considered by the works of Hofstede since the 70s, failed to show significance in a more current experiment, when being applied outside of the IBM study (Schmitz & Weber, 2014). On the contrary, studies still build upon the hypothesis that cultures express different levels of "uncertainty avoidance" (Hofstede, 2001) and succeeded in finding correlations, e.g. participation in decision-making (Jang, Shen, Allen, & Zhang, 2018). Nevertheless, when talking about problem-solving, "uncertainty" has to be considered: a model linking uncertainty and cognition has shown that despite complete certainty over some final stage of a decision-making process, happening in a vast cognitive space representing complexity, uncertainty will not stop growing (Hadfi & Ito, 2013). To cope with the inevitable persistence of uncertainty in algorithms and heuristic problem-solving, it was suggested to translate "complex problem solving" to "finding ways of reducing uncertainty" (Osman, 2017).

2.2   The Role of Information in Decision-Making

In order to understand "information" it might be meaningful to ask "How much information do I acquire, when I learn something new?". According to the "Kullback-Leibler divergence" the amount of information gained depends on what the agent had believed before (Baez & Pollard, 2016). If the agent assumed a fair coin-toss, or 50% chance of heads, it will gain one bit of information. When the agent expects a 25% chance to see heads, it will gain two bits of information when head actually appears.

This example helps defining "information". Just as "uncertainty" and "complexity", the term "information" is used in every-day language and in scientific contexts in many ways. The following chapters will show different perspectives and definitions of information, how information can lead to uncertainty and to what extend information influences 21st century decision-making.

2.2.1   Definitions of Information

Mentioned coin-toss example builds upon the Shannon and Weaver model, where the information content is expressed in "bits". The amount of information (I) is computed by $I = \log_2 n$, with n being the number of different output values. This model can be seen as translating the coin-tossing process into bits, a process which receives as input some belief about the future and translates it to some output, expressed in bits by the Shannon model. From this perspective, information reveals something about the input and its linked process. However, information is not the process itself, neither the input nor the output per se—the output expressed in bits merely is information *about* the input (belief) and the process (coin-toss and model) (Losee, 1998). However, the Shannon and Weaver model is limited to functional terms.

In physics information is commonly described as the entropy of a system. When nothing is known about a certain system, its entropy equals the logarithm of the number of possible states. Whether or not the observer of a system has to be included into the description of information and whether the observer can be seen in isolation is still debated in physics to this day (Brukner, 2018). While the problems and methods used in quantum physics might seem be too far-fetched and abstract for day-to-day economic decision-making, the intellectual basis for developing models used in problem-solving is identical in the two fields of study. "Bayesian-inference" is used in the thought experiment described by Brukner (2018), which is also common in game-theory and neuroscientific models about the human mind and brain. Knowledge or belief about a certain system and knowledge about the knowledge of others is part of game-theoretical analysis, as described in "The Dirty Faces and the Sage" (Fudenberg & Tirole, 1991, p. 547).

Using the "Hierarchical Model of Information Transmission" more abstract notions such as human perceptions, observation, belief, knowledge, as well as the influence of errors, misinformation and bad data can be considered (Losee, 1998). Based on this model, a discipline independent definition of information was provided by the author Losee (1998), who defined information as some output coming from some process, where the output tells something about both the input and process from which it originated (Losee, 1998).

This definition links the meaning of information to some process that might have an impact on the behavior of some agent being aware of the output of this process. An analogue definition describes information as "a stimulus which expands or amends the World View of the informed." (Madden, 2004, p. 9), the stimulus being the impact following the perception of some signal, altering the agent's "World View". The introducing Gedankenexperiment about the tribe holding different belief-groups is also based on the latter definition. Whatever information is, it leads to constant updates about some agent's world-view. When multiple agents are influencing each other's decision-making, game-theoretical models come into play.

In game-theory, information is considered "private information" when it is only obtainable by an individual agent, such as "a random thought or intrinsic motives". "Public information" refers to information, which is potentially obtainable by all agents, who are part of the "game" or decision-making frame. A typical assumption of game theory is that agents hold common knowledge about the given information structure of the game, and about the co-agents' rationality. It is further assumed that agents do so by conducting complicated mathematical calculations, i.e. applying Bayes theorem without error when updating their beliefs (McKelvey

& Page, 1990). McKelvey and Page (1990) show that this game-theoretical assumption on human behavior is approximated by experienced subjects with 85% efficiency and by inexperienced subjects with 69% efficiency. The concept of the "Bayesian-Brain" is often considered by psychologists, neuroscientists and cognitivists. The model assumes that the human brain is constantly predicting possible events and deviations from what is expected, by performing Bayesian inferences, and in doing so, the brain is limited by the requirement to minimize costs stemming from error (Hutchinson & Barrett, 2019, p. 280).

Hutchinson and Barrett (2019) hypothesize that mental events are not arising independently, but are always dependent on prior events. This hypothesis can be linked to the understanding of Durlauf (1998) that "history matters" for complex systems, such as cognitive agents. Opposing the more "simplistic model" of some cognitive agents receiving a "stimulus", translating it by perceptive senses into some "response", Hutchinson and Barrett (2019) offer a different model on both mind and brain, defining "information flow" from a novel psychological and neuroscientific view.

As shown in figure 2.5 both mind and brain are in a constant fluent state. Each state consists of a non-linear, complex system of neuronal activities (green arrows) and feedback (purple arrow), which are to be separated in mind and brain activities. In short, neurons activate memory from which certain "maps" of strategies are derived. Just like a scientific hypothesis, neurons try strategies in accordance to this map, choosing paths which deemed useful in the past and are then corrected by feedback. In a way, the brain simulates strategies by predicting the future based upon past experiences, hence "Bayesian Brain". When the distance between the chosen path and the correcting feedback is too great, this distance can be considered an "error" and the neuron can correct this error by altering its path, i.e. correcting a prediction-error. When the chosen path equals the feedback, the predicting neuron already is on its correct path (prediction) and the hypothesis was correct.

In a certain way, the brain constantly predicts the future and is constantly corrected by the environmental feedback and more importantly: the human brain is also corrected by *anticipated* prediction-error, and therefore not exclusively by environmental feedback. Each combined mind- and brain-state can be considered a "screenshot" of the agent's "World-View". A complex, non-linear network of trial- and error, constantly working on reducing uncertainty by choosing strategies that fits the current context.

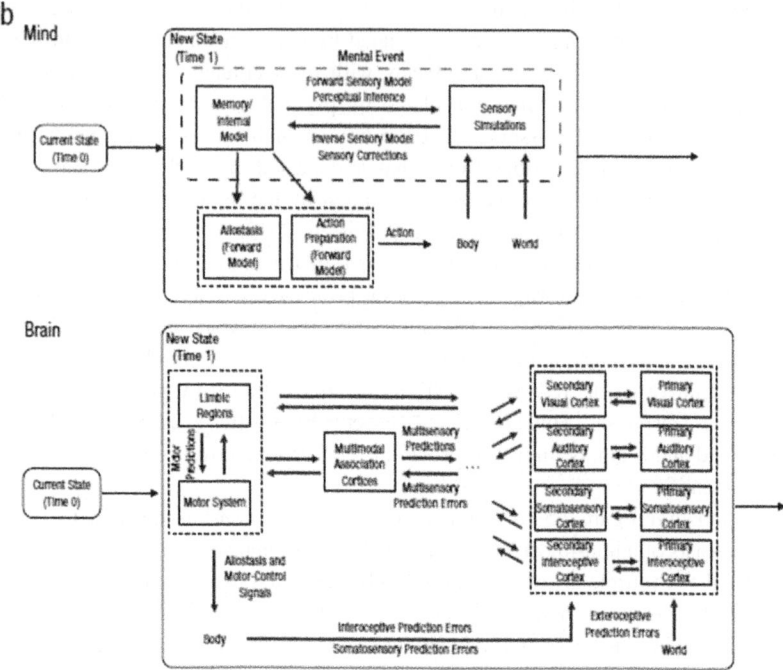

Figure 2.5 Model of the human brain functionality as a fluent state. *Source* Hutchinson & Barrett, 2019, p. 283

2.2.2   Derivation of a Definition for Information

These examples show that "information" can be described as a fluent process, which itself can be described by "packages", such as bits and providing an evaluation of the agent's "belief and reality distance". Physics, informatics and neurosciences can be combined in order to better understand information and its influence on human decision-making. In the end, a clear definition of information cannot be given; however, this thesis relies on the definitions of information by Losee (1998) and Madden (2004), integrating them into the novel predictive processing-framework by Hutchinson and Barrett (2019). Losee (1998) believes that information can be expressed by some value. While this value itself is not information, the value is informative about the input and process from which it is derived. As an internal model or "World View" can be both altered by a stimulus and by the mere anticipation of a stimulus as shown by Hutchinson and Barrett (2019), information is not solely regarded as a stimulus as defined by Madden (2004). The predictive processing-framework (PPF) shows that each internal model is both input and process, so input and process cannot be clearly distinguished in PPF, as required by Losee (1998) to make sense of the information value. In accordance to PPF, a state is linked to a new state by a fluent transition process consisting of frequent updating of prediction and prediction-error distance, while this "linkage" also serves as the process. In PPF each state is both input and process or best described as fluent states.

Building upon the core statements of Losee (1998) that information can be expressed by some informative value, of Madden (2004) that information alters the internal model of some cognitive system and of Hutchinson and Berrett (2019) that cognitive agents both react to external stimuli and stimulated anticipation, the following is derived:

If each of these complex fluent states of some observer were grasped in isolation at time t_n and labelled by some integer, indicating its order of experience and an information theoretical function was applied to receive an informative value (e.g. based on $\log_2$), then—in theory—a string of these fluent states would be identical to the entire experiences and all possible prediction results of the observing agent at time t_n. Information can then be regarded as a redundant function operating on itself, embedding an uncertainty value on possible outcomes, with this value being dependent on the agent's experience (chain of information states) and its belief (prediction vs. prediction-error).

2.2.3 Information Perturbing Events in Behavioral Experiments

Fudenberg and Tirole (1991) close their work "Game Theory" with a remarkable insight. First, they explain that finite state space games are not outmatched by infinite-state-space models approximations, as the latter can have a very different set of equilibria. Second, uncertainty about another's information can lead to state spaces that are even unaccountably infinite. Therefore, in real life economic decision-making, where uncertainty is inevitable and can only be reduced to zero by accepting some "deception potential", a game-theoretical model will either have to cope with uncountable infinity or potentially unprecise and therefore unreliable approximations. Third, while in practical applications of game-theoretical models finite state-spaces are used, their sensitivity to perturbations leading to entirely different outcomes

> *"is another reason to think seriously about the robustness of one's conclusions to the information structure of the game."*

(Fudenberg & Tirole, 1991).

In other words, human decision-making is hardly grasped and simulated by game-theoretical models, as "doubt", mathematically expressed by perturbing some integer, can lead to entirely different outcomes. Even "heuristic approaches" are not immune to such perturbing events. Uncertainty or "doubt" stemming from deception or by how information is presented are important influencers for experiments in the field of behavioral economics and psychology. In the following, three major perturbing events will be briefly described: deception, the "frame effect" and the "order effect".

In short, while deception is commonly used in psychological experiments, deception is far less, if at all, accepted in the domain of economics (Krawczyk, 2019). The "frame effect" describes how human decision-making is influenced by how different choice options are presented (Tversky & Kahneman, 1981), whereas the "order effect" analyzes belief updating (Trueblood & Busemeyer, 2011). Deception, "frame effects" and "order effects" can have an influence on the maintenance and refutation of some agent's belief, which is a critical process in sequential decision-making (Yoshida & Ishii, 2006). All three effects can be manipulated in order to experience different decision-making results or to "nudge" agents, e.g. using the "frame effect" to display information provided by a search engine's result page in such a way that the agent's choices can be improved (Benkert & Netzer, 2018) or using the "order effect" to make agents perform riskier decisions (Aimone, Ball, & King-Casa, 2016). According to most economists, "deception" leads to noisy data and is considered unethical (Houser & McCabe, 2013), while no few psychologists saw deception as a way to produce useful results (Christensen, 1988). More recent research has shown that experimental economists' aversion towards deception is justified (Ortmann & Hertwig, 2005), however, to this day no clear definition of deception exists nor agreement on when deception appears to be used in some experiment (Krawczyk, 2019).

2.2.4   Making Decisions in a VUCA World

As mentioned before, most real world problems are ill-defined. Human agents solve problems by ignoring information (heuristics), which works well to reduce complexity and to solve problems under uncertainty. In order to successfully apply heuristic decision-making or ignore information effectively, information has to be collected first. Information was characterized in this thesis i) as modelled by fluent states, ii) as being linked to an informative value building upon information theory, iii) as being observer-dependent, iv) as a redundant function to alter uncertainty. In the final chapters it was noted that models, experiments and therefore decision-making outcomes are sensitive to information perturbing events caused by deception, the "order" or "framing" of information and that behavioral experiments disregard deception, as it leads to noisy data. All of these circumstances surrounding real economic problems and the complex role of information lead to the conclusion that today's world inhibits characteristics, rendering reliable long-term predictions challenging. This conclusion is expressed by the term "VUCA-world".

"VUCA" stands for "volatility, uncertainty, complexity and ambiguity" (Dörner & Funke, 2017, pp. 2–3) and is commonly used in economic contexts, referring to the unpredictable nature of today's economic decision-making domain. Its four features are similar to the attributes of complex systems, complexity, connectivity, dynamics and goal conflicts (Dörner & Funke, 2017). The term VUCA has been used in a variety of contexts such as to describe modern battlefield- (Nindl et al., 2018), work- (Seow, Pan, & Koh, 2019) and decision-making-environments (Giones, Brem, & Berger, 2019). The VUCA acronym has been misused i.e. providing the impression that leadership was powerless to plan ahead and strategize (Bennett & Lemoine, 2014). On the contrary, the VUCA framework can help to strategize and plan ahead effectively, even when the decision-making environment is inhibiting features of a complex system.

As shown in figure 2.6 (Green, Page, De'ath, Pei, & Lam, 2019, p. 2), two simple questions can be derived by the VUCA framework and consequently asked to categorize a complex system: "How well can you predict the results of your actions?" and "How much do you know about the situation?".

The contents of these two questions can be linked to "expert knowledge". In their famous work "Human Problem Solving", Simon & Newell (1971) found expert chess players to outperform novice chess players in recalling and reproducing the positions of chess pieces after 5 seconds viewing. Experts would remember and thus hold more knowledge about the chess game. Consequently, experts seem to outperform novices when it comes to the question "How much is

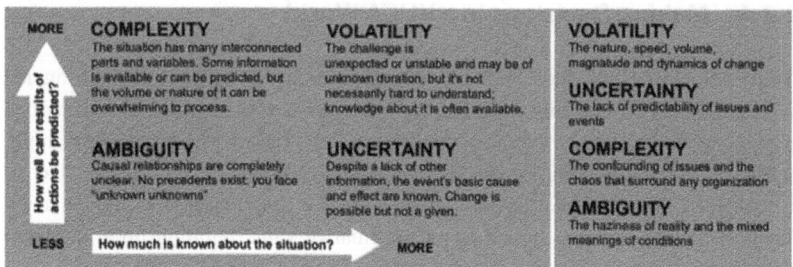

Figure 1 Bennet & Lemoine[2] (left) & Pasmore, O'Shea & Horney [9] VUCA definitions
(right)

Figure 2.6   Dimensions of complex systems. *Source* Green, Page, De'ath, Pei, & Lam, 2019, p. 2

known about the situation?". Perceptual-Cognitive research has shown that expert surfers were more likely to predict waves as being too risky than amateur surfers (Furley & Dörr, 2016). Experts might then outperform novices in complex problem solving when answering "How well can results of actions be predicted?". The overall question is then, how expert knowledge can be defined and whether or not expert knowledge helps in problem solving in a VUCA world. This question is to be answered in detail in the next chapter.

2.3   Expert Knowledge and Problem-Solving

According to Zeleny (2005) information is only symbolic acting, whereas knowledge is true acting, which cannot be replaced by any amount of information. Information is seen by the author as a necessary ingredient, but insufficient recipe for effective volition (Zeleny, 2005). This is because codified knowledge became information, and information technology did not replace social interaction; it was necessary to transform information into effective action and not the other way around (Zeleny, 2005). The author further states that while there can be "too much information" there cannot be "too much knowledge". These statements suit mentioned problems arising from information-based models with high degrees of complexity, ultimately producing uncertainty, instead of reducing it. Just like the model by Hutchinson and Barrett (2019) distinguished between mind and brain or modelling and acting, there exists an analogue distinction between information and knowledge. Knowledge relies on operative acts of measurable volition, rather than on words or letters (Zeleny, 2005).

Just as knowledge is not captured by information systems by these claims, there exists perspectives on expertise not being captured by knowledge management systems: expertise was mainly the result of tens of thousands of hours of acting (Trevelyan, 2014). According to Trevelyan (2014) expertise has to pass three tests in order to be considered as such: First, expertise has to lead to constant sub-par performance. Second, expertise has to lead to volition or concrete outcomes. And third, expertise has to be measurable.

Therefore, action or volition seems to be the key factor combining "knowledge" and "expertise". The resulting term of "Expert knowledge" is now to be defined in more detail, followed by a short description on expert knowledge being used as a resource, and how it is linked to learning.

2.3.1   Definition of Knowledge, Expertise and Expert Knowledge

Theoretical philosophy, building upon ancient Greek philosophy, defines "knowledge" as

"justified true belief, or true opinion combined with reason"

(Hilpinen, 1970, p. 109). This abstract approach in defining "knowledge" leads to logical discussions, whether the information I_1 of person A knowing some event p_1, which includes some uncertainty c that this knowledge was wrong, and the information I_2 of person A knowing that A himself knows that p_1, was the same information ($I_1 == I_2$) or not ($I_1 <> I_2$), I_2 also containing c. It also leads to "ad infinitum problems", such as whether "A knowing A knowing A knowing … knowing p", containing c, or paradox problems that there cannot exist knowledge since uncertainty c is always part of some information (Hilpinen, 1970).

An adequate definition of "knowledge" for the business environment was found to be more suitable, when being modelled less abstract than by attempts stemming from "epistemology". The meaning of "knowledge" is ought to be found in the domain of cognitive sciences (Bolisani & Bratianu, 2018). By defining some discrete system, such as "the static object of knowledge", the "frame problem" would again arise. There also exist studies claiming that knowledge did not find its boundaries from the works of one single agent, but was the result of an intellectual collective, such that knowledge is considered "cognitive contact", where assumptions about reality arise from acts of intellectual confrontation with others (Zagzebski, 2017). To provide a more business oriented definition and to overcome problems arising from the frame problem, when trying to model knowledge with discrete states, so called "fluid flows" are used, leading to the definition of knowledge as "stocks and flows" (Bolisani & Bratianu, 2018, p. 19). This definition applies for both explicit and tacit knowledge and has to be combined with paradigms from physics regarding "entropic uncertainties" (Bolisani & Bratianu, 2018). This leads to the three "rational, emotional, and spiritual fields" defining knowledge (Bolisani & Bratianu, 2018, p. 24). The rational domain of knowledge is defined as being objective and explicit, outlined by language and logic. The emotional dimension of knowledge is subjective and context dependent, being a result of our body responses to the external environment. The spiritual field of knowledge regards ethics and values, which are essential in corporate decision making (Bolisani & Bratianu, 2018).

Decades ago, scientific research in human problem-solving found that expertise requires large amounts of knowledge; the expert has experienced many relevant patterns of some decision-frame and these patterns serve as a guide towards relevant parts of knowledge efficiently (Larkin, McDermott, Simon, & Simon, 1980): This knowledge storages contain varieties of patterns helping with the problem interpretation and problem-solving, while at the same time providing essential and relevant clues (Larkin et al., 1980). Intuition is described by Larkin et al. (1980) as largely being some ability to use "pattern-indexed schemata", distinguishing novices from experts in problem-solving. This broad definition of expertise links to the more recent understanding of "expert performance" reflecting high-level, circumstantial adaptation skills, resulting from long periods of experience and volition (Ericsson & Charness, 1994). Patterns leading to expertise are then automatically acquired in a confined area, where acting happens. Above-average performance is then the result of this iterative process. Defining and selecting "experts" solely based on their years of experience, e.g. for Delphi panels, is a debated selection process, and collective performance in forecasting does not necessarily depend on there being more experienced experts in some decision-making panel. In "Delphi decision-making groups" the total amount of expertise necessary remains uncertain (Baker, Lovell, & Harris, 2006).

Based upon the definitions of knowledge and expertise, expert knowledge is obtained by constant iterative acting in a certain confined domain, where the agent adapts to experienced patterns becoming more efficient in solving problems in the chosen domain, altering rational, emotional and spiritual mental models fluently, and doing so in constant exchange with other people.

Therefore, expert knowledge lives from acting. According to McBridge & Burgman (2012), expert knowledge is important for applied ecology and conservation, as it inhibits complex dynamics, where action is required to reduce uncertainty. When empirical data is lacking, expert knowledge is commonly seen as the optimal source of information; expert knowledge is simply what agents know from practice, training, and experience, and manifests itself in effective recognition of context-relevant information and efficient problem solving (McBride & Burgman, 2012).

2.3.2   Expert Knowledge as a Resource

Making predictions in complex and non-linear decision-environments can benefit from expert knowledge, but is no guarantee for precise forecasts. Age and work experience do not necessarily predict performance, and expert knowledge is context sensitive and has to be embedded in a suitable decision-making domain and framework (McBride & Burgman, 2012). Engineers for example debated many decades, whether or not system design was an intuitive art-form or a scientific process, which had to be systemized; nowadays, engineers rely on a mixed bag of instruments and a more holistic viewpoint when it comes to design, including complexity management, workflows and cognitive systems (Kreimeyer, Lauer, Lindemann, & Heyman, 2006). While iterations of act results in learning, thus building expertise, such iterations have to be minimized in order to reduce costs, as described by the commonly used "Pahl and Beitz Systematic Approach" framework (Kannengiesser & Gero, 2017). Applications of lean and agile software development are growing (Tripp, Saltz, & Turk, 2018) and show that there exists an interest of embedding expert knowledge in more lightweight and flexible frameworks. This is done to reduce costs and in order to be able to react to unpredictable change efficiently (Saini, Arif, & Kulonda, 2017). In other words, in a complex environment, expert knowledge is handled as a resource to save capital, and to better handle uncertainties. This concept is used in "sustainable management" and referred to as "salutogenesis" (Müller-Christ, 2014), which describes that capital can be used in order to stay capable of acting and reacting to unforeseeable events. So even though expert knowledge does not necessarily result in optimal results, it is still considered an important factor when facing dynamical decision-environments and can be effectively included in modern frameworks that save capital, leading to more sustainable problem-solving solutions.

2.3.3   The Role of Learning

According to Simon and Newell (1971), human decision-making consists of cognitive and environmental characteristics (Campitelli & Gobet, 2010). This is called the expertise approach, combining the understanding of expertise and decision-making. Campitelli & Gobet (2010) suggest that Simon's expertise approach should be included into decision-making research: experiments should test for level of expertise and apply different environmental circumstances. Experiments should contain participants with different level of expertise, in order to show whether or not experts and novices show different levels of bias, as predicted by Tversky and Kahneman (1981), and when and why such cognitive illusions disappear, as stated by Gigerenzer (1996). According to the "Simon and colleagues' approach", different environmental circumstances should be applied (Campitelli & Gobet, 2010), such that domain specific expertise can be compared to other domains, in order to test whether or not environmental circumstances have an impact on decision-making, whether this impact correlated to expertise, and if the type of heuristics applied by participants actually changed. Campitelli & Gobet (2010) also suggest that computational models that fit data of human behavior in a multitude of domains are more meaningful than models, which analyze human behavior in more specific cases.

Theories in behavioral economics are seeking generality, adding parameters incrementally, such that results or models can be easily compared to even more general models; even though adding behavioral assumptions to some models describing human behavior makes the model less tractable, behavioral models can outperform traditional ones in precision, when operating in domains of dynamics and strategic interaction (Camerer & Loewenstein, 2004). Behavioral economics relies on field experiments, computer simulation and brain scans, and Camerer & Loewenstein (2004) describe behavioral economists as methodological eclectics, who make use of psychological insights (Camerer & Loewenstein, 2004, p. 7), which distinguishes behavioral economics from experimental economics. "Behavioral Game Theory" generalizes the standard assumptions of game theory, using experimental evidence, and provides a model for "learning" in complex environments, even including neuroscientific evidence to support models about economic behavior (Camerer & Loewenstein, 2004).

The authors Reisch & Zhao (2017) describe behavioral economics as a theory, which does not rely on the view of the consumer acting as a rational Homo oeconomicus, but displaying "bounded rationality", as described by Kahneman (2003) and Simon (1955), where their deviations are predictable "errors". Behavioral economics relies on the "information paradigm" in the sense that consumer behavior is incentivized by the information provided and by their learning progress in the form of preferences, biases and heuristic strategies; however, models building upon this understanding realized that even small incentives can have a big impact on decision-making (Reisch & Zhao, 2017). Key findings of behavioral economics include several biases and heuristics from prospect theory and mental account, and are used to design choice context; as consumers make decisions context-dependently, results by behavioral economic models can be used to nudge consumers (Reisch & Zhao, 2017).

The influence of expert knowledge, the "expertise approach" of decision-making research and behavioral economics find common ground in the domain of "learning". While "expertise" was defined as an "extreme adaption", "learning" too is linked to the concept of adaption, being defined as "ontogenetic adaption", being observed change in behavior of an agent, which stems from making use of regularities surrounding the agent (De Houwer, Barnes-Holmes, & Moors, 2013). To acquire a clear understanding about behavioral changes, it is recommended to rely on this functional definition of "learning", and to acquire information about when exactly learning occurs, so that insights of cognitive nature can also be derived (De Houwer et al., 2013). Experiments should then control *when* learning occurs to effectively measure behavioral changes, stepping away from inefficient models, which understand learning as a "mental mechanism" (De Houwer et al., 2013, p. 641). Experiments can be designed in such a way, as to include the "expertise approach", behavioral economics and "expert knowledge" by this understanding of "learning": the three concepts would meet common ground in software-based experiments, where controlled contextual changes increased the probability in behavioral changes, which can then be compared to novice and expert problem solving performance, having either performed only a few or many iterations of the experiment before, including decades of insights on how biases and heuristics influence decision-making.

The next chapter will introduce the concept of learning, how it is related to measured behavioral changes, which are often influenced by biases and heuristics, and how individual agents can be understood as "disturbances".

2.4   Agents Acting as Disturbances

According to Erev and Roth (2014) mainstream behavioral economics attempts to find deviations from the rational model, offering descriptive models. The authors discuss human learning in order to find domains where people learn fast and

maximize their expected return, to better understand how the structure of an economic environment influences behavior (Erev & Roth, 2014). Important insights
regard feedback and its influence on decisions. When feedback is limited to the
chosen option—that is, when consequences of discarded options are not provided
to the agent—the behavioral impact of negative outcomes last longer than the
impact of good outcomes. This is because bad outcomes reduce the probability
of the agent trying to reevaluate the option (Erev & Roth, 2014). This can lead
to a certain "attitude" towards options through such exploration, where invalid
negative prejudices are hardly overcome (Fazio, Eiser, & Shook, 2004).

Exploration can be described as a requirement to obtain information during
complex problem solving, since in such problem solving scenarios, information
is hidden from the agents on the outset. As most real economic problems are complex or can be considered as problems under uncertainty, this chapter or in fact this
thesis as a whole, will mainly consider problems under uncertainty. There exists a
mathematical expression of the continuum from risk to uncertainty, coming from
the "bias variance theory", written as

$$"total\ error = (bias)^2 + variance + \varepsilon",$$

where "ε" equals noise. The meaning of this continuum is very intuitively explained by Gerd Gigerenzer in his introducing article "Taking Heuristics Seriously" to
the whitepaper "The Behavioral Economics Guide 2016" (Samson & Gigerenzer,
2016).

As depicted in figure 2.7 the left person shows bias towards the bottom right,
next to no variance and overall superior performance as opposed to the right
person, who shows no bias, high variance and a lower score. This intuitive example shows that error can stem from either bias or variance. Fine-tuned complex
models, according to Mousavi & Gigerenzer (2014), lead to high variance when
being applied to different samples, while heuristics with fixed parameters have no
variance, but bias. Still, problems under risk are different from problems under
uncertainty, and while uncertainty is part of many day-to-day situations in real
life, uncertainty has to be reduced to a form of risk, in order to make calculations
dealing with uncertainty compatible to risk calculations. (Mousavi & Gigerenzer, 2014). Anyhow, this thesis wants to assemble more theoretical background
mainly about problems under uncertainty, while not ignoring important aspects of
problems under risk.

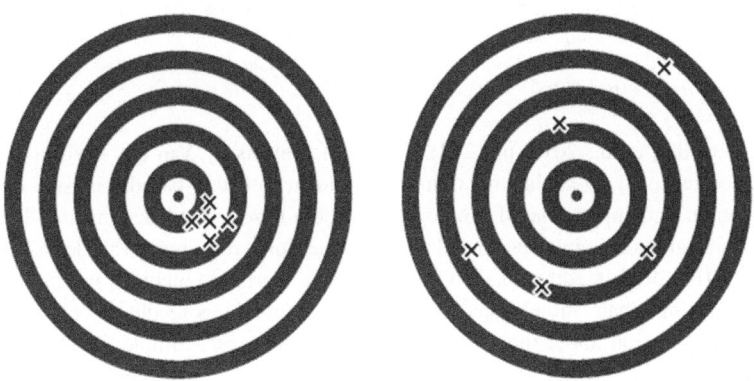

Figure 2: A visual depiction of the two errors in prediction, bias and variance. The bull's eye represents the unknown true value to be predicted. Each dart represents a predicted value, based on different random samples of information. Bias is the distance between the bull's eye and the mean dart location; variance is the variability of the individual darts around their mean.

Figure 2.7   Bias vs. Variance. *Source* Samson & Gigerenzer, 2016, p. VIII

The following sub-chapter will capture the importance of feedback, and its potential influence on following decisions during complex problem-solving under uncertainty, where the agent has to explore, and possibly adapt to contextual changes. Following subchapters will specify the role of non-routine tasks, routine strength in decision-making, derive non-routine problem solving, providing a short summary of these insights by referring to "complexity economics".

2.4.1   The Role of Feedback in Complex Problems Under Uncertainty

According to Van der Kleij, Feskens, & Eggen, 2015 there does not exist a generally accepted model on how learning is created by feedback, but there does exist some evidence regarding the positive relationship of feedback on learning during computerized experiments. However, Van der Kleij et al. (2015) also mention that these conclusions are not sufficient enough for explaining detailed relationships of feedback and learning, defining feedback as follows: "Winne and Butler (1994) suggested *"feedback is information with which a learner can confirm, add to, overwrite, tune, or restructure information in memory, whether that information is domain knowledge, meta-cognitive knowledge, beliefs about self and tasks, or cognitive tactics and strategies" (p. 5740)."*

(Van der Kleij et al., 2015, pp. 2–3). The meta-analysis by Van der Kleij et al. (2015) considered 40 studies regarding the influence of item-based feedback on learning in a computer-based environment. "Item-based" feedback means that agents are granted immediate or delayed feedback on every item (Van der Kleij et al., 2015). Rich feedback led to more effective learning outcomes in "higher order learning" than "simple feedback", which is defined as feedback only providing information about the correctness of some response. Simple feedback is considered to be effective for „lower order learning outcomes" (p. 8). "Lower order learning" is restricted to recalling, recognizing and understanding concepts with no need to actually apply this knowledge. "Higher learning" requires the application of knowledge in novel domains, which is referred to as "transfer" (Van der Kleij et al., 2015, p. 5).

As people tend to think in short-sighted causal relations, commonly assume an effect to have a single cause and halt research for causes upon having found the first satisfying explanation, agents perceive only limited amounts of feedback to self-reinforce or self-correct strategies (Sterman, 2006). Time delays in feedback processes confound the agents' ability to learn, resulting in decision makers to perform corrections, even when enough corrective actions have already been taken "to restore equilibrium" (Sterman, 2006, p. 508).

According to Sterman (2006) "learning is a feedback process", as depictured in figure 2.8, where both dynamics in a complex system and all learning depend on feedback. When deviations from expected states are perceived, agents perform actions from which they think will close the gap. Therefore, strategies are influenced by misperceptions of feedback, unscientific reasoning and biases. In order to learn under conditions of high uncertainty, such as learning under crisis, this " expected states gap" is closed by pre-training, using virtual reality, learning by imitation, communication, information systems, past experiences and operating standards (Moynihan, 2008). It is assumed that knowledge gathered before facing a complex problem under uncertainty helps to better perform in its problem-solving. While Moynihan (2008) stresses that ad-hoc learning during a problem under uncertainty is possible, novel routines should be explored before a network of agents is required to use them.

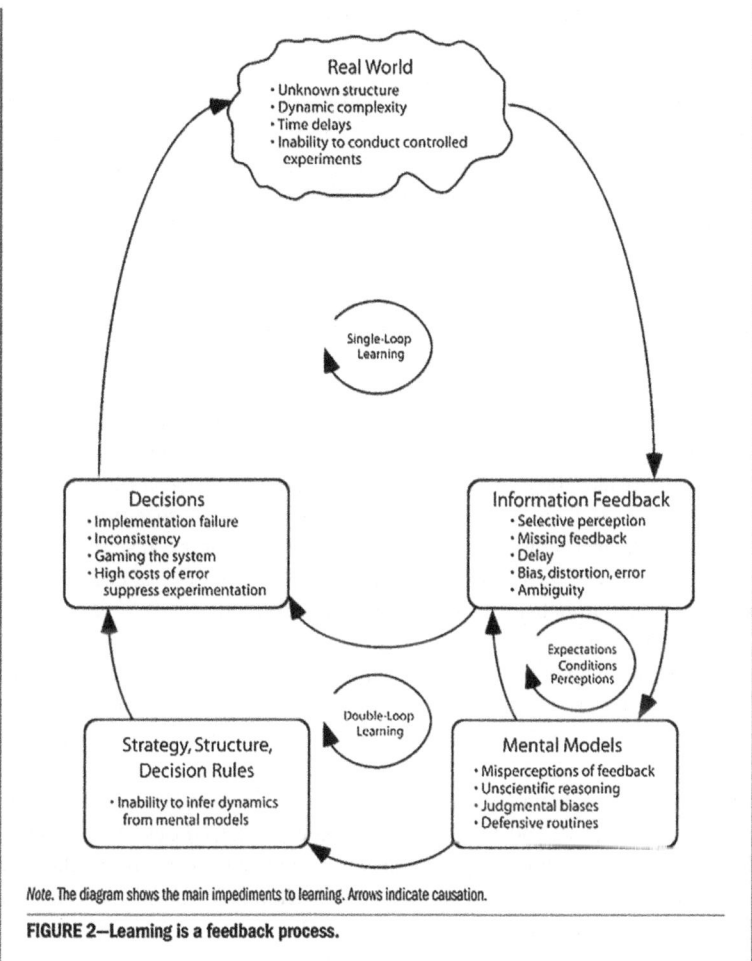

Figure 2.8   All learning is a feedback process. *Source* Sterman, 2006, p. 506

In conclusion, all learning results from feedback, while learning outcomes are influenced by the quality of feedback. Simple learning outcomes already benefit from feedback solely indicating correctness of some response, while transfer requires more sophisticated feedback, i.e.

"hints, additional information, extra study material, and an explanation of the correct answer."

(Van der Kleij et al., 2015, p. 4). In situations of high uncertainty where such additional information cannot be provided, prior knowledge or exploration for new routines can be helpful. The latter real-world problem in crisis management is commonly referred to as "non-routine problem solving". The following sub-chapter will introduce this concept in greater detail.

2.4.2   Novel Problems, Real-World Problems, and Non-routine Tasks

According to thorough experimental results stemming from the "bean fest paradigm", where the relation of exploratory behavior and attitude formation was tested (Fazio et al., 2004), whether or not some novel decision alternative was considered good or bad—at least in a virtual world—is considered by agents in accordance to their weighting bias. Beans could be eaten or not, resulting in either positive or negative effects. Beans would differ in shape and pattern, and participants were able to defeat randomness by clustering the beans' appearances, as shown in figure 2.9.

The experiment attempted various conditions, such as providing feedback to all or only to the chosen bean, framing the experiment by granting points or subtracting life points. In the end, the game was always a performance-based experiment. When a novel alternative in form of some bean is faced by an agent in this experimental environment, where a problem under uncertainty with item-based feedback is simulated, and the agents can learn from feedback (with feedback only provided to the chosen option), agents' choice can partly be predicted by the common "negativity bias". Participants who learned the positive and negative decision alternatives (beans) equally well, tended towards a negative response, generally showing negativity bias towards novel beans (Fazio, Pietri, Rocklage, & Shook, 2015). Agents are influenced by the looks and resemblance of patterns to prior experiences (Fazio et al., 2015). Whether or not an agent had a larger tendency to classify a novel bean as a bad bean, than can be expected by the agent's learning pattern, defines the "valence weighting bias". It is regarded "as a fundamental personality characteristic", as

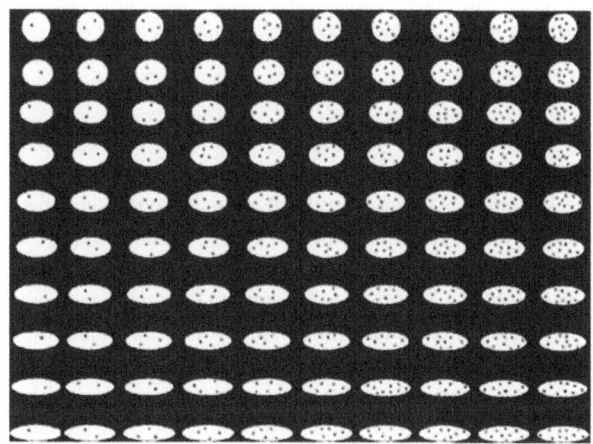

Figure 1 The population of bean stimuli forming the 10 × 10 matrix. *Reprinted from Deutsch and Fazio (2008).*

	Y1	Y2	Y3	Y4	Y5	Y6	Y7	Y8	Y9	Y10
X1	+	+	+			−	−	−		
X2	+	+			−	−	−			
X3						−				
X4									+	+
X5		−						+	+	+
X6	−	−	−						+	
X7	−	−								
X8					+					
X9				+	+	+			−	−
X10			+	+	+			−	−	−

Figure 2 The bean matrix. X refers to shape, from circular (1) to oblong (10); Y refers to the number of speckles, from 1 to 10. The beans presented during the learning phase of the BeanFest procedure are noted with their corresponding positive (+) or negative (−) value. In any given study, the bean values are typically reversed for half the participants. This counterbalancing has not been found to influence outcomes.

Figure 2.9   "Bean-Fest" causal structure. *Source* Fazio et al., 2015, p. 107

"Individuals' valence weighting proclivities have proved relevant to sensitivity to inter-
personal rejection, threat assessment, neophobia, decisions about risky alternatives,
intentions to engage in novel risk behaviors, actual risk behavior, emotional reactivity
to a failure experience, the expansion of friendship networks, and changes in depressive
symptoms."

(Fazio et al., 2015, p. 117). Unfortunately, the authors Fazio et al. (2015) found
the valence weighting bias to not be self-reportable by questionnaires. Also, their
finding are limited to experiments, where decision alternatives give visual clues,
so that the Bayesian brain finds fruitful potential to learning. However, the Bean-
Fest experiment enables to simulate a decision-making environment, where each
problem is novel and different and further shows that individual differences are
key at the very core of problem solving.

According to system theory, problems exist in real life—not only in science:
reality reacts to problems by selection and problems are described as

"real and effective catalysts of social life"

(Luhmann, 2012, p. 173). Chapter 2 defined many aspects of real economic problems so far. Most problems in reality are ill-defined, lack a clear instruction on
how to solve them, happen under uncertainty, are solved by humans via heuristics, are complex, need to be solved by acquiring information or knowledge, are
disturbed by error such as bias, will usually be solved by many interdependent
decisions, require experience and learning to be solved and are embedded in an
opaque network of cause-effect relations, whose feedback signals are not easily
being interpreted correctly by humans.

Studies on learning from feedback in real world problems or economic problems in a complex environment are scarce. Keil et al. (2016) describe learning
from performance feedback in complex environments, where outcomes are observed with time-delay and where a multitude of actions are combined to generate
outcome in different research and development stages of 98 large US pharmaceu-
tical companies during 1993 to 2013 (Keil, Kostopoulos, Syrigos, & Meissner,
2016). Here, the authors focus on a real world "order effect" of information.
Negative feedback, such as performance below aspirations, in an early development stage, are interpreted differently, leading to different actions than negative
feedback in later development stages. In addition, Keil et al. (2016) distance themselves from classical models of experiential learning regarding positive feedback.
They argue that performance above expectations creates a buffer, whose size
favors higher chances of organizational risk-taking. An increasing tolerance of

organizational risk-taking was described to favor search of novelties above aspirations, possibly leading to a shift of the company's core project management (Keil et al., 2016). Organizational recession can also have a positive impact, as it conserves unexplored potential, nourishing firms during times of "uncontrolled exogenous adversity" (Levinthal & March, 1981, p. 309).

Another core finding was that research should concentrate more on the relationship between cognitive biases and behavioral learning (Keil et al., 2016) and that interpretation of information of performance feedback plays an important role in experiential learning in complex processes. Performance feedback is interpreted differently and following action also depends on the "order effect" or stage of R&D process (W.-R. Chen & Miller, 2007), also in accordance to prospect theory (W. Chen, 2008).

From these examples it can be concluded that real-world problems and their related decision-making processes are indeed dependent on both interpretation and order of feedback information. For this very reason, the three information disturbing effects "frame effect", "order effect" and deception were mentioned earlier. Purposeful deception, such as lies, too commonly disturbs feedback information in real world problems and is referred to as "real world deception" (Fuller, Biros, & Delen, 2011).

Due to the high levels of uncertainty in complex environments, pre-training, exploration and routines are essential in coping with real world problems, especially when time pressure does not incentivize investing in reflection time, novel routines or finding new alternative paths. Such a complex decision-making environment with high time pressure is represented by challenges in hospital settings. To reduce costs, the concept of "shared decision-making" and consumer education was tested back in the year 2000 by use of software. Here, treatments were not only chosen by the physician in terms of clinical considerations, but the treatment choice was also influenced by consideration of the patient's values and preferences (Holmes-Rovner et al., 2000). However, as the study showed, the program faced many problems, which can be collectively explained by the effects of "information interpretation", personal bias, and problems stemming from initial hurdles of novel routines: physicians restricted treatments to patients who wanted additional information about the treatment. Physicians also decided not to participate in the randomized study due to personal enthusiasm for the program, and therefore tried to avoid inducing bias by participating. So, physicians did not implement the new shared decision-making process as a routine.

All three problems restricted the implementation of a new routine or in other words, made this task of implementing the non-routine, shared decision-making program a real-world problem and a tough challenge. Individual characteristics facing novelties, the uncertainties stemming from unknown causal relations by misinterpretation of information or order effects and lack of resources to pre-test some novel strategy, render handling non-routine tasks difficult. Despite the difficulties when attempting non-routine tasks, they are considered as being part of important "21st Century Skills" in order to cope with a VUCA world, where circumstances vary frequently, and its features are linked to performance in complex problem solving (Neubert, Mainert, Kretzschmar, & Greiff, 2015).

In order to observe non-routine decision making and measure its related non-routine problem solving performance in an environment that does not incentivize reflection time, i.e. reflecting on a problem when time is cost-assigned, Strunz & Chlupsa (2019) developed a valid application-test scenario in form of a web-browser based online experiment. Its methods and findings are to be described in greater detail in section 2.4.4—in order to do so, problem solving and the role of routine are introduced in the following sub-chapter.

2.4.3   Problem Solving Search and Routine Strength

"In everyday speech the term problem solving refers to activities that are novel and effortful.",

while not all tasks

"feel like problem solving. Some activities, like solving a Tower of Hanoi problem (...) feel like problem solving, whereas other more routine activities, such as using a familiar computer application (...) do not. (...) Newell (1980) argued that the dimension of difference between routine problem solving and real problem solving is the amount of search involved. (...) Newell claimed that we transit smoothly into problem-solving search and indeed that much of human cognition is a mixture of routine problem solving and problem solving that involves search. This claim is realized in his Soar model of cognition (Newell, 1990)"

(Anderson, 1993).

When researching problem solving, the Tower of Hanoi task was one of the first experimental tools being used (Anderson, 1993), and still is applied in research today. Tower of Hanoi has also been used in the psychology of problem solving (Hinz, Kostov, Kneißl, Sürer, & Danek, 2009), in neuroscientific research (Ruiz-Díaz, Hernández-González, Guevara, Amezcua, & Ågmo, 2012), in order to test for executive function and planning (Donnarumma, Maisto, & Pezzulo, 2016), for working memory (Numminen, Lehto, & Ruoppila, 2001), and is being used with children, adolescents, and adults from general and clinical samples (Robin-son & Brewer, 2016). Tower of Hanoi (ToH) consists of simple rules, which are to be explained in greater detail in chapter 3. For now, as can be seen in figure 2.9, all that should be noted about the game is that it always consists of some "state", such as a starting configuration of 5 disks being put on the left most peg. The player than has to apply some "operator" to transform one state into a new state, by e.g. moving a disk onto another rod. In accordance to J.R. Anderson (1993) a "problem space" is then defined by both "state" and "operator". When all pos-sible connections between states are modelled, by applying only valid operators, the entire state space represents the problem-space (Anderson, 1993). Whether humans hold a similar mental representation of this problem-space is still of inte-rest to recent research and results show that the total time required to solve a ToH problem is proportional to its complexity; complexity is defined as the problem-space distance between the game's start and goal state, as well as the complexity of solution and its associated computational costs (Donnarumma et al., 2016). As Donnarumma et al. (2016) show, humans are having troubles to engage in counter-intuitive moves, which are considered as being more complex, as they require the agent to "look-ahead" when playing ToH. The authors also link "subgoaling" to the possible mental representation of a problem-space, where the problem is divi-ded into smaller portions, which have to be solved. The concept of "subgoals" is based upon scientific evidence that human behavior follows a hierarchical struc-ture, where basic and simple actions are clustered into subtasks, which themselves can be combined for the achievement of high-order goals (Solway et al., 2014). According to Donnarumma et al. (2016), the subgoal concept can explain sub-optimal decisions, during problems that require counterintuitive moves: humans have a tendency to simply draw a "direct path" from start to goal state by only being aware of the perceptual distance; the "subgoal" model forms an implicit metric from the problem space, and this implicit metric has a great impact on the decision-making outcome. Human problem solving or human search, is sensitive to its prior and often suboptimal mental, implicit representation. Implicit measu-res are considered as being useful for predicting behavior and analyzing change of mental problem representations (Blanton & Gawronski, 2019).

Human problem solving is also sensitive to routines. Routine is defined as a

"behavioral option that comes to mind as a solution",

which is not considered being some strategy but a

"behavioral option that is most strongly associated with a specific decision situation"

(Betsch et al., 2001, p. 24). According to Betsch et al. (2001), prior-belief effects stemming from high routine participants resulted in agents being reluctant to overcome routine, despite novel feedback suggesting a change of routine as being a lucrative option. Participants who experienced high success rates acting upon a certain strategy, and who then showed high routine, were adapting at slower rates. However, instant adaption with strong routine induced participants were found, when novel feedback could be understood or correctly interpreted by prior knowledge. In their second experiment Betsch et al. (2001) had shown that strong routine participants were falling for the confirmation bias, when tasks were framed as being similar, but were able to discard old strategies, when a task was being explicitly described as being novel. All in all, routine strength significantly influences decision-making, yielding confirmation biases in information acquisitions, and being sensitive towards how tasks are framed. Still, confirmatory tendencies can be overcome when a task is being described as being novel. Adaption in recurring decision-making is being slowed by strongly induced routine and high values in routine strength correlates with the underestimation or negligence of feedback, which encourages overcoming routine, i.e. change in routine strategy (Betsch et al., 2001).

Extrinsic incentives, such as financial rewards are generally assumed to influence human decision-making performance. McDaniel & Rutström (2001) compared two different theories regarding extrinsic reward, intrinsic reward and performance using a Tower of Hanoi experiment. While extrinsic reward can come in form of bonus pay, intrinsic reward was researched by observing monkeys solving mechanical puzzles repeatedly. The animals did so without extrinsic reward, such as food. Therefore, it was understood that there exist actions, which are motivated intrinsically and are performed for their "own sake", independent of extrinsic incentives (Eisenberger & Cameron, 1996, p. 1154).

The first theory analyzed by McDaniel & Rutström (2001) is the psychological theory of "detrimental reward" effects. It was interpreted by the authors in two different ways: First, whether an increase in extrinsic reward lowered perception of attractiveness of the to-be-solved problem, leading to a reduction in intrinsic reward, followed by a decrease in effort, which led to worse performance overall. Second, whether an increase of extrinsic reward induced a distraction effect, leading to a reduction of productivity. The second theory and third hypothesis were named "costly rationality" theory, and stated that an increase in extrinsic reward led to an increase in effort and performance. Extrinsic reward was implemented as error-costs, which differed in the low- and high-cost treatment. Therefore, an increase in error-costs or an increase in penalty was interpreted as a decrease in external reward. In short, participants reported longer time-use when the penalty was increased. The authors interpreted the increase in time-use as high effort, and the increased penalty as a decrease in extrinsic reward, thus rejecting their first hypothesis (McDaniel & Rutström, 2001). McDaniel & Rutström also found the penalty effect to have an insignificant effect on performance; they observed lots of individual variation in performance, potentially dominating any treatment effect, which they found to be in-line with research—however, whether individual variation was the true cause for treatment insignificance is described as being unclear (McDaniel & Rutström, 2001). The executive function, defined as

"a combination of working memory and inhibition inhibitory processes"

(Zook, Davalos, DeLosh, & Davis, 2004, p. 286), had been found to predict heterogeneous performance in Tower of Hanoi experiments.

Betsch et al. (2001) used a "microworld simulation" to research the influence of routine strength. In order to measure complex problem solving, which includes non-routine problem solving, software-based methods either include mentioned microworlds or "minimal complex systems". Different influencers on non-routine problem performance and their measurement procedures, as well as current scientific debate on their usefulness and how non-routine problem solving (NPS) can be measured, using a software-based "minimal complex system", are explained in the following sub-chapters.

2.4.4 NPS: Adaptation, Beliefs, Response Times and Emotion

In order to research human decision-making in dynamic and complex domains complex, computer-simulated scenarios where proposed, which are to shed light on details of agents performing complex problem solving (CPS) under uncertainty (Funke, 2014). Realistic, computer-simulated problems, including multiple changing and interdependent variables, also referred to as microworlds (Funke, 2014), require a certain order of actions to be performed, in order to efficiently and effectively solve them (Güss, Fadil, & Strohschneider, 2012). Due to the complexity of such problems, the decision-making agent cannot possibly retrieve all causal relations, and therefore has to optimize its strategies through heuristics—here, cultural differences were found. Difference in problem-solving were explained by differences stemming from strategic expertise, which themselves are based on heterogeneous cultural learning environments (Funke, 2014). Significant differences in NPS performance by country origin, being India, US-America and Germany, were confirmed, but whether this difference was related to learning environment characteristics remained unclear (Strunz, 2019).

While recent research on cultural influences in CPS were less clear (Güss, 2011), and the influences of cultural uncertainty avoidance were conflicting at times (Güss et al., 2012), strategy making remains a strong predictor in performance under CPS. This leads to the understanding that complex and knowledge-rich problems not only require the use of heuristic decision rules, but further strengthens the importance of general and domain specific knowledge (Funke, 2014). Experts are found to spend more time exploring, showing higher adaptability and flexibility in their strategy making, which predicted performance (Güss, Devore Edelstein, Badibanga, & Bartow, 2017).

Minimal complex systems are less complex and their causal structure can be obtained by strategies helping with precise causal analyses. For example, the "Vary One Thing At a Time" (VOTAT) strategy can be applied to the minimal complex system "MicroDYN", with its causal structure being displayed in figure 2.10, to successfully obtain full information on structure and behavior of the problem (Funke, 2014, p. 2). There seem to be two schools of thought, when deciding whether or not performance in complex problem solving can be equally measured with less complex simulations or "minimal complex systems". How to clearly define and perform "Complex Problem Solving" (CPS) experiments still is heavily debated (Greiff, Stadler, Sonnleitner, Wolff, & Martin, 2015; Funke, Fischer, & Holt, 2017; Greiff, Stadler, Sonnleitner, Wolff, & Martin, 2017). Agreement on the question how to measure CPS performance exists in that participants have to overcome barriers that arise from opacity of relevant information and uncertainty about true causal relations governing the problem's functionality (Strunz & Chlupsa, 2019).

Two other important influencers on performance under CPS are environmental changes and learning of counterintuitive concepts. Both influencers have been mentioned before. Environmental conditions predict learning and maximization (Erev & Roth, 2014) can lead to confirmation bias and failure to adapt a strategy due to routine strengths (Betsch et al., 2001). According to evidence from CPS simulations, and as found in Strunz & Chlupsa (2019), environmental changes only change participants' behavior when those changes actually meddle with an agent's strategy performance (Cañas, Quesada, Antolí, & Fajardo, 2003).

As explained before, performing counterintuitive actions is troublesome for humans to do (Donnarumma et al., 2016). Even when environmental conditions have an impact on an agent's strategy, overcoming its routine strategy might require counter-intuitive concepts or the realization that one is self-deceiving

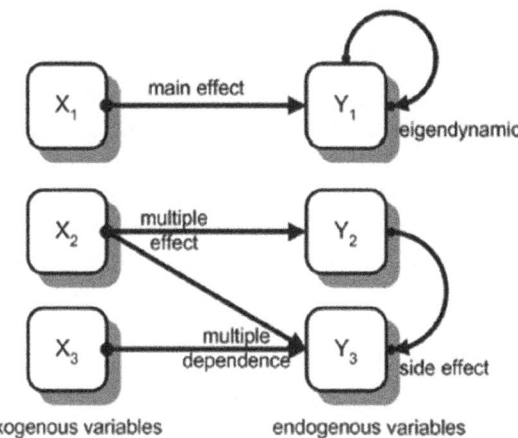

main effect
eigendynamic
multiple
effect
multiple
dependence
side effect
exogenous variables
endogenous variables
FIGURE 1 | A typical MicroDYN item as an example for a more simple system with different kinds of effects. For the selected sets of endogenous and exogenous variables any cover story is possible (from Greiff et al., 2012, p. 192).

Figure 2.10 Causal structure of Minimal Complex System „MicroDYN". *Source* Greiff et al. 2012, p. 192

himself with a mental model, which is by definition always an incorrect representation of reality (Sterman, 2002). Learning and knowledge are described as being essential in order to cope with a change in routine, as described in a study coping with supply chain management (Scholten, Sharkey Scott, & Fynes, 2019). Scholten, Sharkey Scott & Fynes (2019) describe various types of learning and knowledge processes that are to be implemented in order to adapt operating routines towards uncertainties stemming from supply chain disruptions. One aspect found to be of significant importance is to reflect on positive outcomes, in order to use the full potential of knowledge creation (Scholten et al., 2019). As described before, positive performance feedback can result in taking more risks (Keil et al., 2016), meaning that an oversimplification of some above average performance or a misinterpretation of its causal relation leading to the good performance, can result in too risky and costly actions by the decision-makers, who have not spent enough time reflecting on the feedback. However, as described in the former sub-chapter, implicit motives and bias that cannot be self-reported, such as valence weighting bias, deeply influence decision-making. Mathematics (Sidenvall, Jäder, & Sumpter,

2015) and education science (Chong, Shahrill, Putri, & Zulkardi, 2018) are also more and more concerned with non-routine tasks and problems, with both fields coming to the conclusion that non-routine problem solving requires real world knowledge and is being influenced by individual beliefs: Whether a solution to a problem is simply imitated or constructed creatively depends on whether a student felt "secure" enough to do so, and less complex and wrong solutions were favored to the correct and more complex solution, when "it felt too complicated" (Sidenvall et al., 2015, p. 123). This not only applies to the behavior of students. Implicit motives influencing economic decision-making have been confirmed by neuronal evidence, however, this insight is still confronted with resistance in the field of business administration (Chlupsa, 2014).

Beliefs and implicit processes can lead to bias in decision-situations, where the decision-maker is lacking information to make a decision based on former knowledge (Fazio et al., 2015). Following an inner "status-quo" or "inertia" bias, the decision-maker might prefer consistency over positive feedback (Alós-Ferrer, Hügelschäfer, & Li, 2016). In other words, the decision-maker might fail to overcome routine, despite feedback, while others overcome their bias and proceed with non-routine decisions, to effectively react to novel circumstances (Chlupsa & Strunz, 2019; Strunz, 2019; Strunz & Chlupsa, 2019).

Thinking time as a resource, approximately measured as response time, can be helpful to overcome these biases. Response time is defined as the server-side time span between problem activation and client response (Rubinstein, 2007). Research looking at response times in an economic decision-making context, stems from brain studies and neuroeconomics, where brain activity is monitored e.g. via resonance imaging (fMRI). Research regarding response time is also commonly used in psychology (Rubinstein, 2007). While there exists criticism that most neuroeconomic studies resulted in "unimpressive economics" (Harrison, 2008, p. 41), some neuroscientific insights have guided behavioral economic research to this day. Cognitive processes coping with complexity, e.g., answering survey questions of different lengths, are linked to response times (Yan & Tourangeau, 2008), which are a well-researched indicator for overcoming decision biases (Alós-Ferrer, Garagnani, & Hügelschäfer, 2016). Response times have predictive power when decision-makers are facing strategic uncertainty (Kiss, Rodriguez-Lara, & Rosa-Garcia, 2018), e.g. decision-makers show longer response times when multiple options are seen as equally attractive (Krajbich, Oud, & Fehr, 2014). In order to deduce meaningful information from response times, an agent's action has to be identified either as a cognitive action, as an instinctive action, or as a reasonless action. A reasonless action can be the results of some mental decision-making process with low or no logical reasoning (Rubinstein, 2007). Section 4.1.12 "Logic and Expected States" refers to this three-fold distinction later on.

Performance in CPS stems from thinking time, but also from the agents' ability to effectively "identify rules" governing a problem, gaining "rule knowledge" by understanding the problem's internal causal relations (true rule knowledge) and "applying knowledge" by controlling the problem and achieving goals (Wüstenberg, Greiff, & Funke, 2012).

Engaging in non-routine problem solving (NPS) is influenced by a multitude of factors. Very complex decision-making domains will favor heuristic search, while less complex domains will make it possible for the agent to engage in maximization (by algorithmic operators such as VOTAT), obtaining the true causal relations (true rule knowledge about structure and behavior of the domain). Both problem solutions can lead to positive feedback, from which routine can grow, and both solutions benefit from knowledge and learning. When environmental change leads to the routine becoming less favorable, individual valence weighting bias, power of routine, time pressure, beliefs and intrinsic metrics can either hinder or favor a change in strategy. In this case reflection time evidently is a good predictor in overcoming these mental hurdles. Less than 10% of mixed-country participants, about 10% of US-American participants, about 5% of Indian and slightly more than 20% of German participants (Strunz, 2019; Strunz & Chlupsa, 2019) were able to overcome mental hurdles in the NPS experiment "Flag Run", engaging in a change of strategy, built upon a mental model "closer" to the true rules governing the complex problem or in other words: obtaining true rules. Rules do not change throughout the "Flag Run" experiment. However, the starting levels of the experiment "Flag Run" were constructed in such a way that agents would be nudged into building a routine, based upon a wrong mental model of the causal relations. Agents were nudged into thinking that they were able to control the direction of some playing piece, where in fact the direction of the playing piece was always set by default towards "left". As can be seen in figure 2.11, the distance from the playing piece to the goal field is "two steps", when counting from going left, jumping edges, or when counting right, going to the goal field using the more intuitive and visible path. Therefore, the left- and right-hand distance to the goal field are identical. The problem space of "Flag Run" is simple and the true causal relations are even simpler than in most "Minimal Complex Systems". However, not a single agent has proven from its behavior to having understood the true causal relations. The reason for this can only be speculated upon, however, Strunz & Chlupsa (2019) suspect that the implicit mental model of causally relating "direction buttons" and "controlling directions" is very strongly embedded, leading to a very high strength in routine. As the experiment was short, not enough time was given for most agents to find out all "hidden rules" governing the decision-making system's structure and behavior. Strunz & Chlupsa (2019) also tested for a possible correlation between overcoming routine and self-reported levels in "Joyous Exploration", which is part of the multi-dimensional emotion "Curiosity". However, no relation between any of the 5 curiosity dimensions (Kashdan et al., 2018) and NPS performance was found. Participants who gained true rule knowledge did not report higher scores in "Joyous Exploration" and in fact, no correlation to any of the remaining 4 curiosity-dimension were found. The study did confirm that reflection time—that is thinking time measured as response time—did pay off.

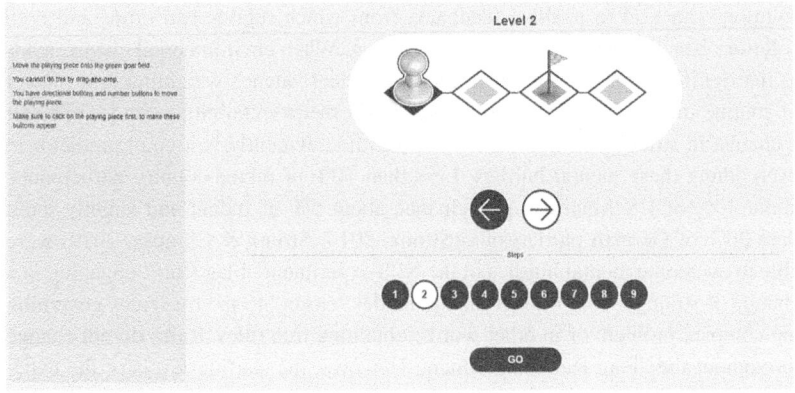

Figure 2.11 Client-side view of "Flag Run" experiment. *Source* Strunz & Chlupsa, 2019, p. 116

Participants consisted of Amazon Mechanical Turk freelancers (MTurks), who benefit financially from solving any task as fast as possible. Studies have shown that the main motivation of any MTurk was "compensation" (Lovett, Bajaba, Lovett, & Simmering, 2018), so that MTurks are suitable participants for experiments, where thinking time was associated with costs and is not incentivized (Strunz & Chlupsa, 2019). Noise from cultural differences in uncertainty avoidance, influenced by the cultural learning environment (Funke, 2014), all MTurks were expected, and differences in NPS performance by country-origin were indeed found (Strunz, 2019).

In all "Flag Run" experiments, agents who started investing in reflection time where more likely to find true rule knowledge (Chlupsa & Strunz, 2019; Strunz, 2019; Strunz & Chlupsa, 2019). This was true for all country origins. Agents who obtained true rule knowledge solved the overall experiment with less operators or "actions" and in a shorter timeframe, therefore being more efficient, even though having invested more time. Agents who obtained true rule knowledge showed less meaningless or random operators. Strunz & Chlupsa (2019) assume that these agents outperformed in learning from uncertainty or learning from unexpected feedback:

> *"While many researches and economists press the importance of skills that enhance adaption to changing conditions, it has to be understood that overcoming routine and its linked set of behavioral biases is not easily performed, and can probably only be done by a small fraction of leaders and employees, when there is not much time to reflect on the problem at hand"*

(p. 122).

While "Flag Run" is less complex in its causal structure than any Microworld experiment, and its causal structure is even simpler than most Minimal Complex Systems, "Flag Run" still is very knowledge-rich. Its hidden rules, making it a CPS task, have to be explored by overcoming a mental model, stemming from strong a-priori routine, to simulate real economic problems, where decisions have to be made quickly and in a non-routine manner, to adapt to the ever-changing VUCA world. Agents had to use heuristics as in ignoring information learnt before and also had to adapt a strategy similar to an algorithmic procedure. "Flag Run" has learnt from the advantages of both worlds: the simplicity of Minimal Complex Systems and the necessity of knowledge-rich structures of Microworlds. As a NPS task, "Flag Run" builds upon the understanding of "All models are wrong" (Sterman, 2002), and that experiments building upon this simple rule will probably further confirm the realization "Complexity from Simplicity", once beautifully shown by John Horton Conway's "Game of Life". Nature's true complexity is simulated in "Flag Run", as even simple structures can result in complex problems either due to our resistance in recognizing "being in error", human overconfidence or due to the circumstance of life that with unavoidable uncertainty comes immanent potential of self-deception. Being overconfident was shown to be influenced by testosterone (Dalton & Ghosal, 2018), which can result in socially beneficial values such as reduction of anxiety or providing information. Being overconfident can also have negative consequences when it is mostly the result of self-deception, not carrying any psychological benefits—the social benefit from overconfidence mainly depends on the environment and private information (Schwardmann & Van der Weele, 2017).

This brings the current sub-chapter to the final conclusion that uncertainty can only be fully reduced by self-deception. An agent can either invest in some decision frame by communication, which is associated with costs, to reduce uncertainty with some risk-averse strategy. The agent can mentally nullify uncertainty by self-deception, risking potential follow-up costs, or in other words accepting "deception potential" by building upon some mental "truth". As this thesis remains upon the understanding that uncertainty cannot be fully "eradicated" and that "all models are wrong", deception potential is understood as being immanent. A full recap of section 2.4 will follow in section 2.4.5

2.4.5   The Human Class: An Unbounded Set of Strategies

In order to neither fall for the "bias bias" (Brighton & Gigerenzer, 2015), nor for unrealistic assumptions of agents always maximizing, the "middle ground" should not be ignored, as agents seem to be able to maximize under certain circumstances (Erev & Roth, 2014), while still forming biased attitudes (Fazio et al., 2004, 2015; Rocklage & Fazio, 2014) towards problems by exploration, reducing uncertainty. Problems under uncertainty and risk are to be separated, whereas risk and uncertainty can be linked in a continuum (Samson & Gigerenzer, 2016), controlling both ends by learning from feedback (Van der Kleij et al., 2015). Feedback is easily misinterpreted, and all learning is a feedback process (Sterman, 2006). In complex environments learning from feedback is also influenced by framing or interpreting information, the order of information coming from feedback (Keil et al., 2016) and real world deception (Fuller et al., 2011). Individual characteristics, fear of uncertainty or lack of resources (Chong et al., 2018; Holmes-Rovner et al., 2000) render adaption to new conditions a challenge, due to routine strength (Betsch et al., 2001) and cognitive dissonance facing counter-intuitive problems (Donnarumma et al., 2016). In order to measure CPS which is linked to NPS (Neubert et al., 2015) it is important to realize that strategy change will only occur when change actually interferes with an agent's strategy (Cañas, Quesada, Antolí, & Fajardo, 2003). Experiments should measure the critical success factor for NPS, being experiential learning (Scholten et al., 2019), by looking at *when* behavioral changes occurs (De Houwer et al., 2013). Thus, the experimenter can observe each performed action of all agents live, as shown in figure 2.12.

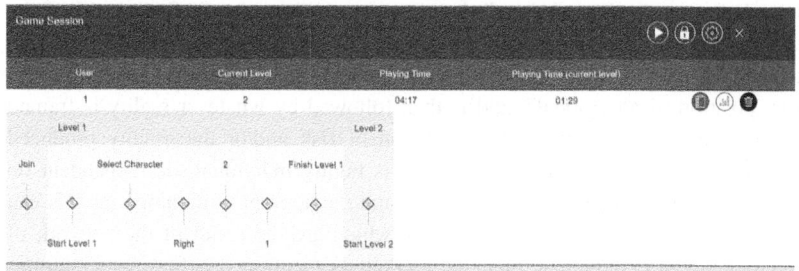

Figure 2.12   Paticipant's actions can be watched live via Curiosity IO backend. *Source* own source

Reflection time was found to be an effective predictor for overcoming "wrong" mental models (Strunz & Chlupsa, 2019), while this thesis remains upon the understanding that all mental models are wrong (Sterman, 2002), and that uncertainty can only be nullified by self-deception, which comes along with advantages and disadvantages (Schwardmann & Van der Weele, 2017). Therefore, deception potential is regarded as being immanent. For this reason, complexity can grow from very simple problem spaces, with "Flag Run" combining all advantages from both Microworlds and Minimal Complex Systems, when trying to measure whether or not some agent is able to find hidden information, and is able to adapt its strategy based upon novel knowledge under circumstances, where time is considered a resource.

Combining all mentioned insights agents are seen analogue to disturbances, which are able to inhibit special features leading to outcomes that are more than just a nonconformity to some anticipated value. Agents are regarded as an "unbounded set of strategies", producing perturbing deviations. As any model is wrong, no theory nor decision-making agent can ultimately nullify uncertainty (creating the bound of some set), and when it does, it can only do so by self-deception (defining some set with a bound), meaning that some theory predicting human behavior will always be wrong, given the right circumstances (redefining the set's boundary). Defining some model as being either "descriptive", "normative" or "prescriptive" seems to avoid this problem at first hand, but whether this differentiation led to sustainable "normative" models, more efficient "descriptive" re-evaluations or more precise "prescriptions" is to be discussed in section 2.5. In mathematics, problems which arise from set theory, which are much alike the problems in trying to establish various "types" of decision-making categories for models (normative, descriptive, prescriptive etc.), are elegantly solved by introducing an "unbounded set", better expressed as "class": Getting rid of the more primitive "set theoretical" understanding, by basing mathematics on "category theory". In this understanding, a "human class" is always placed "at the first position of any model", and is then followed by whatever reality is framed by this very agent, with its interpretation of risk and/or uncertainty produced by some expert system. Framing reality is highly individualistic, dependent on beliefs, stemming from intrinsic motives and the attempt to combine models can always lead to unexpected disturbances, which are the result of the network of interdependent beliefs. The financial market, as mentioned before, was interpreted by W. Brian Arthur (1995) as such a network of interdependent beliefs. All of the above is expressed in "Complexity Economics". Complexity economics does not assume an economy necessarily to be in equilibrium. Agents change their actions and strategies according to the outcome, which they collectively create. This will constantly favor change, to which they adapt their strategy anew. In a complex economy, agents' strategies and beliefs are frequently tested, with the entire system being best described as a redundant, ever-changing function—analogue to the described definition of "information". Therefore, complexity economics defines an economy not as something physically existing, but rather as a network of contingent states, being embedded in indeterminacy, where outcome is based upon interdependent sense-making, with the entire system necessarily being open to change (Arthur, 1999).

Section 2.5 will focus on how agents' decision making is altered in a network where they can assume feedback being either random, machine- or human-made, can communicate with or deceive others, perform in problem-solving when communication is impossible. Putting the cart before the horse, section 2.5 will begin with a more precise definition of "model" and its linked categories from decision-making theory.

2.5   A Network of Interdependent Beliefs

Models in decision-making theory can be distinguished by three categories or types: normative, descriptive, and prescriptive. "The three-way distinction emerged clearly in the 1980s (Freeling, 1984; Baron, 1985; Bell et al., 1988)—all of whom wrote independently of each other), although various parts of it were implicit in the writing of Herbert Simon and many philosophers (such as J. S. Mill)." (Baron, 2012).

Descriptive models are interested in why agents decide as they do, while normative models try to describe how agents ideally behave, and prescriptive models are concerned in prescribing enhancing feature for a certain decision-making process (Mandel, Navarrete, Dieckmann, & Nelson, 2019).

According to Baron (2012), normative models do not have to be or even must not be justified by observations, as long as enough data was acquired by observation to clearly frame the normative model; less obvious normative models i.e. simple correspondence are justified due by philosophical or mathematical argument.

Baron (2012) describes descriptive models as psychological theories, often explaining in cognitive ways how agents behave. These models include heuristics, strategies, and formal mathematical models. When observations depart from normative models, useful descriptive models can explain these departures, referring to such deviations in behavior as "bias" when such departure is systematic.

Prescriptive models are defined by Baron (2012) as engineering models, originally thought of including mathematical tools to analyze decisions or being educational interventions, such as teaching agents various heuristics to exclude certain decision-making strategies that can lead to bias during certain circumstances. Prescriptive models include the idea of nudging people for them to perform normatively better choices.

It is argued that this three-fold distinction is necessary, and none of the three model types should be combined, so that judgements and decisions can be improved or at least preserved in their quality (Baron, 2012); in order to do so, it has to be understood what makes judgements "good". Baron (2012) suggests the introduction of such distinguishing categories regarding quality, so that data can be collected on the "goodness" of certain judgements, monitored, and tested for improvement potential (Baron, 2012).

By the concept of "Judgment and decision making", models are to be defined in order to improve judgements and decisions, have to be re-evaluated by the three-fold criteria of a model, define what "good" judgements are and what circumstances alter them in a more positive or negative way. In this chapter, judgements in an interdependent network of beliefs are to be considered.

Section 2.5.1 introduces the theoretical approach to multiplayer decision-making and section 2.5.2 will focus on multiplayer experiments in behavioral economics.

2.5.1   From Game Theory to Behavioral Game Theory

Game theory has not only become a fundamental economic tool for theoretical, but also empirical science (Fudenberg & Levine, 2016). Game Theory is looking at multiplayer decision-making scenarios, referred to as "games", and is not only some abstract economical model. According to Fudenberg & Tirole (1991), game theory was for example applied in theoretical biology, considering animals as being agents, who follow a set of pure strategies.

The most important aspect of game theory is that individual decisions and "games" are distinguished. While isolated agents are only concerned about uncertainties stemming from their surrounding environment, interdependent decisions by multiple agents being part of a common decision-making domain also have to consider uncertainties coming from their co-agents' behavior, whose behavior can potentially influence the actions of all agents (Fudenberg & Tirole, 1991). Another key difference between individual decisions and games are "zero probabilities" or decision potential, which are irrelevant for decisions but are an intrinsic cornerstone for games (Fudenberg & Tirole, 1991). In order to make predictions about how a game will play out or change its path, "Nash-Equilibria" are used. Nash equilibria describe a certain path or recipe on how a game will unfold, and if all agents figured out this Nash equilibrium to be reached, no agent had any reason not to behave as described by the prescribed recipe. According to this logic, only a Nash equilibrium can be predicted by agents, and can be assumed to be predicted by co-agents. Any prediction that comes to the conclusion that an equilibrium other than a Nash equilibrium is reached, the agent or another co-agent has to perform a "mistake" or "error" (Fudenberg & Tirole, 1991).

Fudenberg & Tirole (1991) follow up by stating that "errors", such as "mistakes", may likely occur, and in order to predict them requires the game theorists to know more about the outcome of the game than its participants. The authors state that "Nash equilibria" cannot be considered "good predictions" in all situations, as not all information is contained in the game theoretical model, such as individual experiences of the participants, which can be influenced by culture.

The authors state that in order to define a complete theory, "error" can be regarded as a human-made mistake "with small probability". Error can also find its origin in "Payoff Uncertainty". The latter renders both modeller and player being unable to be fully certain about any "payoff" value, as suggested by "Fudenberg, Kreps and Levine" (Fudenberg & Tirole, 1991, p. 467). Allowing small payoff uncertainty can have large effects. According to Fudenberg, Kreps and Levine no economically interesting situation is lacking payoff uncertainty, and thought-experiments excluding payoff uncertainty may not be reasonable. This is referred to as the "uncertainty problem". How the cause for "error" is defined by a certain model to be the most likely cause, defines the best model for this specific set of data, however, even small causes have the power to shift an equilibrium (Fudenberg & Tirole, 1991).

With the introduction of constant uncertainty, common knowledge is defined, which not only includes payoff uncertainty, but also the initial uncertainty of each agent about the game's structure (Fudenberg & Tirole, 1991). This formal definition of knowledge leads to "technical and philosophical problems" (Fudenberg & Tirole, 1991, p. 547), some of which were already noted with reference to the "frame problem". However, small changes (perturbations) in a game's information structure (common knowledge in an informal sense) has the power to change an agent's knowledge and therefore alters common knowledge, rendering an exact description of common knowledge to be fuzzy (Fudenberg & Tirole, 1991). A fuzzy common knowledge solution is the "almost common knowledge" concept by Monderer and Samet (1989), which "requires that all players be "pretty sure" that their opponents are "pretty sure" about payoffs (...)" (Fudenberg & Tirole, 1991, p. 564).

The authors show how Nash equilibria are changed entirely by perturbations in their information structure and that the sensitivity

> *"of even the Nash-equilibrium set to low-probability infinite-state perturbations is another reason to think seriously about the robustness of one's conclusions to the information structure of the game."*

(Fudenberg & Tirole, 1991, p. 570).

In more modern approaches of game theory, payoff uncertainty is usually always part of testing models for stability. To enhance game theory, several behavioral models where formed to establish "Behavioral Game Theory", such as the cognitive hierarchy (CH) model, used to predict initial conditions in a repeated game, the quantal response equilibrium (QRE), where agents may perform small mistakes, maintaining correct belief about co-agents' intentions, the Experience-Weighted Attraction Learning (EWA), which predict a decision path as a function operating on initial conditions, and various learning models, which include the understanding of the learning progress of co-agents, strategic teaching and reputation-building, leading to games outside of equilibrium (Camerer & Ho, 2015).

The term "behavioral" is being described by economical, psychological and decision sciences roughly as "being about mental processes" (Gavetti, 2012, p. 267). Modern behavioral economics still study "noise" in coordination games, where agents deviate from their routine because of mistakes, wrong perceptions, inertia or trial-and-error (Mäs & Nax, 2016). Mäs & Nax (2016) constructed a complex experiment, where agents played coordination games with multiple network partners, in games consisting of 20 subjects playing coordination games 150 times: The subjects were neither informed about the game's causal structure nor about their co-agents' types; agents were informed about their own payoff, the last round's choice of their co-agents, but not about the payoff of their opponents. The experiment found 96% of decisions to be myopic best responses, and being highly sensitive to their costs.

Costs and feedback create boundaries which have to be overcome in order to maximize by learning. A study by Bayer & Chan (2007) researched the famous "Dirty-Faces" game by a laboratory experiment, where iterative thinking ("He knows, that I know, that He knows…") is required in order follow common rationality. They authors arrived at the conclusion that a threshold exists between participants performing more than one and two or more meta-levels of iteration, due to the individuals being limited in their ability to apply such meta-cognitive thinking or because the agents considered higher order meta-level thinking to be useless, as their co-agents were expected to be unable to perform higher order meta-level thinking themselves (Bayer & Chan, 2007).

The cognitive hierarchy (CH) model attempts to anticipate human behavior in one-shot games, building upon the number of meta-thinking levels a participant performs (Camerer, Ho, & Chong, 2001). Agents who perform zero steps of thinking are considered behaving random, irrational or not strategically. With performing one level of iterated thinking, participants are considered to behave strategic. The CH model requires some estimate on how meta-level thinking is distributed amongst the participants. For this purpose, the efficient Poisson distribution is used, and participants' heterogeneity is modelled into a thinking-steps model, which calculates the initial probability of individual choice. The model was fitted to data from three studies with a 2558 subject-games (Camerer & Ho, 2001). The thinking-steps model outperformed the quantal response equilibrium model, which assumed only one type per participant. The strength of the thinking-steps model was considered to be its modelling of a multitude of types per participant, i.e. agent heterogeneity. The behavioral game theory model was compared to the classic Nash equilibrium predictions, where the thinking-model predictions were closer to data than Nash equilibrium predictions. The equilibrium predictions by Nash equilibrium were mostly distributed amongst the limits, being either "0" or "1". This is shown in figure 2.13 (Camerer & Ho, 2001).

Still, game theoretical assumptions about common knowledge and rationality have not been shown to be followed by participants in interactive games in real life experiments, and common knowledge and rationality were disregarded as being a model for social interaction (Colman, 2003). Drew Fudenberg and David K. Levine (2016) suggested to enhance game theory with learning theory by simulation, using belief-based learning models, maintaining simplicity, by embedding complex learning theory into game theory and establishing breadth by combining static game theory and dynamic learning theory (Fudenberg & Levine, 2016).

128   *Behavioural Game Theory: Thinking/Learning/Teaching*

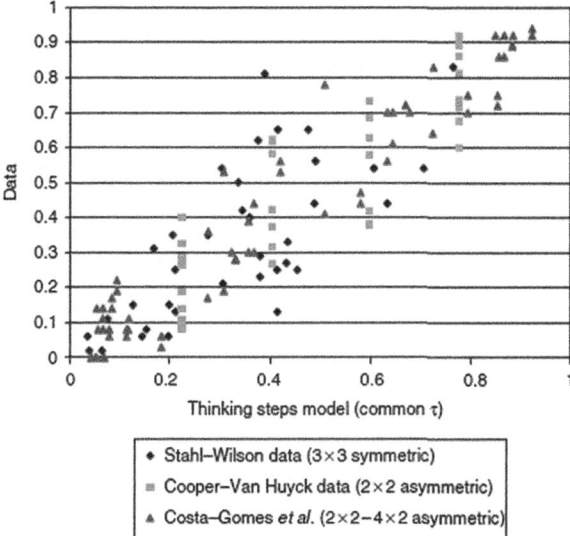

Figure 8.2   Fit of thinking-steps model to three games ($R^2 = 0.84$)

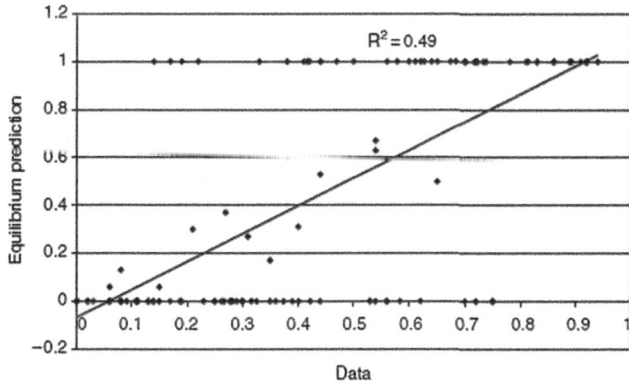

Figure 8.3   Nash equilibrium predictions versus data in three games

Figure 2.13   Behavioral game theory vs. game theory, experimental results. *Source* C. Camerer & Ho, 2001, p. 128

Today, there also exist claims that game theorists wrongly assume the uncertainty problem to be solved by agents accumulating information, even going as far as stating that the game-theoretical object of rationality cannot be described with persisting uncertainty, rendering game theory to be "irrelevant and useless", while the true challenge was to explain the existence of heterogeneous transactions and social interactions by accepting ever-remaining uncertainty (Syll, 2018). In another very critical article, the economist Berhard Guerrien (2018) quotes Andrew Schotter, a former Morgenstern student, to show that game theory has more fruitful potential in the domain of "cooperative", instead of "non-cooperative" game theory. According to this quote by Schotter, von Neumann and Morgenstern were originally trying to break problems stemming from the infinite chain of meta-thinking by introducing strategically interdependent situations that are independent of their expectation of their co-agent (Guerrien, 2018). Guerrien (2018) further states that game theoretical constraints concerning which information is available to participants, were unrealistic and never verified by experiments.

In total, game theory marks an important backbone for behavioral economics, from which many fruitful concepts, realizations and ideas were born. Learning, as a feedback process, benefits from knowledge. As stated before, knowledge cannot be formalized by any instant, game theory included, because such a process would render it instantly as information instead. A formalization of knowledge results in paradoxes, ad infinitum problems and logical debates, similar to the problems of old-fashioned "set theory" or as explained by the "frame problem". Therefore, game theory is constrained in its possibilities as is any other way to model reality: it offers normative models for efficient computations, can be used as a platform for useful explanations in form of descriptive models or used as a "language" to build decision-making enhancing predictive models. Game theory has also shown the importance of sensitivity to perturbations in any normative model that builds upon the concept of an information structure. To the understanding of the author, game theory does not claim having solved the uncertainty problem, at least not exceptionally. Fudenberg and Tirole (1991), one of the golden standards of game theory, summing up the entirety of game theoretical insights until 1989 in one book, have claimed various times that models assuming perfect information or zero uncertainty are not even meaningful—even as a Gedankenexperiment.

The next sub-chapter will concentrate on a few examples of group behavior phenomena observed under experimental conditions and described by game theoretical normative models.

2.5.2   Group Behavior

As stated before, this thesis is interested in group behavior changes, when being confronted with different types of information. Specifically, this thesis' experiment simulates group decision making under uncertainty, where communication between agents is *not* possible. In order to describe scientific research in such a domain, several phenomena of group decision making where communication *is* possible are also listed, in order to exclude such behavioral instances further on.

Decision problems including more than one decision maker are studied in the domain of group decision making (GDM) (G. Li, Kou, & Peng, 2018). Studies on GDM are usually considering how much communication is allowed and how the final outcome is created by group decision making (Tindale & Winget, 2019). Several insights from GDM are listed by Tindale & Winget (2019): groups holding members of high expertise on the task at hand can improve overall group performance; individual motivation for the whole group to perform "accurate decisions" has a positive impact on group performance; groups can perform well without communication; communication will decrease group performance in situations where members are "less than wise"; shared group bias on the decision environment will "exacerbate" these biases (p. 28). When communication between agents is possible, imitation and herding behavior are popular examples of group behavior.

Imitation and innovation have been described as the "dual engines of cultural learning" (Legare & Nielsen, 2015). It is known that humans imitate each other during social interactions, which positively influences action comprehension such as improving language comprehension (Adank, Hagoort, & Bekkering, 2010). Even emotions can be "imitated" in form of emotional contagion, which can improve perceptions of task performance (Barsade, 2002). "Imitate-the-best" and "imitate-the-majority" has been found to speed up individual learning under uncertainty (Garcia-Retamero, Takezawa, & Gigerenzer, 2009).

In a software based experiment it was found that groups were able to find novel solutions to problems that would have been missed by individuals, since interpersonal imitation shifts the group towards the urge to find more promising solutions; however, the size of the group can have significant and nonlinear impact on the groups behavior and performance using imitation (Wisdom & Goldstone, 2011).

Next to imitation, the herding effect is especially relevant for analysis in crowd psychology, where irrationality can arise from group behavior, accumulating deception potential, leading to such phenomena like "exploding market bubbles", which is also referred to as "information cascades" (Samson & Gigerenzer,

2016, p. 109). Herding describes individual agents to imitate group behavior as a whole, rather than following own strategies (Hwang & Salmon, 2004). It has been shown by game theoretical analysis that time and frequency of public information can impact the collective learning process, and that public information can help a herd to overcome a wrong belief and inefficient paths (Bohren, 2014). Neuroscientific models suggest that social alignment is mediated by a system that monitors misalignment and rewards actions leading back to alignment (Shamay-Tsoory, Saporta, Marton-Alper, & Gvirts, 2019). For this purpose, information is required. In international markets, herding was found to depend on the level of information transparency (Choi & Skiba, 2015).

When communication between agents is not possible, due to costs, security, technical problems or language barriers, coordination and cooperation without communication in some problem-space can be performed by "focal" real life decision influencers or prominent solutions, referred to as "focal points" or "Schelling points" (Zuckerman, Kraus, & Rosenschein, 2011). They are defined as "a point of convergence of expectations or beliefs without communication" (Teng, 2018, p. 250). Such Schelling points were proposed as equilibrium refinements of the Nash equilibrium, where the ideal game theoretical strategy has to both consider actions of cooperation and coordination of potential conflict (Teng, 2018). Experiments found groups to outperform individuals in coordination games with focal points, when individual interests of the group were compatible and cognitive input was helpful for controlling the coordination problem (Sitzia & Zheng, 2019); groups report worse levels of coordination when interests are not aligned. In coordination games, groups are also more sensitive to salience (Sitzia & Zheng, 2019).

Group planning behavior differs from individual planning behavior in decision environments governed by either objective risk or subjective risk, the latter being referred to as "ambiguity" (Carbone, Georgalos, & Infante, 2019). In their study, Carbone, Georgalos & Infante (2019) focused on sequential group decision making behavior reacting to novel information. In the objective risk treatment, participants were informed about the statistical chances of their income, i.e. agents were informed about the amount of balls being hidden in urns, such that agents could manifest a realistic mental model of the experiment's creation of risk. During the subjective risk treatment, no such information was provided to the participants. While individuals and groups were found to "substantially" deviate from the optimal, theoretical strategy, facing a stochastic and dynamic problem, individuals outperformed groups under objective risk, whereas groups outperformed individuals under subjective risk (Carbone et al., 2019). Furthermore, both group and individual were found to make myopic decisions under objective and subjective risk (Carbone et al., 2019). When tested for planning, groups were closer to rationality under ambiguity, creating more welfare (Carbone et al., 2019). The study comes to the conclusion that there exists a non-neutral attitude towards ambiguity (Carbone et al., 2019), which affects trust decisions. A negative attitude towards ambiguity correlated with a more negative attitude towards trusting options, while agents who considered themselves as trustworthy, were more likely to trust other agents (C. Li, Turmunkh, & Wakker, 2019). Therefore, subjective belief about others can have a crucial influence in group decision making. It is suggested to not model subjective belief simply as subjective probability (Andersen, Fountain, Harrison, & Rutström, 2014), as risk attitudes of individual agents have to be carefully considered first (Andersen et al., 2014). How to model subjective belief is described as an open question, and agents may not only hold a traditional type of aversion towards risk, but also towards uncertainty, when decisions are made in a domain being governed by subjective instead of objective uncertainties (Andersen et al., 2014).

A good example on individual behavior towards uncertainty comes from random group matching procedures. Multiplayer experiments which match participants randomly, can result in the participants feeling to be treated unfairly, when their partners behave suboptimal towards them. This was in fact experienced during pre-tests of the thesis' experiment. Ballinger, Hudson, Karkoviata, & Wilcox (2011) claim that "working memory capacity" (WMC) mediates the ability of participants to react to such situations with more or less sovereignty, with WMC working as a mental buffer (Ballinger et al., 2011). WMC also supposedly predicts performance on how agents can adapt their "depth of reasoning" throughout experiments with growing structural complexity (Ballinger et al., 2011; Strunz, 2019).

Improved performance by groups compared to individual decision-making is commonly achieved by interpersonal communication (Charness, Cooper, & Grossman, 2015). When subjects work together via computer interfaces, communication costs can counterintuitively enhance group performance; while higher costs in communication reduces message quantity, they enhance message quality in groups, so that groups facing communication costs outperform individuals significantly (Charness et al., 2015). However, in cases when communication likely introduces error, more communication is not always better than less. In such cases, assigning costs to communication enhances performance (Charness et al., 2015).

Group decision making under uncertainty profits from communication, as shared information will increase decision quality, when information is sufficiently processed by the group; when shared information is insufficiently processed, groups tend to be overconfident in their decision making (Sniezek, 1992). Social factors such as face-to-face discussions and the goal to reach consensus are described to influence group confidence (Sniezek, 1992).

Experimental research about the influence of expertise and information in GDM under uncertainty in an environment, where no communication is possible, is scarce. Such a domain could be thought of multiple agents working with a personal computer, making decisions by investing in a certain market, where each agent does not know its co-agents. Still, all of the agents' decisions are interdependent and all agents will collectively see the same market results. Uncertainties might arise from different sources, such as uncertainty about the number of co-agents, causal relationship of group invest and market results or whether own action is of effective relevance. Uncertainties can stem from doubt, e.g. by asking the question whether there was an optimal group strategy, if such a strategy could actually be achieved and if maximization was possible with limited information about the causal relations. In general, two kinds of uncertainties in group decision making are considered: environmental and social uncertainty (Messick, Allison, & Samuelson, 1988).

It has been shown that communication highly reduces environmental and social uncertainties "by enhancing group coordination and performance" (Messick et al., 1988, p. 678). Furthermore, it was experimentally shown that agents are risk-averse regarding environmental uncertainty, are less influenced by social uncertainty, while individual risk aversion was not influenced by communication at all (Messick et al., 1988).

Individual experience, such as proficiency, also mediates how external information is interpreted and which measures are ultimately taken, as shown by disaster risk reduction decision-making: risk expressed by numbers or by verbal clues differed in their impact, while its impact also depended on whether or not an agent was a scientist or not, as scientists had more experience with risk expressed via numerical probabilities (Doyle, McClure, Paton, & Johnston, 2014). However, verbal clues were consistently found to be regarded as more ambiguous than numerical terms (Doyle et al., 2014). In addition, probabilities were found to be commonly misinterpreted by the participants (Doyle et al., 2014).

In summary, GDM under uncertainty without the ability to communicate with other agents will be influenced by individual expertise regarding performance, due to routine strength and their interpretation of information. The lack of communication does not necessarily lead to worse group performance, which depends on the collective status of "wise" decision making, the decision-domain's resistance to error-perturbation, and individual motivation to let the group make accurate decisions. Biases stemming from communication such as social influences, herd behavior, imitation, collective bias and overconfidence can be excluded. Prominent solutions or Schelling points can be expected, when all agents have had similar "single-player" experience and expertise. Ideally, working memory capacity is measured in such an experiment in order to understand individual stress resistance to "unfair" group constellations. The individual types of risk-aversion should not be influenced by the lack of communication. In the example of GDM under uncertainty, risk is seen as the individual attempt to try a strategy which deviates from a strategy that has been shown to be effective in the past. As participants in GDM have shown to be less risk averse towards social uncertainty, and are more risk averse to environmental uncertainty, information that is interpreted by an agent as there being good reason to belief that other agents are influencing the game, will more likely lead to deviation from the former "effective" strategy than with information that is interpreted by an agent as there being good reason to belief that random or uncontrollable instances are influencing the game.

General Research Objectives 3

In order to formulate specific research objectives, this chapter condenses insights from the theoretical background, deriving key objectives that are to be analyzed empirically. Following the "Engaged Scholarship Diamond Model", designed to close the theory-practice gap (Ntounis & Parker, 2017), the four domains "Theory Building", "Problem Formulation", "Problem Solving" and "Research Design" are to be fulfilled in any preferred order by the researcher (Van de Ven, 2007). This thesis' conclusion serves as "Problem Solving" and will bridge real world problems ("Reality") and empirical results from empirical research ("Solution"). Heading from reality to theory, problem formulation included potential rise in complexity by globalization and the limitations of humans performing complex problem-solving. Information and expert knowledge were then identified by theory as being critical influencers in individual and group decision-making. The following first sub-chapter sums up key findings of the theoretical background. The resulting model, which is linked to some solution via the experimental research design, is to be explained in the second sub-chapter. A brief framework of a suitable experiment is provided in the third sub-chapter (Figure 3.1).

3.1   Summary of Key Findings

Besides limitations in financial resources, change and human resources were described as being the fundamental problems for interconnected institutions, engaged in complex problems of global proportions. In order to better cope with unpredictable change, expert knowledge is increasingly embedded in decision-making processes. Routine-strength can inhibit decision-makers to adapt to change effectively, while knowledge and feedback interpretation are influencing success in

© The Author(s) 2021   67
U. G. Strunz, *The Impact of Individual Expertise and Public Information on Group Decision-Making*, FOM-Edition Research,
https://doi.org/10.1007/978-3-658-33139-9_3

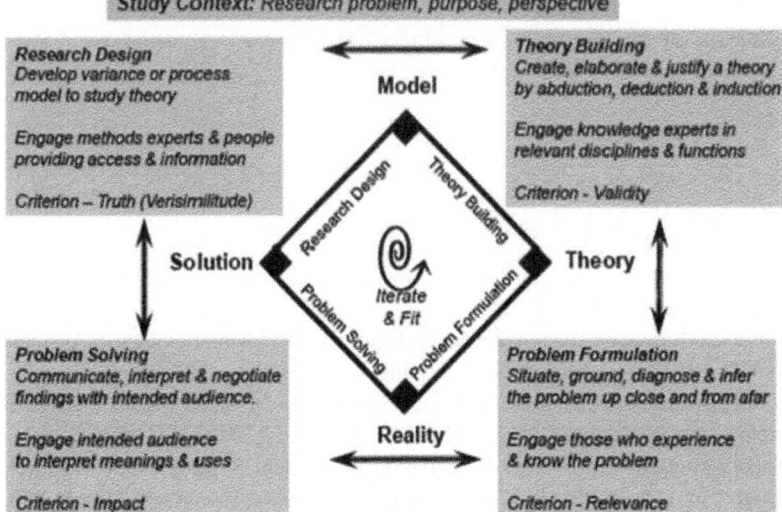

Figure 3.1 The Engaged Scholarship Diamond Model by Van de Ven (2007). *Source* Ntounis & Parker, 2017, p. 353

overcoming routine. Expertise is formed by many iterations of acting in a certain domain, with heterogeneous feedback coming from this domain, and is therefore a learning process, as all learning is a feedback process. The environment of such a domain is a predictor for maximization and learning itself, and can also lead to bias and to self-deception building upon illogical or even logical mental models. This can either make adaption to a novel, more efficient and effective strategy harder or easier. Experiments have shown that environmental conditions only influence a change in an agent's strategy, when feedback or the agent's interpretation of feedback confirms that the new environmental conditions lead to a performance downswing, when the routine strategy is not altered. Environmental conditions generally lead to different behavior when being formulated as being either man-made or its source being stochastic. Social or man-made change leads to agents trying to optimize via pattern recognition, whereas stochastic change leads to agents trying maximization via logical rationale. Risk, being expressed as either verbal or numerical probabilities are being interpreted differently, depending on the agent's knowledge—however, humans tend to not behave optimal when probabilities are provided. Groups and individuals behave differently facing problems under uncertainty, also depending on whether or not groups are able to communicate within. Group performance is also influenced by its member's expertise and performance, while individual expertise is hard to predict reliably via knowledge span, e.g. years of experience.

Two major aspects are then to be researched: the impact of public information and expertise on group decision-making, when facing a problem under uncertainty. Public information will either be communicated actively via text messages, which are actively announced via pop-up notifications or passively via visual clues. In both cases, public information is therefore considered change. There will also be a case, where change is neither announced actively, nor passively, and agents will have to figure out change themselves via feedback interpretation. Change will either impede strategy performance or not. The dependent variables will not only focus on decision-making performance but also behavior, and therefore strategy changes or accordingly strategy persistence. In no case will an agent be deceived by public information, a distinguishing aspect of the model for empirical research from psychological attempts including deception.

3.2 Model for Empirical Research

In order to test the influence of expert knowledge or expertise, the experiment has to be designed in such a way for participants being able to maximize in a domain, where feedback is part of a stable, well-defined problem. Participants can then use their optimal strategy in a second well-defined domain including little change, and then adopt their strategy in an ill-defined but metastable domain, with lots of change hidden from them, where the strategy from the well-defined domain still leads to maximization. During the well-defined stages, all agents act alone in isolation. In the ill-defined stages, agents will act as a group. The experiment will be based on the thoroughly researched puzzle game "Tower of Hanoi". The multiplayer version of "Tower of Hanoi" is designed by a deterministic 64-state algorithm, which ensures that every agent of a group has influence over the outcome, but does not necessarily impact the outcome. The algorithm does not change during the ill-defined stages. Also, without communication, no participant can gain full control over the outcome. Therefore, even if the true rules governing the experiment during the multiplayer version are known, the outcome of some action remains unknown, making these stages ill-defined. However, a group can outperform randomness by sticking to the ideal strategy from the well-defined stages. Finally, the metastable, ill-defined domain will inhibit little change at some point, which vastly changes the inner dynamics and feedback becomes "chaotic" with high certainty. In theory however, all stages, including well-defined and ill-defined stages, can be solved in the same number of moves. Feedback itself will remain stable, i.e. logical from some strategic perspective during the well-defined domain. If the strategy is not altered in the well-defined domain after little change was introduced, performance will be worse, and feedback will remain logical from some strategic perspective. Feedback will remain seemingly logical from some strategic perspective during the metastable and ill-defined domain, but can also become chaotic from the perspective of some strategic perspective if some agents behaved "less than wise". Feedback will be chaotic with high certainty during the instable and ill-defined stages. This might lead to participants interpreting chaotic feedback as being purely random, and any action being equally bad, leading to a state of mind as being "indifferent". This can lead to agents acting blindly in accordance to their routine strategy or seemingly random. Feedback and therefore interpretation itself is then used as the defining "atoms" of the system, in accordance to some system being described by its system-states as "instable", "indifferent", "stable" and "metastable" (Jeschke & Mahnke, 2013). Figure 3.2 pictures these system states with intuitive diagrams.

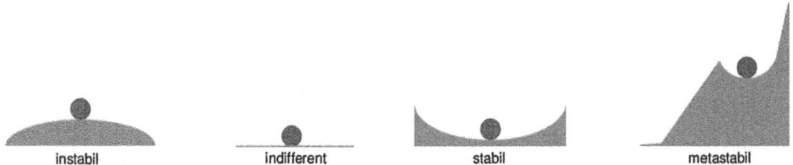

Figure 3.2 Considered system states: instable, indifferent, stable, metastable. *Source* Jeschke & Mahnke, 2013, p. 17

Passive change is performed by visual clues, being the "goal rod" of the "Tower of Hanoi" stages. Agents will have to solve Tower of Hanoi three times in a row with the rightmost rod being the goal rod, and then three times in a row with the center rod being the goal rod. The change will not be "actively" communicated, but will be communicated "passively" by visual clues, which are corrected for color-blind people, i.e. not only by color but also by non-announced text. During the well-defined stages, expertise in solving Tower of Hanoi will be measured. The passive change is considered as non-social environmental change. Participants who are not immediately aware of the goal rod change will perform worse. After a certain number of well-defined stages, participants will face ill-defined stages, where the "Tower of Hanoi" game is in fact a multiplayer-version.

Different types of public information, also including no public information are tested in various information conditions. Again, the goal rod will be changed after the same amount of stages as in the well-defined stages. Throughout the entire ill-defined stages, the same hidden rules apply. This experimental setup is further specified in table 3.1.

Table 3.1   Model for empirical research: system conditions of online experiment. *Source* own source

	Before (passive) **change**	**After** (passive) **change**
Well-defined (single-player)	Stable system, logical feedback.	Stable system, logical feedback.
Ill-defined (multiplayer)	Metastable system, seemingly logical feedback.	Instable system, seemingly chaotic feedback, possibly leading to indifference.

3.3   Experimental Framework for Research Objectives

In order to measure the impact of public information and expertise, various information conditions and various forms of logic models have to be categorized. In other words, various information conditions and strategies have to be considered. Even well-defined problems of reality can usually be solved in more than one way. In order to enable two forms of logic being valid during the well-defined Tower of Hanoi game, the disks can "jump edges" just like in the "Flag Run" experiments. Therefore, even the well-defined stages can be solved in more than one way of thinking. Also, the direction cannot be influenced by the direction buttons during the ill-defined stages of the multiplayer version of Tower of Hanoi. As assumed by Strunz & Chlupsa (2019), direction buttons attract a deep intrinsic motive to be part of an agent's strategy, being ideal for testing non-routine problem-solving performance. In addition, the disks also jump edges during the ill-defined stages, and are collectively controlled by all agents of one group. Three agents per group were chosen, however, the number of agents per group can be chosen arbitrarily in accordance with the algorithm.

In summary, the experiment will research the following general research objectives: i) the impact of active public information about change on group problem-solving behavior, when such change does not have an influence on strategy performance, ii) the impact of passive public information about change on group problem-solving behavior, when such change does have an influence on strategy performance, iii) the impact of various forms of active public information, e.g. social change or stochastic change, on agents changing their routine strategy, iv) the impact of active public information about hidden rules on agents changing their routine strategy, v) the influence of individual expertise stemming from well-defined learning environments in ill-defined problem-solving domains regarding overcoming routine strategy and overall performance.

The experiment measuring these general research objectives is explained in the following chapter, after which the specific research questions and hypotheses are listed.

Empirical Research Design

4

The experiment consisted of three parts: the login-stage, the experiment and an after-survey. The experiment starts with 6 single-player Tower of Hanoi games to enable learning and to induce routine, referred to as "individual decision-making expertise in routine-strategy". The single-player rounds are followed by 6 three-player Tower of Hanoi games, where the first three multiplayer-games can be solved perfectly by the agents when sticking to the single player strategy.

This chapter is divided into three parts. The first part describes the software used to measure behavior changes in a complex problem-solving game. As two different versions of the software existed, emphasis on software development process will be laid upon and an overview of the evolutionary process of the experiment is described. The second part describes the participants of the study—details about their background, and where they were recruited from are provided. The third part will explain what participants had to do during the experiment, how data was collected and in which order the experiment was structured.

4.1 Development and Materials

Two different software versions of the experiment exist. The first version was programmed with "zTree",

> "a software package for developing and carrying out economic experiments."

Electronic supplementary material The online version of this chapter (https://doi.org/10.1007/978-3-658-33139-9_4) contains supplementary material, which is available to authorized users.

U. G. Strunz, *The Impact of Individual Expertise and Public Information on Group Decision-Making*, FOM-Edition Research,
https://doi.org/10.1007/978-3-658-33139-9_4

(Fischbacher, 2007, p. 172). The software running on zTree was developed in cooperation with a local German IT company. The second version was developed from scrap with same company and embedded in an also self-developed framework for behavioral experiments called "Curiosity IO".

4.1.1   Software Development Process

Development processes for both software versions oriented themselves at a combination of the classic "Waterfall" software development process and "scrum", using "Waterfall" as a framework, and embedding e.g. the face-to-face meetings suggested by scrum.

The software development method scrum

> *"assumes that the systems development process is an unpredictable, complicated process that can only be roughly described as an overall progression."*

(Schwaber, 1997, p. 1). "Water-Scrum-Fall" is a hybrid approach, where "Hybrid Agile methods are a reality in most Agile implementations" (West, 2011, p. 9) and the "Water-Scrum-Fall" approach offers a "simple set of principles, working practices, and roles for teams to execute (…) and guidance on team organization and transparency" (West, 2011, p. 11), while not excluding traditional development milestones. Here the "hybrid method in which traditional and agile approaches are combined seemingly provides the "win-win" situation." (Theocharis, Kuhrmann, Münch, & Diebold, 2015, p. 13). The simple Figure 4.1 from West et al. (2011) precisely shows the software development process for both experiments. After an extensive meeting ("Water"), the IT company developed the software via scrum, with weekly meetings ("Scrum"), and offered support with bug-fixing, and performance testing ("Fall") (West, 2011, p. 10). The development of Curiosity IO relied less on weekly meetings however and face-to-face meetings were no longer recorded in written form.

All milestones of the software development process are being listed in chronological order in the appendix table "Software Development Milestones" (see annex 1).

Figure 6 Water-Scrum-Fall Is The Reality

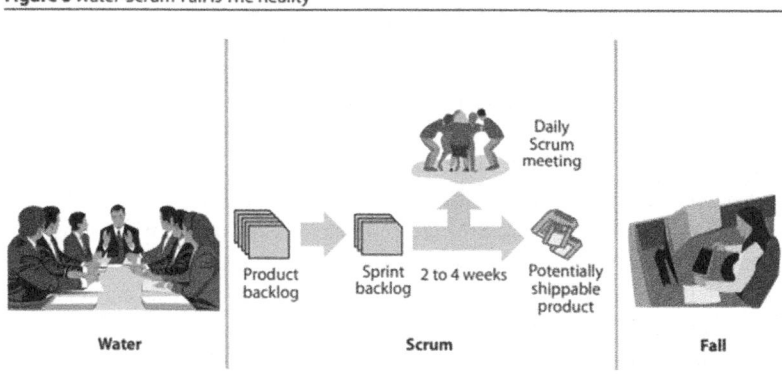

60109   Source: Forrester Research, Inc.

Figure 4.1   Software development process Water-Scrum-Fall. *Source* West, 2011, p. 10

4.1.2   Legacy Version of Experiment

While an experiment using the zTree program had been conducted and data was collected, both program and data were not used. Instead, Curiosity IO was developed, with an identical experiment, and its resulting data had been used for evaluation. The software development process of the zTree experiment, its application and the reasoning process for abolishing this program and its data will be described, before coming to Curiosity IO and its results. As this "failed" experiment led to new insights and improvement ideas concerning Curiosity IO, it is a fundamental cornerstone of the entire theoretical and practical process. As this legacy experiment was conducted in the historic "Hopfenpost" building in Munich, the experiment is referred to as the "Hopfenpost experiment". The Hopfenpost experiment will first be described, followed by critical analysis and its problems, ultimately leading to the decision to dismiss the experiment. Software documentation of the zTree software is attached in the appendix (see annex 1).

The first experiment was conducted with the zTree software version from 18th to 22th of June 2018 in a rented room located in the historic "Hopfenpost" Munich. This experiment was conducted "offline" with 264 participants, recruited by two hired companies. The only requirement for all participants was being fluent in German. Before, a website was created, attracting potential college participants with prizes and participation fees. However, this approach deemed to be ineffective to recruit participants. The two companies recruited 169 female, and 95 male participants for the experiment, with no further restrictions on the participants, such as graduation degrees, age or monthly income. Due to technical difficulties 210 data sets remain useful for analysis. During the five-day timespan, experiments had been conducted from 10 am to 5:30 pm in four groups, in one room, using 18 rented laptops, a 28-port switch, and 3 backup laptops. Due to hot weather, participants had access to water throughout the experiment. Fees were handed out in cash to each participant after the experiment.

Figure 4.2 shows the process of the Hopfenpost experiment, which was conducted via the zTree version of the Tower of Hanoi game. Players were first instructed to take a seat, and to self-report age and sex. Providing an email address was optional, and only necessary, if one was interested in winning a prize. Every experiment was assigned to either group 1 or group 2. Every group's experiment consisted of 4 stages. Before the first stage, participants were orally informed about their task. They had to solve several rounds of "Tower of Hanoi", iteratively answer a questionnaire, and were told about how to correctly use GUI elements in order to do so. They were not deceived by any wrong statement. In the first stage, both groups started with the regular one-player version of ToH, followed by a questionnaire, in order to self-report data on perceived stress (Cohen & Williamson, 1988) and self-reported uncertainty (Clampitt & Williams, 2000). Minor changes were made to both questionnaires to adapt their content to the experiment's context, e.g. replacing "months" by "rounds". The questionnaires were also translated into German and participants were instructed to use the German versions. These two questionnaires were answered after every stage. The second stage started with three rounds of three-player version Tower of Hanoi. Three rounds of three-player version Tower of Hanoi, being referred to as "Tower of Europe", is being played three times in a row as well during stages three and four. The global information between both groups differed in stage two. Global information was always provided orally, and in German. The first group was informed about the fact that they were now sharing control with two other people in this room. The second group did not receive any other information, other than there now being a "Please wait." screen popping up after each input, as output calculation differs. In stage three, the first group was told that the directional buttons did not and will not influence the game at all and in fact, had no influence at all during the past three games, and only change color when being pressed. The second group in stage three was now provided the same information as group 1 during stage two—that they are sharing control with two others in their room. The final stage four offered no new information to group 1 but did provide group

2 with the insight about the "dummy-effect" of the directional buttons, just like group 1 during stage three.

The experiment produced more than 400.csv files of data about the participant's choices made and self-reported items. However, the experiment was flawed for many reasons, which are now to be explained.

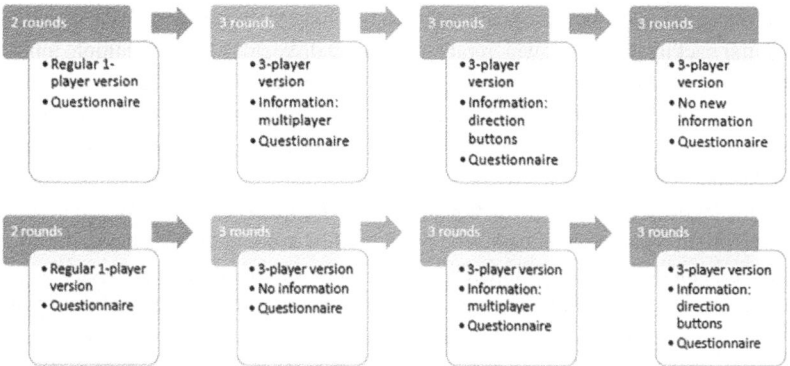

Figure 4.2 Process model of the legacy "Hopfenpost" experiment. *Source* own source

4.1.3 Problems with Legacy Experiment

Throughout the experiment, participants were able to communicate with each other. While the participants were instructed to remain silent, vocal signals such as sighing and moaning, eye contact and clicking sounds could not be avoided, and their potential influence on the data cannot be estimated. Another problem was the high effort in dealing with raw data. As the individual data sets are not linked to the individual seat ID written on each paper, where participants self-reported age and sex, but to the zTree ID, many references would have to be made by hand first. When zTree IDs were "shuffled" in order to randomize groups, it had to be written down by hand, *who-is-who*. In order to being able to truthfully report back to the companies who hired the participants and how many actually arrived, the self-reporting part about sex and age using paper was also done in order to know, from which company the individual participant was recruited from, as both companies offered different wages. Therefore, the experiment was not fully automated in order to have solid evidence "in paper form".

Another problem was that zTree is not a very suitable software for GUI heavy experiments. While it is astonishing that a single player and multiplayer Tower of Hanoi game can be programmed using zTree's rudimentary architecture, it is not graphically convincing. Furthermore, zTree does not offer redundant functions, so that the entire game was programmed with one huge iterative function. This led to the first backup notebook, which ran on an HDD drive, to calculate multiple inputs from more than 9 participants so slowly that participants started complaining, and with more than 10 participants, the entire experiment crashed. A notebook, running on an SSD, had to be used in order to run the experiment with enough efficiency.

During the experiment the actions of each participants could not be monitored. Therefore, the participants had to be monitored by walking behind them, in order to being able to see their computer screens. This was sometimes necessary when participants reported problems with mouse-control, accidentally closed the application or other problems which laid outside of experimental relevance. However, when walking past participants back, some of them reported that being a huge issue and that they will probably behave differently, when being observed from behind. Participants who took a long time to finish the single player version game also reported orally that the presence of others who finished the game faster, made them feel uncomfortable, altering their cognitive stability to the worse.

Due to zTree's software restrictions, and security concerns, not all inputs could be saved, such as individual presses and clicks on the directional buttons. A group could have solved a stage with only seven actions, but with hundreds of inputs, the latter not being saved, distorting information.

Since global information was reported orally, no recordings of each non-automated part of the experiment exist, and the participants were not isolated, the experiment is hard to defend against accusations of "use of deception", modeler bias, and noise from communication between participants. In addition, technical problems and bugs resulted in biased data. When a game-group was only containing one or two participants instead of the required three, the software would show unusual behavior, which even crashed the entire experiment. While the latter only happened once, it could have happened every time, when an experiment did not include a number of participants dividable by three.

The questionnaires were slightly changed and translated into German. Therefore, it was not clear whether these questionnaires still validly measured self-reported stress and uncertainty. The latter survey's quality is debatable, as the study is a rather unknown proceedings manuscript.

The "offline" participant acquisition and entire experimental process was very resource demanding. Due to this reason, and all mentioned problems above, an "online" version of "Tower of Europe"—that is the three-player version of Tower of Hanoi—was developed. While in the beginning the software "oTree" was considered, which is an "online software for implementing interactive experiments in the laboratory" (D. L. Chen, Schonger, & Wickens, 2016, p. 88), which runs on any web-browser without any application requisites, again "oTree" was found to lack graphical requirements, and modern software development language.

4.1.4 Curiosity IO—Structure and Functionality

Software development of Curiosity IO started in November 2018, and was mainly finished August 2019. The software framework contains a number of classic game theoretical experiments such as "Prisoner's Dilemma", "Battle of the Sexes", "Nash Bargaining Game", "Optional Prisoner Dilemma", "Public Goods", "Trust Game", "Ultimatum Game", "Dictators Game", "Public Goods (3 Player)". It also contains "Flag Run" (Strunz & Chlupsa, 2019), "Dynamic Flag Run", and "Tower of Hanoi". Extensive bug-testing and prototype testing of the two main experiments, being "Flag Run" and "Tower of Hanoi", had taken place. Since the 18th January 2019, multiple pre-tests and experiments were conducted. Using the "Flag Run" und "Dynamic Flag Run" game, 13 sessions with 1.459 participants from "Amazon Mechanical Turk" in total were performed, as well as 4 "Tower of Hanoi" sessions with a total of 150 participants—prior to the main experiment. Raw data of all experiments remain saved, and a selection of raw data can instantly be exported in.csv file format. Most screenshots of the software are added to the electronic appendix, and is referred to as "e-appendix" in the following.

Curiosity IO is a framework for online behavior experiments, which can be run on any device and web-browser. Participants can login to an experiment-session by entering the URL https://www.curiosity-data.com. Participants then have to type in the experiment's "Session Code" (see e-appendix chapter3_1_participant_login). When an experiment-session is "open", and the participant has entered the correct "Session Code", the participant will automatically begin with the experiment. What comes next, e.g. a label for the participant to provide age and sex, a questionnaire or game theoretical experiment depends on how the experiment was designed by the experimenter.

Experimenters can reach the admin panel via https://admin.curiosity-data.com. It is password protected (see e-appendix chapter3_2_experimenter_login). After entering the correct password, the main menu of Curiosity IO is unlocked. It consists of three panels: "Sessions—Create and analyze test runs", "Level Editor—Create and edit level configurations" and "Survey Editor—Create and edit surveys" (see e-appendix chapter3_3_main-menu).

Choosing "Sessions" leads to a list of all performed experiments (see e-appendix chapter3_4_gamesessions). The list displays the experiment's name, type of experiment, date, number of users, and the session code. Pressing the red "X" icon on the top right will lead back to the main menu. Choosing the icon "New Session" will open up the "Create Session" screen (see e-appendix chapter3_5_session).

The "Create Session" popup offers various options to design a session. Entire "experiments" are referred to as "sessions". It can be closed with the red "X" icon, a "Cancel" button, and a session can be created pressing a "Save" button. In the first two empty text fields, a "Session Name" and a "Player Password", formerly referred to as "Session Code" is to be entered. A checkbox enables the experimenter to activate or disable the panel, which enforces the participant to self-report their sex and age, before being able to start with a session. Each session can consist of three parts: a pre-survey, an experiment and an after-survey. Pre- and after-survey are questionnaires, which can be designed in the "Survey Editor". Experiments include all listed game-theoretical experiments, as well as "Flag Run", "Dynamic Flag Run" and "Tower of Hanoi". All these experiments can be chosen from the dropdown menu "Select Game". A session can also consist only of surveys—in this case "No Game" has to be chosen.

Depending on the chosen experiment, various options are now enabled, disabled or added. The two dropdown menus "Select Pre Survey" and "Select Post Survey" are always enabled, and list all pre-defined questionnaires created via the "Survey Editor". When the experiments "Flag Run" or "Dynamic Flag Run" are selected, the dropdown menu "Select Level Configuration" is enabled, and lists all pre-defined level configurations created via the "Level Editor". When the experiment "Tower of Hanoi" is chosen, multiple elements are added: a button "Add TOH Configuration", three empty text-fields named "Single-Player Timer", "Multi-Player Timer", "Give-Up Timer" and a checkbox labelled "Bot" (see e-appendix chapter3_11_createsession_2). Selecting "Add TOH Configuration" opens makes the "TOH CONFIG" popup appear (see e-appendix chapter3_12_tohconfig_1).

The "TOH CONFIG" popup can be closed with the red "X" icon, a "Cancel" button, and a "Tower of Hanoi" procedure can be created pressing the "Save" button. Such a procedure has to consist of at least one group. Each group can experience a different procedure. Participants will be put into groups (experiment-group) automatically, without being explicitly informed, by the group number. This will explained later in greater detail. "Add Group" adds a new group, which can be deleted by pressing the "Delete" icon or edited by clicking on its entry label (see e-appendix chapter3_13_tohconfig_2). When editing a group, consisting of at least one "game", a list of its games are displayed (see e-appendix chapter3_14_tohconfig_3). The group "edit" menu can be closed with the red "X" icon, a "Cancel" button, and a group procedure can be created pressing the "Save" button. One game is always filled in by default. The edit list contains information about the game ID, number of discs used (min. 3 to max. 10), starting state, goal state, single- or three-player, and whether or not help-text and popup are used. Each "Tower of Hanoi" game consists of three rods. While there exist ToH experiments with more than three rods, Curiosity IO does not offer more than three for the time being. "Add Game" adds a new game, which can be deleted by pressing the "Delete" icon or edited by clicking on its entry label. When editing a game, popup menus and text fields can be used to alter number of discs, start state, goal state, single- or three-player, and whether a popup should be visible (see e-appendix chapter3_15_tohconfig_3). Help-text and popup-text can be entered via the empty text-fields. When a popup is active, it has to be closed by the participant, in order to engage with the experiment. This can be used in order to announce help-text changes or report other important information to the participant.

Going back to the "Create Session" menu, various timers can be set. The "Single-Player Timer" is the amount of time in minutes each participant is provided to solve a Single-Player ToH game. The timer is displayed to the participant during the game, even on the popup. When the timer reaches 0, the next level is automatically started. The "Multi-Player Timer" is the analogue time for each participant to solve the three-player version of "Tower of Hanoi", also referred to as "Tower of Europe" (ToE). The ToE timer starts after each participant has provided an input. The "Give-Up Timer" is the number of minutes after which a "Give-Up" button appears during ToE. Since each ToE game requires three participants, these three players are called a "game-group". When the "Give-Up" button is being pressed by any participant of a game-group, the experiment for the entire game-group ends. When the bot checkbox is marked, it will activate the "bot-system". For the bot-system to work, "Start Wait" or "In Game Wait" have to be filled with an integer. When the ToH experiment comes with ToE games, game-groups of three players are required.

Considering an experiment has only one experiment-group: When participants join such an experiment, they have to wait until two other participants have joined. Those three participants are then put automatically in one game-group, when this experiment has only one experiment-group. This game-group is then automatically assigned to the first experiment-group. The next three participants who joined will be assigned to the second game-group. This game-group will automatically join the next experiment-group, if such an experiment-group exists. "Start Wait" indicates the number of minutes a player has to wait before bots will fill the game-group with either one or two bots. This feature was implemented so that MTurks do not have to wait too long, in order to still offer ethical pay.

Considering an experiment has more than one experiment-group: When participants join such an experiment, they will join, in successive order, each experiment-group.

"In Game Wait" is the number of minutes a player has to wait before bots will fill the game-group with either one or two bots during the game. This feature was implemented so that participants of a game-group could still end the experiment, when a game-group co-player disconnected. This is a good alternative to the more rigid "Give-Up" button concept, as it still allows to produce decision-making data of the entire experiment.

Bots only solve ToE games. Each bot is a simple algorithm using a "random-function". A "random-function" is usually "pseudo-random", as it uses various uncorrelated signals of a computer to produce e.g. a random integer. In this case, using this random-function, the algorithm chooses with a 50%-pseudo-random chance the small disk or with a 50%-pseudo-random chance the middle/large sized disk. When ToH or ToE is played with three rods, only the small or any other disk can be moved. Therefore, it is always a binary choice, with only three exceptions: when all disks are placed on one rod, only the small disk can be moved. After having "chosen" either small or middle/large sized disk, the algorithm chooses by 50%-pseudo-random chances whether or not a disk's moving distance is either 1 or 2 spaces. As there are only three rods, and disks cannot be moved 0 or 3 spaces, this also is a binary choice. How these two binary choices by three agents lead to a single output in ToE will be explained later.

A click on a listed experiment in the "Sessions" menu opens the session overview (see e-appendix chapter3_5_session). The session overview lists all participants. Each session overview displays four icons on the top right of the screen. The leftmost icon triggers an experiment as being "active". While participants are able to log in to an "inactive" session, and start with a pre-survey (when the session is set to "open", see below), they will be faced with a waiting screen when reaching an actual experiment, such as "Tower of Hanoi". Only when an experiment is set to "active" will the actual experiment start. Therefore, the "active" button does not influence pre-surveys, but only experiments. Once active, an experiment cannot be set to "inactive". After the leftmost icon, the second icon from the left "opens" or "closes" are session with a single click. When an experiment is "closed", participants can not join a session by entering their session code. The "Proceed" button at the "Join Session" screen will simple not work. When an experiment is "open", participants are able to join the session by enter their session code, and can begin e.g. with a pre-survey. When a session is both "active" and "open", participants can come and join the experiment, without the experimenter having to manually open and close the experiment. This feature has been implemented when experiments have to be conducted over the course of days and using e.g. Amazon Mechanical Turk, where participants might come from different time zones. When experiments are performed with people sitting in one room, the "active" feature is useful, so that participants all start with the experiment simultaneously after having filled out the questionnaire. In order to make sure that no further participants can join an experiment, it can be "locked". The two buttons combined features are explained in Table 4.1 (own source) for better understanding.

Table 4.1 All permutations of lock and play buttons with effect explanation

active/inactive button	locked/unlocked button	effect
inactive	locked	Default state. No participant can join session. No already joined participant can start with experiment
inactive	unlocked	Participants can join session, and start with pre-survey. No participant can start with experiment
active	unlocked	Participants can join session. Participants can start with experiment
active	locked	No participant can join session. Already joined participants can start with experiment

The third icon opens the "Game Session" options menu or "Session Configuration". Depending on the experiment, the options menu might differ. The following will explain the option menu as it appears, when a "Tower of Hanoi" experiment is chosen (see e-appendix chapter3_16_sessionconfiguration). The "Session Configuration" can be closed via the red "X" or the "Cancel" button. "Restart Session" will make each participant start over from the very beginning of the entire session, e.g. participants have to re-do their pre-survey. Data created is saved server-side, but cannot be downloaded via the options menu any longer (see below "Download Level Data or "Download Survey"). "Kick all and restart Session" will have the same effect as "Restart Session", but all participants will have to rejoin the session via the "Join Session" screen. "Clone Session" will make create an identical copy of a session in the "Game Sessions" list. The new session will appear with the original session name followed by "_clone". This comes in handy, when a session is complex and takes much time to create. This way multiple clones with e.g. slightly altered timer times can be tested, before a main experiment is conducted. In order to do so, a session can be edited. This can be done via "Edit Session" in the "Session Configuration" menu. A session cannot be edited as soon as it was set "active". When an experimenter wants to edit an already "active" session, the session can be cloned first, and then edited. Any session can be deleted by pressing "Delete Session". A popup will then ask "Are you sure you want to delete this session?". In order to remove the session from the "Game Sessions" list, this action has to be confirmed by pressing "Proceed". Choosing "Download Level Data" will download a.csv file with the experiment's raw data, which differs from game to game. When a "Tower of Hanoi" session included ToH and ToE, a single- and multiplayer.csv will separate raw data from one-player and three-player games. "Download Survey" will download a.csv file with the sessions' questionnaire raw data, which differs according to surveys' structure and content.

During an experiment, each participant can be monitored "live". The "Game Session" overview displays the participant ID, the current level or stage the participant is in, the total playing time, and the playing time in the current stage. Clicking on a listed participant during or after the experiment, will display three different icons (see e-appendix chapter3_6_session-user-options). Choosing the leftmost icon displays survey answers, which can also be monitored "live" during the experiment (see e-appendix chapter3_7_user-options_1). The center icon opens the experiment monitoring tool, where each input of the participant during the experiment is listed, and can also be observed "live" during the experiment (see e-appendix chapter3_8_user-options_2). The rightmost icon removes a participant from the experiment. The session overview also displays an icon "AddBotGroup" when the experiment is of type "Tower of Hanoi" (see e-appendix chapter3_9_session-bot). A "bot" is a simple algorithm, which randomly chooses inputs, as explained before. Clicking this icon adds a group of three bots, which will solve any ToE game. This feature was added to receive data about how many steps are required to solve "Tower of Europe" when the agents acts randomly.

This concludes the main menu's "Sessions" part. The "Level editor" is only used for "Flag Run" and "Dynamic Flag Run" games. Since this thesis builds upon raw data from the experiment "Tower of Hanoi", this main menu option is skipped.

The next main menu option is the "Survey Editor". Choosing "Survey Editor" leads to a list of all created surveys (see e-appendix chapter3_17_surveylist). The list displays the survey's name, date of creation, last date being modified and last date being used. Pressing the red "X" icon on the top right will lead back to the main menu. Choosing the icon "New Survey" will open up the "Survey Editor" screen (see e-appendix chapter3_18_surveyeditor_1).

The "Survey Editor" can be closed via the red "X" or being closed and saved via the "Save" button. By default, a single question already exists. Each question is listed in the "Survey Editor". Each question can be assigned to a group. Groups can be created, edited and deleted by clicking the "Groups" button. The "Groups" feature has yet only be tested with the "Dynamic Flag Run" game, and will not be explained in further detail. The listed questions can be ordered with the grey arrow buttons, and can be deleted with the trash-bin button. Pressing "New Questions" adds a new question. A question can be designed with right-hand side features. A question can be of type "One Choice", "Multiple Choice", "Scale" or "Free Text".

Each question of type "One Choice" and "Multiple Choice" can be formulated via a text-field and can consist of multiple answers. Pressing "New Answer" will make a text field appear, where the answer can be formulated. Order of answers can be rearranged via two direction buttons. Special features to an answer can be added. Those features have yet only be used in the "Dynamic Flag Run" game, and its description is to be skipped here. An answer can also be deleted via the trash-bin symbol.

Questions of type "Scale" only have one answer. Its lower and upper end, with according description, can be modified via text-fields. An example would be "very low, 1, 10, very high" (see e-appendix chapter3_19_surveyeditor_2). Questions of type "Free Text" will automatically provide a text-field for each participant.

This concludes the main menu's "Survey Editor" part and the entire options available to the experimenter via Curiosity IO admin panel. In the following, a "Tower of Hanoi" experiment from the perspective of a participant is shown, in order to discuss their features and functionality.

4.1.5 "Tower of Hanoi" Example Session

The session consists of a pre-survey, a "Tower of Hanoi" experiment and an after-survey. The experiment consists of one experiment-group, consisting of one game-group with one human agent and two bot. The experiment will have two games. One classic single-player ToH game and the three-player version (ToE).

In detail, the pre-survey and after-survey are identical questionnaires consisting of one "One Choice" question with two possible answers and are created using the "Survey Editor" (see e-appendix chapter3_25_phdexample_6). The sessions' experiment (see e-appendix chapter3_20_phdexample_1 and chapter3_21_phdexample_2) is called "PhD Thesis Example Session" with session code "phd". Sex and age is chosen to be a mandatory choice for each participant. ToH and ToE timers are set to 1 minute. The bot was activated, and its activation or waiting time set to 1 minute before the experiment, and set to 1 minute during the experiment. The described surveys, named "Done_Before", are chosen to be pre- and after-surveys. There is only one experiment-group (see e-appendix chapter3_26_phdexample_7). The experiment-group holds two games, with three discs, starting rod being the leftmost rod (Start $==$ 1). The goal rod of the ToH game is set to be the middle rod (Goal $==$ 2), and the goal rod of the ToE game is set to be the right rod (Goal $==$ 3). Both games have a help text and a popup (see e-appendix chapter3_22_phdexample_3). Help-texts and popup context were set to be different for this example (see e-appendix chapter3_23_phdexample_4 and chapter3_24_phdexample_5).

The session is set to be "inactive" and "open". The participant types in the session code "phd" to join the session (see e-appendix chapter3_27_joinsession). After that the participant provides sex and age (see e-appendix chapter3_28_joinsession) and is immediately brought to the pre-survey after submitting these details (see e-appendix chapter3_29_phdexample_10). Upon having provided an answer, the participant is now facing the "waiting screen" (see e-appendix chapter3_30_phdexample_11), as the session's experiment is set to "inactive". The experimenter sets the experiment to "active", which also automatically "closes" the session (see e-appendix chapter3_31_phdexample_12). The participant is still only seeing the "waiting screen", since two more participants have to join in order to form one game-group. The "Tower of Hanoi" experiment groups participants at the very beginning, even before a ToH game, when at least one ToE game is part of the experiment. Thus, it is defined from the beginning, who will face who in the second ToE game. After 1 minute a bot called "10000" joins the game-group. After another minute a second bot called "10001" joins the game-group (see e-appendix chapter3_32_phdexample_13). At this moment, three agents are part of the game-group, starting the experiment immediately. The participant no longer sees the "waiting screen" but is looking at the instructions popup, with the text "This is the popup.", a popup "OK" button to close the popup, the timer displayed on the popup, and the "helptext label" next to the popup (see e-appendix chapter3_33_phdexample_14). After closing the popup by pressing "OK", the participant can see the actual "Tower of Hanoi" game: a caption titled "Tower of Hanoi", with the timer now displayed below, three rods placed on platforms, a red marked goal rod with "Goal" written below to also address colorblind participants, and the three disks on the left rod in start-state setup (see e-appendix chapter3_34_phdexample_15). The participant has to press the small disk in order to make the "Steps" buttons, "Direction" buttons and "GO" button appear (see e-appendix chapter3_35_phdexample_16). After having chosen number of steps and direction, the participant can confirm the selection made by pressing "GO", upon which the resulting state will be displayed. When the participant manages to solve the game by positioning the three disks onto the goal rod or when the timer runs out, the "Level Completed" screen is displayed (see e-appendix chapter3_36_phdexample_17). This screen can be skipped by pressing "Next Level"—however the screen is automatically skipped when the participant reached the "Level Completed" screen not by solving the game but because the timer ran out. After the ToH game the participant now looks at the ToE game, with an instructions popup "This is the second popup", a "OK" button to close the popup and the "helptext label" with "This is the helptext label with different information now." written on it (see e-appendix chapter3_37_phdexample_18). No timer is displayed, since the timer starts after all three agents of the same game-group have to provide an input first during a ToE game. This is done as agents of the same game-group might have to wait for their co-agents to reach the ToE game; e.g. when two agents are still playing the first ToH game and the third agent has already reached the second game (ToE), and provides an input selection (disk/number of steps/direction, and pressing "GO"), this agent will face the "Waiting Screen", until all members of the same game-group have provided an input selection. After closing the popup, the participant can choose an input just like in the first game. This time, the goal rod is the very right one (see e-appendix chapter3_38_phdexample_19). After confirming disk, steps and direction selection, the timer starts (see e-appendix chapter3_39_phdexample_20). The output is the product of the one human and of the two bot agents input selections. After the ToE stage, no "Next Level" screen is displayed, as it was the final game. Instead, the after-survey is shown, which in this example, is identical to the pre-survey (see e-appendix chapter3_40_phdexample_21). When completing the after-survey, the "Thank You" screen with the participant ID is displayed (see e-appendix chapter3_41_phdexample_22). MTurks for example are instructed to provide the experimenter with this ID, so that the experimenter can check whether or not the MTurk has actually finished the session.

This concludes the example experiment. In the next sub-chapter, data output is described and explained.

4.1.6   Example Session Data Output

Using the options icon in the "Game Session" menu, and pressing "Download Level Data" and "Download Survey" several.csv files are downloaded (see e-appendix chapter3_42_phdexample_23):   "PhD_Thesis_Example_Session_single_player" (ToH.csv), which contains raw data about all ToH games that were part of the "Tower of Hanoi" experiment. "PhD_Thesis_Example_Session_three_player" (ToE.csv), which contains raw data about all ToE games that were part of the "Tower of Hanoi" experiment. "PhD_Thesis_Example_Session_survey" (Survey.csv), which contains raw data about all surveys that were part of the session. For more efficient statistical analysis of the thesis specific hypotheses, two additional.csv files were added after having conducted the main experiment. Tables explaining their variables are added to the appendix, being referred to as "Master.csv" and "Progress.csv" (see annex 5 and annex 6). The content of Progress.csv and Master.csv is not explained in further detail in this chapter, as their content is explained by the description of independent and dependent variables.

Survey.csv lists several raw data (see e-appendix chapter3_43_phdexample_24), all summed up and explained in the according table in the appendix (see annex 2). All types of raw data being saved in Survey.csv, an explanation of its meaning, and how the raw data looks like in the example Survey.csv output file.

ToH.csv lists several raw data all summed up and explained in the according table in the appendix (see annex 3). The table lists all types of raw data being saved in ToH.csv, an explanation of its meaning, and how the raw data looks like in the example ToH.csv output file. Some raw data will be explained in greater detail in the following sub-chapter.

ToE.csv lists several raw data all summed up and explained in the according table in the appendix (see annex 4). The table lists all types of raw data being saved in ToE.csv, an explanation of its meaning, and how the raw data looks like in the example ToE.csv output file. Long raw data names were cut to save table space. Some raw data will be explained in greater detail in the following sub-chapter.

Tables in the appendix (see annex 2–6) show all raw data being exported to.csv format. The next sub-chapter will explain listed data in more detail, such as how data is created—this is supported by data examples derived from the Curiosity IO example session described in the former chapters.

4.1.7 Response Time and Input

Response time creation differs for human and bot agents. While response times for bot agents are simulated, as their input order is randomly assigned, response times by humans are always server-dependent. Due to technical issues response times are not reliable enough to make precise statistical analyses. Response times are therefore disregarded.

4.1.8 States Derived from State-Space

Data such as "start_state" in ToH.csv and ToE.csv require a state-space of the experiment. When including operators, the state-space between ToH and ToE differs, as the former only requires a single action to produce an operator, and the latter requires three actions to produce an operator. However, the resulting output states of ToE are identical; if the three actions which produce an operator in ToE are ignored or modelled as being "intrinsic" to the operator, ToH and ToE state spaces are isomorphic.

Figure 4.3 shows the state-space of both ToH and ToE (Knoblock, 2000, p. 3), with integers added to each knot. It consists of 27 knots, representing all possible states, which are visually represented in the "Tower of Hanoi" experiment. It also contains directed, double-headed graphs, representing all possible transitions between states by the according operator. At 24 knots three different operators exist. This is not the case in all possible "start" states (not to be confused with start_state), which are states 1, 8 and 15. Here, only two operators exist. From each state there exists a path of seven operators leading to states 1, 8 and 15. Since only these three states can be set to goal states, there always exists an ideal path of seven operators towards the goal state.

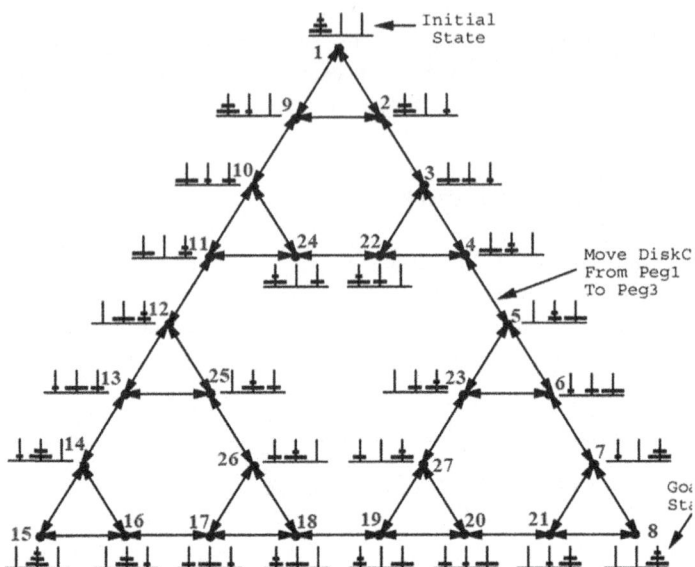

Figure 4.3 Tower of Hanoi state space model with their according integers. *Source* Knoblock, 2000, p. 3, red integers added by author

4.1.9 Move States

In ToE.csv the "move_state" data is an integer from 1 to 64 referring to all possible three-player action combinations leading to an operator (see e-appendix chapter3_Algorithm-States_new_appendix_44). An action consists of a chosen disk and number of steps. Chosen direction is only important when assigning a certain type of logic, which will be explained in a later sub-chapter.

In states 1, 8 and 15 only the small disk can be chosen. In any other state, agents can either choose the small disk or one of the remaining larger disks. With three rods, there is not state where an agent can choose between more than two disks in total. Therefore, each agent is confronted with a binary choice when deciding which disk to move—exceptions are state 1, 8, and 15. Each agents can choose between 1 or 2 steps, at any state, making it a binary choice. Therefore, an individual action can be described by two symbols. "S" representing "Small Disk", "M" representing "Medium or Large Disk", 1 representing "One Step" and

2 representing "Two Steps". Any operator consists of three actions. The operator being referred to by "move_state" 1 is "S1, S1, S1", meaning that all three agents have chosen to move the small disk one step. Another example would be "move_state" 55, with actions "M1, S2, M2". Here, the first action selection was "Move medium or large disk one space", the second action selection was "Move small disk two spaces", and the third action selection was "Move medium or large disk two spaces".

4.1.10 Operator Output Function

Each set of three actions lead to one specific operator (see e-appendix chapter3_Algorithm-States_new_appendix_44). The idea of ToE was that each agent held control over the game, and that the direction buttons were not influencing the game at all. The order of information or the order of actions matters for calculating the operator. It was important that no participant would be able to gain advantage over others, meaning that the algorithm was implemented in such a way that no agent would be able to gain more control than other players. This was achieved by restricting communication. As the order of information matters, no agent can be sure at which position its action will be listed. The algorithm was also built in such a way that it can be used for more complex games or state-spaces than "Tower of Hanoi", e.g. a 4-rod version of "Tower of Hanoi". The ruleset for the algorithm is derived from a meta-logic and adjusted to the experiment's degree of complexity. How the algorithm (function) determines the operator (output) by three actions (input) is now explained.

Three inputs are received, e.g. "S1, M2, S2" listed here in chronological order. Only the first two inputs are regarded, and only checked for "choice of disk", e.g. in this case "S, M" By doing so "The Decider" and "Direction-Deciders" are obtained. The Decider's action indicates which disk is being moved and how far it is being moved. Table 4.2 (own source) shows all possible permutations.

By example, the input "S1, M2, S2" leads to "S1" being the "Decider" action, meaning that the small disk will be moved one space. Now, the direction has to be obtained. In order to do so, inputs by the "Direction-Deciders" have to be regarded. Direction-Deciders are the two agents who are both not the "Decider", e.g. in this example, the 2nd and 3rd actions are Direction-Decider actions, as the 1st action is regarded as Decider action. By doing so, each agents has an influence on the game, with nearly eliminating the chance of any agent using a strategy to always be the Decider or always be the Direction-Decider, also never holding "full power" over disk-, steps- and direction-selection.

Table 4.2 All possible input combinations leading to resulting „direction-deciders"

Possible "choice of disk" input (first two, by time)	Resulting "Decider" action	Resulting "Direction-Decider" actions
S, S	2nd action committed	1st & 3rd action com
S, M	1st action committed	2nd & 3rd action com
M, S	3rd action committed	1st & 2nd action com
M, M	2nd action committed	1st & 3rd action com

In order to define in which direction a disk moves, the two Direction-Decider inputs are regarded. Now the inputs are only checked for "choice of steps", in this example "M2, S2" are the Direction-Decider inputs, and the two inputs checked are "2, 2". The Direction-Deciders' actions indirectly indicate in which direction the disk is moved, as the Decider's Choice of Range is also considered. Table 4.3 (own source) shows all possible permutations that decide the direction of the disk.

By mentioned example, Direction-Deciders input "2, 2" and Deciders input "1" leads to the direction of the disk being "left". The resulting operator equals "move_state" 29, where the Small Disk is being moved 1 step to the left.

Table 4.3 All possible input combinations of direction-deciders leading to direction of disk

Possible "choice of steps" input by Direction-Deciders	Possible "choice of steps" input by Decider	Resulting direction
11	1	left
	2	right
12	1	right
	2	left
21	1	right
	2	left
22	1	left
	2	right

The algorithm to determine the operator is purposefully more complex than required to fairly share control, in order to being used for more complex state-spaces as well. Since an operator can lead to an illegal state, such as a bigger disk lying on top of a smaller disk, the next sub-chapter will explain, how an operator leads to the resulting output state, which can be observed by the agents.

For this, a more fundamental definition of a "Tower of Hanoi" game is provided, and differences in handling illegal moves in a ToH and ToE game are shown.

4.1.11 State Output Function

When designing the ToE game, several choices had to made, how closely related ToE should be to ToH. The core idea designing ToE was to "still play a Tower of Hanoi" game. Therefore, the core rules that make a game a "Tower of Hanoi game" had to be defined. Those "axioms" of ToH are:

– A move is a state, which differs from the last state
– No state may show a larger disk lying on a smaller disk
– The game consists of three rods

The first axiom leads to the impossibility to move a disk and bring it back to the original position. The second axiom never allows a move resulting in some state, where a bigger disk lies on top of a smaller disk. The third axiom limits the games complexity and state-space greatly.

In addition to these axioms, each agents of ToE was supposed to have an influence on the game, and this control should be fairly distributed. However, in some situations playing ToE, individual, legal moves, can result in collective illegal moves. In the ToH game what defines an illegal move differs from a ToE game, since in the latter the direction-buttons do not influence the game, and the game is played alone.

During a ToH game, pressing the "GO" button with number of steps but not direction being chosen, results in a "No Direction" error message (see e-appendix chapter3_45_nodirection_error). During a ToH game, trying to move a bigger disk onto a smaller disk results in a "Wrong Move" error message (see e-appendix chapter3_46_wrongmove_error).

During a ToE game, pressing the "GO" button with number of steps but not direction being chosen, does not result in an error message. This is because such an error message can be regarded as deception. As the direction buttons do not influence the game, such an error message would state that the direction buttons have to be selected, implicitly saying that they actually do influence the game. Therefore, no such error message will pop up when no direction buttons are chosen. During a ToE game, when the resulting operator, consisting of three individual actions, would result in an illegal move, axiom number two would be violated. Following the meta-logic of the algorithm, such an operator will be "corrected". Ignoring the more complex meta-logic, the resulting solution is that a "M" disk will simply "follow its direction" until a rod is being reached, where it can be placed. This must not be the original rod, as this would violate axiom one. Therefore, there does not exist any error message for this case. This approach differs from the legacy zTree version, where in one instance such an error message was displayed to the ToE agents—however, this was due to a wrong implementation of the algorithm; another reason for discarding the legacy experiment.

In both ToH and ToE games, disks can jump edges. In other words, when the small disk is moved two steps to the right, the resulting state will always equal if the disk was moved one step to the left. For example, when starting the game (ToH and ToE) in state 1, an operator equal to "S2 right" will result in state 2 just as an operator equal to "S1 left". No error message, for both ToH and ToE will popup, when a disk is moved "out-of-bounds". In other words, there are "no borders" between the left rod and the right rod, as the graphical representation of the "Tower of Hanoi" experiment might suggest. This feature was introduced to make the ToH more similar to the ToE game, as the latter requires there to be "no borders" in order to make the algorithm work. A similar ruleset was used in the "Flag Run" game, as this experiments rests on the same meta-logic.

An example showing the correction of an illegal move during a ToE game is provided in the following. For instance, consider state 17 is reached and the goal rod was the center rod. The ideal ToH operator would be "M1 right" or "M2 left" applying "no borders" logic. During a ToE game, all three agents could use their single player logic and choose "M1, M1, M1", which is "move_state" 43, and results in the middle disk being moved one step to the left. The middle disk would jump edges from the left rod and land on the right rod, counting as "one step to the left". This would result in an illegal state, as the small disks rests on the right rod. The medium sized disk therefore goes left one more step, landing on the center rod, where it may "legally" be positioned. This results in state 16, ultimately desired by the three agents. Therefore, the middle or large sized disks will always land on the only legal spot, when being chosen. This is not because the algorithm was designed in that way, but because the "playing field", being just three rods, is so limited that it may look this way. The third axiom works in favor for the agents. This is because when all three agents agree on one disk being moved, such as "Sx_1, Sx_2, Sx_3" or "Mx_1, Mx_2, Mx_3", the disk agreed upon will always be moved. If that chosen disk has to be selected in order to follow the most efficient path, and if that disk was a medium or large sized disk, it will always result in the ideal state, disregarding the choice of steps. This is the reason why sticking to the ToH logic during a ToE game, will outperform randomness, as will be explained later.

Individual inputs can differ from the collective operator, as being shown in the following example. Consider state 14 being reached, the center rod being the goal rod. The ideal single player solution would be "S1 right" or "S2 left" applying the "no borders" logic. During a ToE game, all three agents could use their single player logic and choose "S1, S1, S1", assuming no one had figured out that disks jump edges. This action input equals "move_state" 1, and results in the small disk being moved one step to the left. The small disk would jump edges from the left rod and land on the right rod, counting as "one step to the left". This would result in state 16, which was probably neither desired nor expected by the three agents.

It is clear by the two former examples that during a ToE game, several "logical" perspectives exist and that a ToE operator does not necessarily equal what an agent expected to happen. Whether or not an individual action equals some logic or whether or not the individual action results in some expected state is also expressed by raw data. The following sub-chapter will explain logic and expected state data.

4.1.12 Logic and Expected States

The "Flag Run" experiment had shown that participants developed different strategies, all stemming from a different logic, but all effective strategies relied on having obtained "true rules" governing the game (Strunz & Chlupsa, 2019). During the "Flag Run" game, some participants even came up with effective strategies not anticipated by the experimenters; still, they also had to build their strategy upon having figured out a "true rule". Such a "true rule" was that during the "Flag Run" game, the game-piece can jump edges or that the direction buttons did not influence the game at all. These two "true rules" are also implemented in the "Tower of Hanoi" experiment. During a ToH or ToE experiment, the disks can jump edges and the ToE game is not influenced by the direction buttons. Another "true rule" for ToE is that the disk, steps and direction are decided by all three agents as a collective, calculated by a complex algorithm, making it very unlikely or even impossible for one individual agent to control the game alone. However, participants can beat randomness by sticking to the ToH logic, as three actions that agree on a disk will result in this disk being moved.

Given the two examples from the former sub-chapter, it has already been described that different "logical" approaches can be identified, by which participants act. As the results of the "Flag Run" experiment had shown, most participants who effectively solved the NRP stick with a single form of logic, as soon as feedback confirms this logic to be effective. Again, consider state 14 being reached, the center rod being the goal rod. The ideal single player solution would be "S1 right" or "S2 left" applying the "no borders" logic. When no agent had figured out during the ToH game that pieces "jump edges" and that there was "no borders" between the left and right rod, the "S2 left" solution might seem illogical. This is because the agent is only locally informed and is missing information about the true nature of the game, analogue to the island Gedankenexperiment. This might lead to all agents providing inputs "S1, S1, S1", direction "right", leading to state 16, which is unfavorable. However, it might just be that one agent had figured out the "no border" logic, applying "S2", direction "left". If the agents were able to inspect their co-agents' inputs, the two remaining agents would find "S2", direction "left" as being an illogical move. As a reminder, during a ToE game, the directions chosen by the players does not have any effect whatsoever. Assuming one agent chooses "S2", and two agents choose "S1", depending on the order of information, three different "move_states" are possible: move_state 2 ("S2, S1, S1") moves the small disk one step to the right, leading to the desired goal state 15; move_state 5 ("S1, S2, S1") moves the small disk two steps to the right, leading to the unfavorable state 16; move_state 17 ("S1, S1, S2") moves the small disk one step to the right, leading to the desired goal state 15.

Assuming move_state 2 and 17 occurred, could lead to a confirmation of a locally logical, but globally illogical strategy. The two agents who had chosen input "S1", direction "right", who had not figured out the true rule of "disks jumping edges" would find the input "S2", direction "left", as being an illogical input. From the perspective of the single agent, who used the "no border" strategy, both inputs are logical solutions. However, all logics are globally imperfect as the direction of disks cannot be influenced by pressing the direction buttons. This example shows the analogy to the island Gedankenexperiment. Depending on the individual experience, individual logics are applied, which can be either confirmed or denied by environmental conditions. However, since the agents decide collectively, negative feedback cannot be assigned to a wrong strategy with certainty. Group performance still can benefit from the "traditional strategy", being acquired in the first ToH game, since agreement on the optimal disk outperforms randomness. While the rules of the game do not change, the goal rod's position, simulating an environmental condition, can have a major influence on the strategy's performance. A game-group can solve a ToE game optimally in 7 moves by applying the most intuitive "border" ToH logic, when the goal rod is the right rod (goal == 3). Since agents cannot communicate, even having obtained the excel sheet with all 64 input permutations, agents could not control the game fully, as they had to communicate their input order. With the goal rod being the center rod, the most intuitive "border" ToH logic will fail to solve the game in 7 moves, and would lead to—probably—unfavorable and unexpected results. This environmental condition (goal $==$ 2) will have an impact on any strategy's performance. Depending on the game setup, feedback, valence weighting bias, routine strength, logic applied and intrinsic motives, a human agent will alter its strategy or remain using the strategy. It is therefore important to cover as many "logics" as possible, in order to make sense of the agent's strategy, and to measure if an input lead to an "expected" output state.

All different logic models and "expected" output states are saved as a Boolean in ToH.csv and ToE.csv (see e-appendix chapter3_dir_or_nodir_states_appendix_47 and chapter3_exp_states_appendix_48). With their necessity being explained, the following will explain which models of logic are saved, how they are created and how "expected" and "unexpected" states are distinguished.

During a single player ToH game, two different "logic models" are being measured. These two logic models are saved in ToH.csv as a Boolean with "logic" and "no_border_logic". When the Boolean of the according "logic model" equals 1, the action is regarded as being equal to this "logic model". When the Boolean equals 0, the action is regarded as not being equal to this "logic model".

In ToH an action is saved as being equal to "logic", with Boolean equal to 1, when the output state follows the ideal path, without the disk "jumping edges". This path depends on "start" and "goal" rod position, "start_state", "input" and "direction". In ToH an action is saved as being equal to "no_border_logic", with Boolean equal to 1, when the output state follows the ideal path, with the disk "jumping edges". The ideal path is the path were the goal is being reached in 7 moves. When the playing piece deviates from the ideal path, both "logic models" assign a Boolean of 0. When the "start_state" is a state, which is the result of such a deviation, the following move is given a Boolean of 1, when it follows the ideal parh again. The latter is to be shown by example in the following. All possible configurations that lead to "logic" or "no_border_logic" are listed in the electronic appendix (see e-appendix chapter3_dir_or_nodir_states_appendix_47).

For instance, consider a ToH game with the starting rod being the left rod, the goal rod being the right rod and three disks. In this case, the ideal path would lead to "state" 2, and the ideal operator for "logic $==$ 1" would be "S2 right", and the ideal operator for "no_border_logic $==$ 1" would be "S1 left". Studies about "Tower of Hanoi" performance showed that the first move is often the move, deviating from the ideal path the most. Assuming the agent deviates from the ideal path at the first move, choosing action "S1 right". State 9 is reached and Booleans for both "logic models" are then assigned a value of 0. The ideal path would now lead to "state" 2, and the ideal operator for "logic $==$ 1" would be "S1 right". Assuming the agent chooses to correct its deviation by "S1 right", state 2 is reached and a Boolean of 1 is assigned to "logic", even though the "start_state" was outside of the original ideal path. A Boolean of 0 is assigned to "no_border_logic", since the disk did not jump edges.

During a three player ToE game, where the direction buttons do not influence the disks, several different "logic models" are being measured. Players can also choose to confirm an input without having pressed a direction button—being saved as "n" or "none". ToE logic models are saved in ToE.csv with a Boolean assigned to them. When the Boolean of the according "logic model" equals 1, the action is regarded as being equal to this "logic model". When the Boolean equals 0, the action is regarded as not being equal to this "logic model".

The ToE "logic models" are: "framed_logic", distinguished by "dir", "nodir" and "ideal"; "no_border", distinguished by "dir", "nodir", and "ideal". Each "logic model" evaluates individual actions, and not the collective operator. Written in front of each "logic model" attribute, "first_player", "second_player" or "third_player" refer to which agent's action is considered.

The logic model "frame_logic" with "dir", short for "direction", is isomorphic to ToH "logic". When participants play one or multiple games of ToH, routine strength by feedback leads to human agents probably "carrying" the single player ToH logic into the three player ToE domain.

A Boolean of 1 is assigned to "framed_logic" with "nodir", short for "no direction", when an action equals "framed_logic_dir", disregarding direction. For example, consider a ToE game with the starting rod being the left rod, the goal rod being the right rod and three disks. In this case, the ideal path would lead to "state" 2, and the action for "framed_logic_dir $==$ 1" would be "S2 right", and the action for "framed_logic_nodir $==$ 1" would be "S2 left" or "S2 right" or "S2 none". This logic is measured because during the legacy experiment, participants had orally reported to the experimenter that they kept on pressing direction buttons, even though they were informed that they did not influence the game. They remained pressing the direction buttons arbitrarily, either always or frequently, without using "framed_logic_dir". They reported to do so to "stay in rhythm" or "out of routine" or "because they did not feel like ignoring the direction buttons altogether".

A Boolean of 1 is assigned to "framed_logic" with "ideal", when an action equals "framed_logic_dir", and direction "none" is chosen. For example, consider a ToE game with the starting rod being the left rod, the goal rod being the right rod and three disks. In this case, the ideal path would lead to "state" 2, and the action for "framed_logic_dir $==$ 1" would be "S2 right", and the action for "framed_logic_ideal == 1" would be "S2 none". This logic is measured to identify players, who stick with the "framed_logic" but regarded the direction buttons as being useless.

The three remaining "logic models" are analogous to the three mentioned "logic models", however, they identify players who make the disk "jump edges". All three versions of "no_border logic models" were introduced to identify players, who had obtained the "true rule" that "disks jump edges".

Assuming a ToE game with the starting rod being the left rod, the goal rod being the right rod and three disks. In this case, the ideal path would lead to "state" 2, and the action for "no_border_dir == 1" would be "S1 left", the action for "no_border_nodir == 1" would be "S1 left" or "S1 right" or "S1 none", and the action for "no_border_ideal == 1" would be "S1 none".

The following Table 4.4 (own source) will list all mentioned examples of ToE "logic models".

Table 4.4 All possible input combinations resulting in according logic category booleans

ToE, with starting rod being left rod, goal rod being right rod, first move

Individual input	Logic model	Boolean
S2 right	framed_logic_dir/nodir/ideal no_border_dir/nodir/ideal	1/1/0 0/0/0
S2 left	framed_logic_dir/nodir/ideal no_border_dir/nodir/ideal	0/1/0 0/0/0
S2 none	framed_logic_dir/nodir/ideal no_border_dir/nodir/ideal	0/1/1 0/0/0
S1 right	framed_logic_dir/nodir/ideal no_border_dir/nodir/ideal	0/0/0 0/1/0
S1 left	framed_logic_dir/nodir/ideal no_border_dir/nodir/ideal	0/0/0 1/1/0
S1 none	framed_logic_dir/nodir/ideal no_border_dir/nodir/ideal	0/0/0 0/1/1

With models of logic explained, i.e. how they are created, saved and for which purpose they were introduced, "expected" and "unexpected" states are to be discussed in the following.

In a ToE game unexpected outputs can occur. For this reason, ToE.csv assigns a Boolean to each individual agent's action, depending on the output state, indicating whether (1) or not (0) the individual action lead to the expected outcome.

This measurement was introduced to obtain data about individual decision-making correlating with feedback or in other words, to obtain information about whether or not participants alter their strategy when they "do not see what they expected" or stick to a strategy when they "do see what they expected". In order to make an assumption about, whether or not some output state was expected by a participant, several data attributes have to be known: start_state, output state, input, and direction. A data sheet lists all possible configurations (see e-appendix chapter3_exp_states_appendix_48).

Several "expectation models" exist, with each assigned a Boolean: FL_exp_dir, short for "framed logic expectation considering direction"; FL_exp_ideal, short for "framed logic expectation not considering direction"; NB_exp_dir, short for "no borders logic expectation considering direction" and NB_exp_ideal, short for "no border logic expectation not considering direction".

For instance, consider a ToE game with the starting state being equal to state 1, as modelled in the state-space (see Figure 4.4). Some game-group operator results in the output state equal to state 2, as modelled in the state-space. An input equal to "S2 right" leads to Boolean 1 being assigned to "FL_exp_dir". An input equal to "S2 none" leads to Boolean 1 being assigned to "FL_exp_ideal". Both "expectation models" assume the "framed logic model". When the "no border logical model" is assumed, two other "expectation models" are distinguished. Considering the same example start and output state by some game-group operator, an input equal to "S1 left" leads to Boolean 1 being assigned to "NB_exp_dir". An input equal to "S1 none" leads to Boolean 1 being assigned to "NB_exp_ideal".

How logic models and expectation models are to be interpreted depends on many factors. To reduce complexity, a heuristic approach is being taken: it is assumed that every input is being chosen deliberately. Therefore, with "expected models", there does not exist an "exp_nodir" distinction. This, of course, excludes errors and deviations stemming from misclicking or non-deliberate inputs. It also makes data of "expectation models" meaningless, when the participant expected "nothing" or just "randomly" provided inputs. It is assumed such deviations occur rare enough, so that their number have a neglectable impact on the overall experiment. However, when a participant shows many "framed_logic_nodir" actions, and next to no "dir" or "ideal" data, it can be assumed that data of "expectation models" will not be very meaningful, as they assume the direction to be selected with purpose.

Building upon Rubinstein (2007) an action can be considered "reasonless", when response times are short, and also by analyzing the actions' logic and expected states, i.e. a set of actions that jump between different logic states, and has an expected state outcome similar to the randomizer bot results, can efficiently regarded as being "reasonless". An action can be considered "instinctive" when response time are short, and e.g. both logic and expected states show that the agent still sticks with the single-player logic routine, being "framed" by its own mental model. While Rubinstein (2007) categorized actions intuitively, this thesis follows Rubinstein's suggestion and base the categorization of actions between cognitive, instinctive and reasonless with "on other sources of information", being the logic and expected states data (Rubinstein, 2007, p. 1258). This also reduces the risk to falsely interpret agent deviations from optimal behavior, e.g. by simple misklicking as non-standard preferences (Cason & Plott, 2014).

This concludes all logic and expected states models. With all raw data and their creation explained, the next sub-chapter will focus on the participants, who conducted the main experiment.

4.2 Participants

180 Amazon Mechanical Turk workers (MTurk) were recruited via "Amazon Mechanical Turk", where online freelancers can be hired for various tasks, such as online questionnaires and experiments. From these 180 participants, data of 87 MTurks could be used for statistical analysis. As indicated in Strunz & Chlupsa (2019), MTurks "are commonly recruited for behavioral experiments due to AMT's workers pool size, low costs and being able to produce high-quality data fast (Buhrmester, Kwang, & Gosling, 2011)" (p. 114). Freelancers recruited via this platform show comparable bias and heuristic behavior as participants recruited by more traditional methods (Paolacci, Chandler, & Ipeirotis, 2010). MTurks are mainly motivated monetary compensation (Lovett et al., 2018), such that realistic working conditions can be simulated with these participants, where thinking-time is associated with costs.

There exist possible cultural influence on complex problem solving and adaptive decision making (Güss, 2011; Güss et al., 2012)—differences which are supposed to stem from different learning environments (Funke, 2014). Highly significant differences in non-routine problem solving performance and response times by country origin have been measured comparing 290 Indian, 262 US-American and 51 German participants via the "Flag Run" experiment (Strunz, 2019). For this reason, all 180 MTurks were restricted to US American MTurks. In order to ensure that MTurks were actually human and not automatically working machines, so called "bots", approval rating, reflecting the MTurk's „repution" was set to "high levels" to ensure high quality data. High levels of MTurk reputation are defined to be the case with an approval rating above 95% (Peer, Vosgerau,

& Acquisti, 2013). When a task, referred to as "HIT" is opened to US American freelancers with a mandatory HIT approval rate of higher than 95%, 11.126 freelancers were "captured" in a study from 2015 (Stewart et al., 2015) and a more recent study stated there being 12.000 MTurk freelancers on average (Difallah, Filatova, & Ipeirotis, 2018). However, according to Difallah, Filatova & Ipeirotis (2018), these numbers are extreme underestimates due to variation. When correcting for propensities at least 100.000 to 200.000 freelancers are actively working.

Even though no differences in NPS performance were measured regarding sex, and only low correlation regarding age were found in Strunz & Chlupsa (2019), age and sex was again asked for during the login-stage, as the reflective cognitive state was described as being influenced by age (Liebherr, Schiebener, Averbeck, & Brand, 2017) and as female participants have shown to change to a better strategy less efficiently in experiments under feedback (Casal, DellaValle, Mittone, & Soraperra, 2017).

As MTurks' behavior vary over the course of a 24hour day, with participants behaving less reflective on the weekends (Arechar, Kraft-Todd, & Rand, 2017), the final study was conducted on a regular working day, being the 6th of December. According to an online tracker showing hourly demographics of AMT Workers (Difallah et al., 2018; Paolacci et al., 2010), the most recent data available at the time when the experiment was conducted, showed variation of US American freelancers throughout the entire month of September 2019 ranging between 52.58% and 85.42%. The the majority of MTurks consisted of US Americans. Regarding sex, 49.04% female and 50.96% male US American MTurks participated from September 1st 2019 to September 30th 2019 according to the online tracker (Paolacci et al., 2010), indicating well balanced monthly sex distribution. Dates for December, when the experiment was conducted, were not available at the time of research.

Age distribution over workdays, being Monday to Friday, from the 1st of September 2019 to 30th of September 2019 retrieved from the online tracking tool (Paolacci et al., 2010) are listed in Table 4.5.

MTurk demographics from 2018 (Difallah et al., 2018) reported 55% of US female participants and 45% of US male participants. Household income for US MTurks were found to be below the average of the US population: with the US household median being "$57K" and the US MTurks household median being "around $47K", and "while 26.5% of US households make more than $100K per year, for MTurk workers this percentage falls at 12.5%." (Difallah et al., 2018, p. 4).

Table 4.5 Year of Birth distribution of MTurks on workdays Mo-Fr, from 01.09.2019 to 30.09.2019. *Source* data acquired via online tracking tool by Paolacci et al., 2010

Year of Birth	Percentage	Age (as of 10/2019)
2000–2010	1,268%	9–18
1990–2000	34,232%	19–28
1980–1990	36,87%	29–38
1970–1980	14,758%	39–48
1960–1970	9,46%	49–48
1950–1960	2,604%	59–58
1940–1950	0,598%	69–78
1910–1940	0,21%	79–108

From 87 MTurks 29 self-reported being female and 58 self-reported being male, with an average of 33.16 years for both sexes.

Actively monitoring the MTurk forums is recommended by researchers, in order to find out whether or not a HIT was discussed amongst the MTurks, which could have a negative influence on the experiment's data quality (Cheung, Burns, Sinclair, & Sliter, 2017). When a pre-test of the main experiment was performed, minor information about the experiment was found to be shared online. A single participant rated the experiment as "fair" but also stated the disadvantage that one of his partner's bad performance made her wait longer than necessary. Information being shared online cannot be avoided. For this reason, an after-survey was included, asking participants, whether or not they had already participated in this experiment before.

As most participants are informed about playing in a group anyways, information being shared online was observed to be very limited, and as certainly not all MTurks are actively monitoring the MTurk forums, treatment diffusion effects are regarded as potentially low. For this reason, more transparency was regarded to outweigh its potential negative side-effects, and an official profile on "TurkerView" was created, where MTurks are able to retrieve information about the experimenter's former payments, communication, number of rejections, approval response times, and number of blocked participants.

As studies have found 40% of MTurks working with "Amazon Mechanical Turk" as their primary job, the practical recommendation to act as "reputable employers" was followed (Brawley & Pury, 2016, p. 542), and more than 45 USD per hour was paid to MTurks on average over the course of 26 HITs. Since "unfair wages, and inaccurately listed time requirements were among the top five worst Requester behaviors" (Brawley & Pury, 2016, p. 542), calculating MTurks average pay was always aimed way above US minimum wage, when experience in early experiments was missing. For this reason, the high average hourly pay was achieved.

In conclusion, from 180 participants, data of 87 US American MTurks was randomly selected from an online pool of potential participants. How many MTurks can ultimately be reached is debated and dependent on the model used to approximate it. According to literature, certainly more than 11-thousand freelancers via "Amazon Mechanical Turk" were reached, and numbers could extent to more than 100-thousand. In order to being able to rely on the most recent statistical results, data from September 2019 was used to determine US female/male distribution, and age during working days.

4.3   Procedure

Participants were provided with in-depth instructions and a text field, where the according participants ID was supposed to be entered, as shown in Figure 4.4.

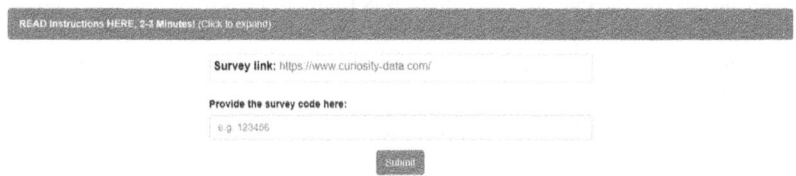

Figure 4.4 MTurk client side view of HIT. *Source* own source

Upon having clicked on "(Click to expand)" each participant was provided with the following instructions:

Survey Instructions reading time: 2–3 minutes. Trouble Shooting section included. Make sure to read.
Complete an online experiment consisting of 12 levels of Tower of Hanoi. Instructions are included ingame. Bonus pay for best 10%.
= When experiment lasts longer than 51 minutes, submit with Worker ID and time played, you will be approved if you did not idle on purpose. =

Go to https://www.curiosity-data.com/ and enter **1992** as "Session Code".

Please provide us with your sex and age. You will be given an ID at the end. Enter this ID as your Surveycode. Do **not** provide me with your worker ID.

This experiment may easily last longer than 30 minutes. Do not start this HIT when you do not have enough time.

You may have to **wait up to 10 min** at the beginning.

You may have to **wait up to 14 min** during the experiment.

Do not leave the game unattended. If you are kicked due to inactivity, I will **under no circumstances** approve your work.

Check the information box on the left of your screen during the game. Its contents may change and are important.

Make sure to leave this window open as you complete the survey. When you are finished, you will return to this page to paste the ID into the box. **Not** your worker ID.

About me:

I am registered on TurkerView (Ulrich Strunz), if you want to leave a rating.

You can easily reach me via email, I will answer.

My experiments are unique. Thanks for helping me out.

Compensation:

In case you are unable to submit in time, I offer compensation in some cases. My time is limited. I am also human. Please be patient in this case, I am working with hundreds of MTurks simultaneously, alone. Leave me a reminder Email in case you did not receive funds. Screenshots help, so you can prove your progress.

= When experiment lasts longer than 51 minutes, submit with Worker ID and time played, you will be approved if you did not idle on purpose. =

Please do not spam me with multiple emails, I will listen to your explanations in case something went wrong.

Survey:

There is a pre-survey included. Please make sure to answer it. I need to know if you are from USA.

There is an after-survey included. Please make sure to answer it. I need to know if you have played this experiment before.

Experiment:
Using a tablet or notebook will be ideal. Mobile phones might have a too small screen to display all information properly.

The experiment is not bugged. It has been tested with more than 200 participants by now. I have no influence over the setup you are using. Old hardware or missing drivers may result in bad latency. Check the trouble shooting section for more details.

Trouble-Shooting:

!!! Some MTurks experience problems when using Google Chrome since its last update. Clearing your cache might be necessary before starting the game. !!!

The game has been tested with Chrome, IE, Firefox, Yandex Browsers. No trouble was experienced.

In case you accidentally close your browser, just come back. Your experiment progress will be saved.

Several Turkers reported a problem with the publish button not working. This is an AMT specific problem. The best option is to:

1) Inform me via Email when an error occurs.

2) Wait. Sometimes the button will function after 5 min of waiting time.

In case the proceed button does not work:

1) Make sure you have typed in **1992** as session code.

2) Make sure to have chosen your SEX using the drop-down menu and have provided us with your AGE using integers.

3) Since the latest Chrome update, some unsolvable (from my side) issues were reported, when using this Web-Browser.

After going to https://www.curiosity-data.com/, participants had to self-report their sex and age. After a valid input they could start the experiment by clicking the "Proceed" button. The entire experiment consisted of a Tower of Hanoi/Tower of Europe experiment, and an after-survey. The experiment came with five different information conditions, represented by five experiment groups. The participant was assigned to one of the five experiment groups automatically by login order, as explained in the former chapter. Participants were also assigned automatically to game groups by login order, each game group consisting of three players, as explained in the former chapter. Each information condition (experiment group) consisted of 13 games or levels. The first 7 games were single player games. The last 6 games were multiplayer games. The first game was added to give players enough time to read popup and help-text information, and data collected during the first game was not used for analysis. The first game was considered as a buffer level. The second popup showed up at game 8. The goal rod changed during the single player and multiplayer games. Each game was played with three rods, referred to as either left, center or right rod. During the first four single player games (buffer level included) the goal rod was set to be the right rod. During the last three single player games, the goal rod was set to be the center rod. The first three multiplayer games were played with the right rod being the goal rod, while the last three multiplayer games set the goal rod to be the center rod. All games in all information conditions were played with three disks. Figure 4.5 (own source) shows the entire setup.

For each single player game, a timer of 2 minutes was preset. When the timer ran out a level was automatically ended, skipping to a "Level Completed" screen, which was also automatically closed after 1 second, having shown the next game screen. The single player timer automatically started as soon as the game screen was shown.

For each multiplayer game a timer of 3 minutes was preset. When the timer ran out a level was automatically ended, skipping to a "Level Completed" screen, which was also automatically closed after 1 second, having shown the next game screen. If the last game 13 was skipped in such a way, the after-survey was automatically displayed.

When a game group was not filled with three participants before the experiment started, a waiting screen appeared. After 5 min of timeframe an automated bot participant was added to the group. If for some reason a player left a game group during the game, and Curiosity IO registered this player as being disconnected, a bot was added to the group after 10 min. This feature was implemented for ethical reasons, so that MTurks were still able to solve the experiment in time. When a game group was filled with three agents, the actual experiment started with the first game level.

The first level called "Game 0" includes a popup with the following message:

"--- Do not worry about the timer. Take your time to read the following! ---
Your task is to solve 12 games of Tower of Hanoi.

6 training games, and then 6 performance games. An additional game (this game) is added, so you can read these instructions.

For each game a timer will be displayed. When the timer reaches zero, the next game will automatically start.

Game	Discs	Start	Goal	Type	HelpText	Popup	
Game 1	3	1	3	single	Yes	Yes	🗑
Game 2	3	1	3	single	Yes	No	🗑
Game 3	3	1	3	single	Yes	No	🗑
Game 4	3	1	3	single	Yes	No	🗑
Game 5	3	1	2	single	Yes	No	🗑
Game 6	3	1	2	single	Yes	No	🗑
Game 7	3	1	2	single	Yes	No	🗑
Game 8	3	1	3	multi	Yes	Yes	🗑
Game 9	3	1	3	multi	Yes	No	🗑
Game 10	3	1	3	multi	Yes	No	🗑
Game 11	3	1	2	multi	Yes	No	🗑
Game 12	3	1	2	multi	Yes	No	🗑
Game 13	3	1	2	multi	Yes	No	🗑

Figure 4.5 Administrator perspective of entire experimental setup using Curiosity IO framework. *Source* own source

Try to solve each level in as few steps as possible. The best 10% of all participants will win a 2.00 USD bonus (only if you provide me with the ID displayed at the end of the experiment, do NOT provide me with your worker ID).

Your performance will not be measured during the first 6 practice games.

Your performance will be measured during the 6 performance games.

Important:

1) During performance games, the timer will start AFTER your first move. So you can take your time reading pop-up information.

2) Pay close attention to the instructions on the left-hand side as they might change. A pop-up will be displayed when additional information is added to the instructions, to make sure you notice the change.

3) Every piece of information displayed is true. You can trust all written information."

Instructions displayed on the left side included the following text:

"**Instruction Game 0**
(no performance measured)
The objective of the puzzle is to move the entire stack to the indicated goal rod, either center or right rod, obeying the following simple rules:
Only one disk can be moved at a time.
Each move consists of taking the upper disk from one of the stacks and placing it on top of another stack or on an empty rod.
No larger disk may be placed on top of a smaller disk.
Click on the disk you want to move first. Drag-and-Drop does not work.
After that, you will have to figure out the rest for yourself.
With 3 disks, the puzzle can be solved in 7 moves.
Additional information:
No additional information so far."

The instruction text did not change throughout the first 7 games, except in the integer referring to the current level being played.

A second popup appeared in all five conditions with starting of game 8, and instruction texts differed amongst conditions. All instruction texts were altered as follows:

"Performance Game 7 (performance is measured)",

therefore, participants were informed about that their performance was now evaluated during the coming levels.

Instructions texts then differed amongst the five conditions (experiment groups, EG) in the "Additional Information:" part. The second popups differed from the first popup by stating "You are now starting with 6 performance games." and with exception of experiment group 1, the second popup also contained the warning phrase "Attention! Additional information was added to the instructions. Make sure to read!". This warning was implemented in order to make sure that participants actually read the additional information. The additional information contents were written in capital letters to induce disfluency, in order to enhance chances of "promoting more comprehensive consideration of opposing views", as disfluency in writing style has been proven to disrupt confirmation bias (Hernandez & Preston, 2013, p. 178).

Instruction text content is summarized in the following Table 4.6.

Table 4.6 Instruction texts for according information conditions in „ill-defined" stages. *Source* own source

EG	Game 8 instruction text "Additional Information:"	Warning
1	"No additional information."	No
2	"YOU ARE PLAYING IN A TEAM OF THREE HUMANS DURING THE NEXT 6 GAMES. YOU ALL HAVE INFLUENCE ON THE MOVEMENT OF THE DISCS AND SHARE CONTROL OVER THE GAME ACCORDING TO HIDDEN RULES. THE RULES DO NOT CHANGE DURING THE NEXT 6 GAMES."	Yes
3	"YOU ARE PLAYING IN A TEAM OF THREE HUMANS DURING THE NEXT 6 GAMES. YOU ALL HAVE INFLUENCE ON THE MOVEMENT OF THE DISCS AND SHARE CONTROL OVER THE GAME ACCORDING TO HIDDEN RULES. THE RULES DO NOT CHANGE DURING THE NEXT 6 GAMES. SINCE YOU CANNOT COMMUNICATE WITH EACH OTHER, IT IS HIGHLY UNLIKELY FOR YOU TO FIND OUT THESE RULES."	Yes
4	"YOU ARE PLAYING IN A TEAM OF THREE HUMANS DURING THE NEXT 6 GAMES. YOU ALL HAVE INFLUENCE ON THE MOVEMENT OF THE DISCS AND SHARE CONTROL OVER THE GAME ACCORDING TO HIDDEN RULES. THE RULES DO NOT CHANGE DURING THE NEXT 6 GAMES. DURING THE NEXT 6 GAMES THE DIRECTIONAL BUTTONS DO NOT INFLUENCE THE GAME AT ALL. ALL THEY DO IS CHANGE COLOR WHEN BEING PRESSED."	Yes
5	"YOU ARE PLAYING IN A TEAM OF THREE HUMANS DURING THE NEXT 6 GAMES. YOU ALL HAVE INFLUENCE ON THE MOVEMENT OF THE DISCS AND SHARE CONTROL OVER THE GAME ACCORDING TO HIDDEN RULES. THE RULES DO NOT CHANGE DURING THE NEXT 6 GAMES. SINCE YOU CANNOT COMMUNICATE WITH EACH OTHER, IT IS HIGHLY UNLIKELY FOR YOU TO FIND OUT THESE RULES. DURING THE NEXT 6 GAMES THE DIRECTIONAL BUTTONS DO NOT INFLUENCE THE GAME AT ALL. ALL THEY DO IS CHANGE COLOR WHEN BEING PRESSED."	Yes

With game level 8 being reached, participants played 6 rounds of Tower of Europe, in identical manner as explained in the former chapter. Each experiment group contained different additional information, defining the five different information conditions, which are to be explained in the following.

The first information condition (EG: 1) did not contain any further information. Participants were not informed about the fact that they did now share control with two additional agents. This information conditions is now referred to as "no information condition" (N-IC).

The second information condition (EG: 2) informed participants about them sharing control during all 6 performance games with two other agents in accordance to hidden rules, which will not change. This information condition is now referred to as "GDM information condition" (G-IC).

The third information condition (EG: 3) informed participants about them sharing control during all 6 performance games with two other agents in accordance to hidden rules, which will not change. Participants also received the "discouraging" information that due to a lack of communication potential these hidden rules will likely remain hidden. This information condition is now referred to as "disillusioning information condition" (D-IC).

The fourth information condition (EG: 4) informed participants about them sharing control during all 6 performance games with two other agents in accordance to hidden rules, which will not change. Participants also received the information about the directional buttons not having any function besides changing color when being pressed. This information condition is now referred to as "routine information condition" (R-IC).

The fifth information condition (EG: 5) contained all additional information from G-IC, D-IC, R-IC. This information condition is now referred to as "combined information condition" (C-IC).

Additional information content was displayed throughout all ToE games, and did not disappear or alter its contents at any moment.

Having solved all 6 ToE games, participants had to answer an after-survey, simply asking "Have you done the experiment "Flag Run" before?", which participants were able to answer by either choosing "Yes" or "No", after which the experiment ended, and participants were provided with their ID.

The following chapter will derive hypotheses, list dependent and independent variables and how data was treated.

Specific Research Objectives

5

The experiment's purpose was to create a decision-making domain related to a VUCA domain—where agents had to solve a complex problem—and to analyze how their behavior changed when provided different global information. Another major aspect of the experiment was to "train" the agents first in decision-making in isolation (routine-strategy), followed by randomly grouping them into a "game" of three agents afterwards. The agents were unable to communicate, did not receive information about the former actions of their co-agents, but were always able to collectively see the outcome of their shared control over the game. The following research questions are to be answered:

1) Does public information about environmental change ("You are sharing control with humans!") favor change of routine-strategy, when such new environmental conditions do not influence the routine-strategy's performance?
2) Does influence of environmental change (Middle rod is goal rod.) on routine-strategy's performance favor change of routine-strategy?
3) Will deviation distance from routine-strategy depend on the type of public information, i.e. information about man-made uncertainty will lead to higher deviation from routine-strategy than from unspecified uncertainty (no further public information)?
4) Will public information about hidden rules favor overcoming parts of the routine-strategy?

Electronic supplementary material The online version of this chapter (https://doi.org/10.1007/978-3-658-33139-9_5) contains supplementary material, which is available to authorized users.

U. G. Strunz, *The Impact of Individual Expertise and Public Information on Group Decision-Making*, FOM-Edition Research, https://doi.org/10.1007/978-3-658-33139-9_5

5) Is group performance in the complex problem-solving game dependent on individual decision-making expertise in routine-strategy, when the routine-strategy statistically benefits the group's performance in the game where no communication is possible?

5.1   Derivation of Hypotheses

The first research question of this thesis asks, whether information provided in G-IC, D-IC, R-IC and C-IC influences participants in changing their strategy, which they used to solve the ToH games during ToE games 8, 9, and 10. ToE games 8, 9, and 10 can be solved with certainty in seven steps, when all game group agents stick to the framed logic, and can be solved with high probability in seven steps, when all game group agents mostly stick to the framed logic. Therefore, sticking with the framed logic during the first three ToE games will solve the GDM problem under uncertainty efficiently. As experimental results showed that individual strategies are mostly only altered by environmental change, if such change had an influence on the strategy's performance, it was assumed that when participants had proven "framed logic" routine and ToH expertise, participants of such a game group will unlikely change their strategy.

The participants' "routine" was derived from the proportion of either "Framed Logic" or "No Border Logic" level-solving moves or actions. An action solving a ToH game is by definition always either solved via a "Framed Logic" or "No Border Logic" action, and can never be both. When neither a "Framed Logic" nor "No Border Logic" action solved a level, it was because the timer ran out. If a player listed more "Framed Logic" (F-L) or more "No Border Logic" (NB-L) values at actions, which solved a ToH level, the according logic was assumed to be the routine strategy. When a participant listed an equal proportion of F-L and NB-L actions that solved ToH levels, the routine strategy was regarded as unclear and therefore reported as "mixed" (Mx-L).

ToH expertise of each individual was expressed by an index, and was the result of the participant performance measured during ToH games 2 to 7.

ToH expert knowledge levels or ToH expertise was measured by looking at different parameters collected from ToH levels 2 to 7:

– How many ToH levels were solved?
– Did participants solve at least one ToH game in 7 steps?
– What was the least number of steps required in any ToH game?
– How many ToH games were solved with 7 steps?

– How many steps in total were required to solve the ToH games?

Ideally, if an agent solved all six ToH levels (excluding the first game) in 7 steps using F-L, this agent would have proven the highest amount of expertise, and would have shown the F-L to be the routine-strategy. If an agent solved all ToH levels in 7 steps using NB-L, this agent would also have proven the highest amount of expertise, and would have shown the NB-L to be the routine-strategy.

Expertise in F-L routine was expected to have the side-effect that game groups with high levels of F-L expert knowledge would solve the first three ToE levels with higher efficiency. The ToE rules were therefore not expected to affect strategy performance that stem from a framed strategy routine. ToE rules were however expected to influence strategy performance that stem from a no border strategy routine. Information about routine strategy and expertise levels was saved for each participant. Table 5.1 (own source) shows all data mentioned above by example, to express routine strategy used, and according expertise.

Table 5.1 Results of example experiment for explanation, part 1

Information	Value
Strategy proportion	F-L (6) NB-L (0)
Routine strategy (F-L/NB-L/Mx-L)	F-L
Number of failed ToH games	0
Least number of steps required	7
Number of 7-steps games	2
Steps in total	60

In order to create expertise categories, a pretest with 30 participants, all being US-American MTurks, was conducted, using the identical setup as being used in the main experiment. Three participants had idled throughout the entire experiment, and were not considered. The remaining 27 US-American MTurks' results regarding routine strategy were used, and according information about expertise is summarized in table 5.2 (own source).

Average values of strategy proportion regard 189 level-solving actions from 1623 actions in total. From 189 level-actions by 27 participants, only 4 NB-L actions solved a game, performed by three distinct players. By definition all 27 players were using F-L as their routine strategy.

17 out of 27 participants completed all ToH games in time, not failing a single game. 8 out of 27 participants failed at one ToH game, by not completing it in

time. Two out of 27 participants failed at three ToH games, by not completing them in time.

24 out of 27 participants completed at least one ToH game in 7 steps. Three out of 27 participants failed to solve at least one ToH game in 7 steps, having required 8, 9, and 10 steps during their best games.

Table 5.2 Results of example experiment for explanation, part 2

Information (n = 27)	Value (on average)
Strategy proportion, average	F-L (5.33) NB-L (0.15)
Routine strategy (F-L/NB-L/Mx-L)	all used F-L
Number of failed ToH games, average	0.59
Least number of steps required, average	7.22
Number of 7-steps games, average	2.81
Steps in total, average, n = 17	53.53

Results regarding the amount of achieved 7-steps games are listed in the following table 5.3 (own source), 15 out of 27 participants achieved between three and 6 perfect 7-steps ToH games. Only one out of 27 participants managed to solve all ToH games with 7 actions.

When participants who failed to solve at least one ToH game are excluded, the remaining 17 participants required 53.53 actions in total to solve all 6 ToH games. It took the two participants who failed to compete at least one ToH game in 7 steps 65 and 72 steps to complete all stages.

No participant who solved either 5 or 6 ToH games with 7 actions failed to solve a single ToH game. Only one participant who solved 4 ToH games with 7 actions failed to solve at least one ToH game. Two participants who solved three ToH games with 7 actions failed to solve at least one ToH game. Five participants who solved two ToH games with 7 actions failed to solve at least one ToH game. Two participants who solved either none or just one ToH game with 7 actions failed to solve at least one ToH game. No participant who required 60 or more steps in total to solve all ToH games managed to solve more than two games with just 7 actions.

From these results, three expertise categories are established using the number of ToH games solved in 7 steps and number of failed ToH games. The highest

Table 5.3 Results of example experiment for explanation, part 3

Number of 7-steps ToH games	Number of agents (n = 27)
0	3
1	2
2	7
3	5
4	6
5	3
6	1

expert rank is assigned to participants, solving 4 or more ToH games with 7 actions, not having failed more than one ToH game. The medium expert rank is assigned to participants solving two or three ToH games with 7 actions, not having failed more than 1 ToH game. The low expert rank is assigned to participants solving none or one ToH game with 7 actions.

By this definition all 27 out of 27 participants were assigned the routine strategy "F-L". 10 out of 27 participants from the pretest were assigned an expert rank of "high", 10 out of 27 participants were assigned a "medium" expertise, and 7 out of 27 participants were assigned "low" expertise.

The 7 low expertise (L) participants collectively failed to solve 8 ToH games in total. The 10 medium expertise (M) participants collectively failed to solve 5 ToH games in total. The 10 high expertise (H) participants collectively failed to solve only one ToH game. From these 27 participants only 15 produced valuable data, as 12 participants were either part of a bot-agent game group, disconnected or were part of a game group with players who idled throughout the single player phase. From these five game groups, two game groups were in the G-IC, two were in the D-IC, and one group in the R-IC. The according expertise levels are listed in table 5.5 (own source).

From the small pretest alone, only 50 % of data could be used for analysis. Therefore, a rather large number of participants was expected to be required for the main experiment. It was estimated that for more than 180 game groups per condition, about 6000 human agents were required. Accordingly, 300 participants were expected to produce 10 game groups per condition. Even with 6000 human agents, analyzes would have still been limited by many factors, being discussed in chapter 5.

As participants will be assigned to a bot agent after 5 minutes of waiting time due to ethical reasons, a game group that contained a bot-agent and was part of any other information condition other than N-IC was considered as a "deception" condition. This is because participants of such game groups were informed about playing with "human agents". Therefore, game groups having bot-agents in any information condition other than N-IC were considered "deceptive" and were excluded fully from data analysis. In order to enhance chances of filling game groups with human agents, the main experiment was divided into several parts, with each part collecting US-American MTurks at different day times.

Due to the pretest results group expertise levels were expected to be mixed; from five game groups, four showed distinct levels of group expertise. Ten different group expertise levels are possible, rated as "1" for "L, L, L" and "10" for "H, H, H". Group expertise was expected to be normally distributed, confirming experimental studies that while repetition leads to better strategy use, each participant differs greatly in their individual ability to learn ToH rules (Janssen, De Mey, Egger, & Witteman, 2010).

The group expertise level is calculated by individual expertise levels. The order, by which the expertise group ratings are listed, favors "group quality over individual quality". In other words, a group consisting of 2 L experts and 1 H expert ranks lower in group expertise than a group with 1 L expert and 2 M experts. Table 5.4 shows all possible group expertise rankings resulting from individual expertise.

Table 5.4 Group expertise rated as an integer in order from individual expertise levels. *Source* own source

Individual expertise levels in group	Resulting group expertise
L, L, L	1
L, L, M	2
L, L, H	3
L, M, M	4
L, M, H	5
M, M, M	6
M, M, H	7
L, H, H	8
M, H, H	9
H, H, H	10

Another order of preference that should be noted was L, H, H (8) over M, M, H (7). From a set theoretical viewpoint L, H was preferred over M, M. However, M, M, M (6) was preferred over L, M, H (5), where in this context M, M was preferred over L, H. Therefore, from a purely logical viewpoint, a contradiction exits. The reason why M, M, M was preferred over L, M, H is because of consistency of skill in this group, as one single participant, who behaved "less than wise" was able to derail an entire group strategy. This might seem to be a weak argument then for the preference of group expertise 8 over 7, however, to acquire expertise level H requires very high precision in ToH decision-making. A group with expertise level 8 consists of two highly skilled experts, rendering the possibility of "less than wise behavior" of one single participant less likely. Of course, the order of group expertise still is debatable, but thorough thought was certainly put into its creation.

Table 5.5 Results of example experiment for explanation, part 4

Participant IDs	Expertise Levels	IC
4, 5, 6	M, M, L (4)	D-IC
7, 8, 9	H, L, L (3)	R-IC
16, 17, 18	M, H, H (9)	G-IC
31, 32, 33	L, M, H (5)	G-IC
34, 35, 36	L, H, M (5)	D-IC

Coming back to the first research question, several variables were identified. Public information is either lacking in the N-IC or comes in four distinct forms in the G-IC, D-IC, R-IC or C-IC. Environmental conditions are all such circumstances that lie outside of the agent's control. Interpretations are not regarded as being part of the environmental conditions, even when "wrong interpretations" are facilitated by environmental conditions, as explained by two examples: as participants of the N-IC are not informed about playing with other agents, it is expected that participants of the N-IC interpreted outcomes that deviated from their expectation stemming from "error", such as software bugs, glitches, randomizing variables, wrong inputs, and not due to human influences; as participants of the G-IC are not informed about there being next to chance of obtaining the true hidden rules, it is expected that participants of the G-IC interpreted outcomes that deviated from their expectation stemming from "error", such as bad expertise of co-agents, human mistakes or "bad cognitive skill" by co-agents.

The distinct information in each IC are considered public information and being part of the environmental conditions, however, their interpretations are considered as being in control of each agent. Therefore, "public information about environmental change" is part of environmental conditions, lying outside of the agent's control, whereas their interpretation and ultimately their impact on the individual's behavior is considered to be part of each agent's control.

Change stemming from environmental conditions are considered as being interpreted either as environmental or social influences. Environmental influences were defined as all influences which are not "man-made". Social influences were defined as all influences which are "man-made". It was expected that environmental influence interpretations (EI-I) led to participants trying to maximize control over expected outcomes by sticking their routine strategy. It was expected that social influence interpretations (SI-I) led to participants trying to maximize control over expected outcomes by deviating from their routine strategy. The fluent transition from deviation distances stemming from EI-I and SI-I are explained by listing all information conditions.

In the N-IC participants were expected to interpret deviations from expected outcomes mostly stemming from environmental influences, as the N-IC participants were not informed about there being human co-agents.

In the G-IC participants were expected to interpret deviations from expected outcomes mostly stemming from social influences, as the G-IC participants were not informed implicitly that no agent was able to "outsmart" the hidden rules, other than by sticking to the regular single player rules.

In the D-IC participants were expected to interpret deviations from expected outcomes stemming less from social influences than in the G-IC, as the D-IC participants were implicitly informed that all agents were "still putting their trousers on one leg at a time" and that looking for "patterns" to "outsmart" the hidden ruleset was a waste of time. D-IC participants were expected to interpret deviations from expected outcomes stemming less from environmental influences than in the N-IC, as D-IC participants still knew that they had "some control" over the outcomes, and in fact they did.

The algorithm was written in such a way that each participant always had the chance of decisive impact on the group action's outcome, and always had some impact on the group action's outcome, while never having a chance of full control over the outcome, as order of inputs were decisive. Even if the entire algorithm was known, communication would be required in order to synchronize order of inputs with other co-agents, to obtain full control over the group action's outcome. Although not entirely impossible, this thesis expects no game group to optimize control over game group outcomes. When the goal rod was the right rod, a game group could only "seemingly" optimize game group output. When the right rod was set to be the goal rod, a game group could solve ToE in 7 steps, with each individual agents sticking to the F-L, disregarding order of inputs. This was not the case when the goal rod was the center rod. When the center rod was the goal rod, by F-L the optimal move was "S1", with "S1, S1, S1" resulting in the small disc. The only realistic way of doing so without communication was if a game group stuck to a certain "rhythm", meaning that order of information was stable, and at least one participant provided an input outside of F-L at the right moment. It was expected that such a dynamic decision-making equilibrium would not be observed.

In the R-IC participants were expected to behave similar to G-IC participants, if R-IC participants (mostly) did still use directional buttons; should R-IC participants (mostly) refrain from using the directional buttons, then greater deviations than in the G-IC were expected. As the environmental condition "The directional buttons do not influence the game at all" will never influence any strategy performance, some participants in the R-IC were expected to still use the directional buttons due to routine strength. In other words, routine strength of pressing directional buttons was considered to dominate deviations from routine logic in some cases. Due to routine strength it was expected that participants who refrain from using the directional buttons, were still using them in some cases. R-IC participants were expected to deviate more from their routine strategy than N-IC, and more than D-IC, due to SI-I.

In the C-IC participants were expected to behave similar to D-IG participants when directional buttons (mostly) were used, and greater deviations were expected when directional buttons (mostly) were not used. C-IC participants were expected to deviate more from their routine strategy than N-IC participants, less than G-IC participants, and less than R-IC participants.

In order to formulate the according hypotheses, deviation distance from routine strategy has to be defined and expressed by an index in the following. For now all mentioned expected deviation distances (dd) in each condition are ordered as follows:

$$dd(\text{N-IC}) < dd(\text{D-IC}) <= dd(\text{C-IC}) < dd(\text{G-IC}) <= dd(\text{R-IC}).$$

Therefore, the greatest deviations from routine strategy were expected in the R-IC and the least deviations from routine strategy were expected in the N-IC conditions.

The greatest expected distance from routine strategy using the pretest was expected to be observed between D-IC and R-IC, as no N-IC data was available. In order to create the deviation distance from the routine strategy, several steps have to be taken. This is to be explained by example of the pretest again, using data of two game groups.

First the proportion of ToH routine logic actions to the total amount of ToH actions were measured in two ways, being "ToH total" and ToH parts". A ToH total index of e.g. 0.6842 with ToH routine F-L means that ToH games' actions from level 2 to 7 were in 68.42 % of the cases F-L actions. A ToH parts index of "1,0 / 0,5" means that ToH games' actions from level 2 to 4 were in 100 % of the cases F-L actions and from level 5 to 7 were in 0.5 % of the cases F-L actions.

Since in ToH game 5 the goal rod changed from being the right rod to being the center rod, most players failed to solve ToH game 5 as efficiently as ToH game 4, as players would use their level 4 strategy to begin level 5 with actions that deviate from the ideal path. The position of the goal rod was considered being a change of environmental conditions which affects a participant's former routine strategy. Therefore, F-L has sub-routine strategies regarding the position of the goal rod. This effect was also expected in ToE games, since in game 4 the goal rod changed from being the right rod to being the center rod.

The highest proportion of ToH logical actions was achieved by participant 7, who was ranked with high expertise. Lowest ToH logic proportion was achieved by participant 8, who was ranked with low expertise. It was expected that expertise rank and ToH total were to correlate, leading to the first two hypotheses. All hypotheses, dependent and independent variables are to be listed in the following sub-chapter.

5.2   Hypotheses and Variables

As expertise and logic proportions were expected to correlate, and goal rod change was expected to influence performance, the first two hypotheses are as follows:

Hypothesis 1: The higher the individual expertise rank, the higher the logic proportion "ToH total" is.

Hypothesis 2: Change of goal rod during ToH and ToE games in the 4th level leads to the first actions in the same level deviating from the ideal path.

As can be seen in table 5.6, all participants in the D-IC conditions stuck closely to their routine strategy's logic during ToE levels one to three, obtaining logic proportion levels of 95.24 %, 100 % and 100%. Even though participants were facing environmental change, this change did not influence the routine strategy's performance. As expected, the participants did therefore not deviate from their routine strategy at all (participants 5 and 6) or not nearly at all (participant 4). It is expected that participants of the N-IC will show significantly lower values of routine logic deviation than D-IC, leading to the third hypothesis:

Hypothesis 3: Participants in the N-IC condition show the highest logic proportions in ToE levels one to three, expressed by "ToE parts 1", followed by proportions of D-IC participants, then C-IC, G-IC and R-IC.

As expected, routine logic deviations in the R-IC condition were higher than in the D-IC condition. While playing ToE participants 4, 5 and 6 followed their routine logic in 76.27 %, 86.44 % and 74.58 % of all cases, and participants 7, 8, and 9 followed their routine logic in only 23.57 %, 24.29 % and 22.86 % of all cases. N-IC participants were expected to show even higher values in logic proportion than D-IC participants. This leads to the fourth hypothesis:

Hypothesis 4: Participants in the N-IC condition show the highest total ToE logic proportion values, followed by proportions of D-IC participants, then C-IC, G-IC and R-IC.

By example of the small sample sized pretest, routine logic deviations grew in the D-IC condition, which was expected, due to the change of the goal rod position influencing strategy performance. However, the goal rod change during ToE games has to be treated differently from the goal rod change during ToH games. During ToH games the goal rod change will influence performance due to participants e.g. not paying attention to such change, using their F-L logic which would be ideal when the goal rod is "right" not "center". This loss in performance can be quickly corrected during ToH by becoming aware of the goal rod change and adapting the F-L to the new goal rod position. It was expected that participants who deviate from the ideal path in ToH level 5, but performed well during ToH level 4, will either keep on "trembling" throughout ToH levels 5 to 7 where the goal rod was changed to being "center" or quickly learn and adapt their F-L to the new ToH goal rod conditions. However, ToH games participants are not expected to be "surprised" be their actions' output, measured in "expected states" deviation. Goal rod change in ToE level 4 on the other hand also influences the participants' expected states deviation, as for example an individual action input of "S1 r" might result in the small disk "seemingly" travelling to the left or might even result in the medium or large sized disk being moved; such cases are expected to create an "expected states deviation". Such expected states deviation can lead to new interpretation of each individual agent. The influence of the environmental condition "goal rod change" in ToE level 4 is expected to be of lower influence to ToE routine logic deviations in levels 4, 5, and 6 than the "expected states deviation" experience. In order to measure this, ToE parts 1 logic deviations are also considered, where no goal rod change is yet performed. It was expected that "expected states deviation" is a better predictor of ToE logic deviation than the environmental condition "goal rod change", as the former is expected to lead to interpretation changes, inducing deeper uncertainty than by the latter. Therefore, expected states deviations are expected to influence ToE logic deviations in all conditions of the experiment. In addition, higher expected states deviations were considered to lead to individual behavior which increasingly is not "captured" by any logic category, leading to low "logic marker" values. The logic marker reports the amount of actions in ToE games that are "0" in any logic category divided by total amount of actions. In other words, high values of expected states deviations were expected to make participants behave "randomly" from the perspective of the experimenter.

Hypothesis 5: The higher expected states deviation proportion values with respect to routine strategy during all ToE conditions, the higher logic deviation proportion values are.

Hypothesis 6: The higher expected states deviation proportion values with respect to routine strategy during all ToE conditions, the lower the logic marker proportion values are.

Table 5.6 Results of example experiment for explanation, part 5

ID	exp	ToH routine	ToE strategy	condition	ToH total (parts)	ToE total (parts 1 / 2)
4	M	F-L	F-L dir	D-IC	0,6842 (1,0 / 0,5)	0,7627 (**0,9524** / 0,6579)
5	M	F-L	F-L dir	D-IC	0,6111 (0,56 / 0,6552)	0,8644 (**1,0** / 0,7895)
6	L	F-L	F-L dir	D-IC	0,5 (0,5227 / 0,4737)	0,7458 (**1,0** / 0,6053)
7	H	F-L	F-L nodir	R-IC	0,7037 (0,6071 / 0,8077)	0,2357 (0,1806 / 0,2941)
8	L	F-L	F-L nodir	R-IC	0,4386 (0,2692 / 0,5806)	0,2429 (0,2361 / 0,25)
9	L	F-L	F-L nodir	R-IC	0,6250 (0,6757 / 0,5714)	0,2286 (0,1806 / 0,2794)

R-IC and C-IC are expected to create higher expected states deviation from routine strategy as these conditions "take away" the basis for reinforcing the routine strategy, i.e. by informing about the "uselessness" of the direction button. It was expected that during R-IC expected states deviation values with respect to routine strategy were higher during ToE parts 1 than in all other conditions.

As the logic deviation distance of the G-IC was expected to be higher than of the C-IC, but the expected states distance of the C-IC was expected to be higher than of the G-IC, ToE game group performance, measured in total amount of required steps to solve all six ToE games, are considered, to indicate, whether logic deviation or expected states deviation with respect to routine logic is a better predictor of ToE group performance. Expected states deviation can be considered as a measurement of "irritating" feedback when a certain logic is used and was considered to lead to fundamental interpretation changes. Expected states deviation is the result of action. Logic deviation on the other hand expresses already performed action, embedding some former expectation. High expected states deviation distance with respect to some logic is considered as "more random feedback". By Hypothesis 5 and 6 this was considered to lead to higher logic deviation distances, and seemingly random behavior. R-IC was expected to induce radical interpretation problems, inducing participants to feel uncertain about their routine strategy. G-IC was expected to induce uncertainty by social influence, where participants would try to adapt their strategy according to certain "patterns", ultimately adapting their strategy. In G-IC participants were expected to use different forms of logic, not just their routine logic, therefore both using F-L and NB-L, leading to a lower proportion of routine logic used than in the C-IC condition, as only one logic form can be the routine logic.

Routine consistency is the number of routine strategy actions during the ill-defined stages that fall either into the F-L or NB-L category, divided by the total amount of actions during the ill-defined stages; sub-distinguishing elements of logic forms such as dir, nodir and ideal are disregarded for the calculation of routine consistency. When an action falls neither into the F-L or NB-L category, this action still is added to the total amount of actions, by which the number of routine strategy actions during the ill-defined stages is divided. Actions that fall outside of any known logic category are measured by the logic marker. For instance, a player has developed routine logic F-L from the well-defined stages. He has used 100 actions total during the ill-defined stages, with 90 F-L actions (80 times dir, 5 times nodir, 5 times ideal) and 10 NB-L actions (4 times dir, 2 times nodir, 4 times ideal), and therefore has a logic marker of 0 (0.00 %), since all actions are part of known logic categories. The resulting routine consistency is 0.90 (90 %).

Low routine consistency in G-IC ultimately was expected to lead to greater logic deviation distance from routine logic than in the C-IC condition, and due to logic volatility, to also lead to a higher deviation of expected states with respect to the routine logic. In the C-IC condition participants were expected to "stick with one logic" as they were "discouraged" by dissolution, still being induced by a lowered form of social influence and interpretation uncertainty. The D-IC lacks the interpretation uncertainty regarding the direction buttons, and comes with a lowered form of social influence. In other words, participants in the R-IC were expected to use different kinds of logic forms or strategies, and are induced with deep uncertainty with all strategies they tried, perhaps even leading to participants actually performing actions arbitrarily. Participants in the G-IC were expected to use different kinds of strategies, without being induced with deep uncertainty. Participants in C-IC were induced with deep uncertainty, however, were expected to be less volatile in their strategy forming than in G-IC, still deviating more from their routine strategy than in D-IC.

Hypothesis 7: Expected states deviation proportion values during ToE parts 1, ToE parts 2 and ToE total in R-IC are the highest, followed by G-IC, C-IC, D-IC and lastly N-IC.

Hypothesis 8: Routine consistency is the lowest in R-IC, followed by G-IC, C-IC, D-IC and N-IC.

Group performance, measured in numbers of group actions required to solve all ToE games, depends on the order of group actions. The algorithm is implemented in such a way that when all participants of a game-group at least agree on the optimal disk to be moved, this collectively chosen disk will always be moved, and the game group will outperform randomness greatly, even with different strategies in mind on how to move the disk. However, it was expected that even this "fundamental logic" will be dissolved with inducing deep uncertainty by telling participants the truth about "the direction buttons not working". It was expected that the proportion of actions where participants did agree on one disk, disregarding whether it was the optimal choice, was the best predictor for group performance, expressed by the "fundamental index".

Hypothesis 9: The lower the fundamental index the lower game group performance.

Finally, it was expected that group expertise rank explains inter-condition logic deviations amongst groups.

Hypothesis 10: Lower inter-condition group expertise rankings lead to lower logic deviation proportions.

In the following, table 5.7 (own source) will list all dependent and independent variables required for all 10 hypotheses and their according hypothesis (H).

Table 5.7 Independent and dependent variables, with according hypothesis

Independent variable	Dependent variable	H
ind. expertise rank	logic proportion "ToH total"	1
goal rod change, level 4	starting routine logic values of 0 in ToH and ToE, all conditions	2
public information	logic proportion "ToE parts 1" in order N-IC > D-IC > C-IC > G-IC > R-IC	3
public information	logic proportion "ToE total" in order N-IC > D-IC > C-IC > G-IC > R-IC	4
expected state proportion	logic proportion during all ToE conditions	5
expected state proportion	logic marker proportion during all ToE conditions	6
public information	expected state proportion ToE total, ToE parts 1 and ToE parts 2 R-IC < G-IC < C-IC < D-IC < N-IC	7
public information	strategy consistancy index R-IC < G-IC < C-IC < D-IC < N-IC	8
fundamental index	game group performance during all ToE conditions	9
group expertise rank	logic proportion ToE total, ToE parts 1 and ToE parts 2	10

Results

6

An attempt to conduct an experiment with 330 US-American MTurks failed due to server memory capacity with the Amazon AWS "t2.micro 1 GiB". After upgrading the server to 32 GiB of working memory with the Amazon AWS "t2.2xlarge 32 GiB", an experiment with 180 US-American MTurks was conducted, from which data of 87 participants was used. As estimated, more than 50 % of participant data was lost due to connection errors, incorrect raw data, participants leaving the experiment or participants playing in a game group with one or more bots. CPU capacity reached 55 % during the experiment, and it is not advised to try larger numbers of participants with mentioned settings.

29 female and 58 male participants aged 33.16 years on average were analyzed. From 87 participants 9 reported having conducted the experiment before, 63 reported not having conducted the experiment before, while 15 participants did not answer to this question. By comparing MTurk ID tables all 9 participants, who reported having conducted the experiment before, were part of the 330-participants experiment, which crashed before the ToE stages were reached. Therefore, all participants were included. Participants from the example experiment mentioned before were not included.

Chapter 6 will analyze all hypotheses in according sub-chapters, beginning with testing variables for parametric or nonparametric distribution.

6.1 Testing For Nonparametric Distribution

Variables were tested for nonparametric distribution using the One-Sample Kolmogorov-Smirnov Test. Each null hypothesis stating that the variable was distributed normally was rejected for 11 variables with high significance, being listed

© The Author(s) 2021
U. G. Strunz, *The Impact of Individual Expertise and Public Information on Group Decision-Making*, FOM-Edition Research,
https://doi.org/10.1007/978-3-658-33139-9_6

Hypothesis Test Summary

	Null Hypothesis	Test	Sig.	Decision
1	The categories of expertise occur with equal probabilities.	One-Sample Chi-Square Test	,010	Reject the null hypothesis.
2	The distribution of strategy_volatility_marker1 is normal with mean 1 and standard deviation 0,222.	One-Sample Kolmogorov-Smirnov Test	,000[1]	Reject the null hypothesis.
3	The distribution of ToH_tot is normal with mean 0.6989 and standard deviation 0,258.	One-Sample Kolmogorov-Smirnov Test	,003[1]	Reject the null hypothesis.
4	The distribution of ToH_parts1 is normal with mean 0.7323 and standard deviation 0,267.	One-Sample Kolmogorov-Smirnov Test	,000[1]	Reject the null hypothesis.
5	The distribution of ToH_parts2 is normal with mean 0.6833 and standard deviation 0,290.	One-Sample Kolmogorov-Smirnov Test	,000[1]	Reject the null hypothesis.
6	The distribution of ToE_tot is normal with mean 0.7410 and standard deviation 0,224.	One-Sample Kolmogorov-Smirnov Test	,000[1]	Reject the null hypothesis.
7	The distribution of ToE_parts1 is normal with mean 0.7583 and standard deviation 0,255.	One-Sample Kolmogorov-Smirnov Test	,000[1]	Reject the null hypothesis.
8	The distribution of ToE_parts2 is normal with mean 0.7338 and standard deviation 0,240.	One-Sample Kolmogorov-Smirnov Test	,001[1]	Reject the null hypothesis.
9	The distribution of ToE_X_tot is normal with mean 0.4864 and standard deviation 0,225.	One-Sample Kolmogorov-Smirnov Test	,000[1]	Reject the null hypothesis.
10	The distribution of ToE_X_parts1 is normal with mean 0.6013 and standard deviation 0,251.	One-Sample Kolmogorov-Smirnov Test	,000[1]	Reject the null hypothesis.
11	The distribution of ToE_X_parts2 is normal with mean 0.4245 and standard deviation 0,224.	One-Sample Kolmogorov-Smirnov Test	,001[1]	Reject the null hypothesis.
12	The distribution of logic_marker is normal with mean 0.0796 and standard deviation 0,099.	One-Sample Kolmogorov-Smirnov Test	,000[1]	Reject the null hypothesis.

Asymptotic significances are displayed. The significance level is ,05.

[1]Lilliefors Corrected

Figure 6.1   Test results for nonparametric distribution of variables. *Source* own source

in figure 6.1. Distribution of individual expertise occurring with equal probability was rejected at the 0.01 level of significance. The list includes variables for individual expertise, routine consistency, all logic proportions from the well-defined stages, all logic proportions from the ill-defined stages, all expected states from the ill-defined stages and the logic marker index. Using Shapiro-Wilk testing, all 12 null hypotheses stating normal/parametric for the same variable distributions were rejected with very high significance ($p = 0.000$). For this reason, distributions are considered being nonparametric, and therefore, with exception of Hypotheses 2, nonparametric analyses are used.

6.2   Expertise Rank and Logic Proportion

Hypothesis 1: The higher the individual expertise rank, the higher the logic proportion "ToH total" is.

Individual expertise rank was categorized either being „low", „medium" or „high". Agents who failed more than one ToH game due to the timer running out were always part of the "low" expertise rank. Agents who completed 4 or more ToH games in 7 steps were part of the "high" expertise category. Agents who completed two or three ToH games in 7 steps were part of the "medium" category. Agents who completed one or no ToH game in 7 steps were part of the "low" category.

33 agents were part of the „low" expertise group, 16 agens were part of the „medium" expertise group and 38 agents were part of the „high" expertise group.

„ToH total" is the proportion of ideal routine strategy steps used in all ToH games, with exception of the first game. Spearman's rho showed a correlation significant at the 0.01 level (2 tailed), as shown in figure 6.2.

Agents with low ToH expertise (0) had a mean index of 0.4463 ToH total (std. error 0.0338, std. deviation 0.1943). Agents with medium expertise (1) had a mean index of 0.7231 ToH total (std. error 0.03646, std. deviation 0.1458). Agents with high expertise (2) had a mean index of 0.9080 ToH total (std. error 0.0172, std. deviation 0.1063). Figure 6.3 shows specifics as a box-plot diagram.

Kruskal-Wallis H shows group differences in ToH total index by ToH expertise to be highly significant ($H(33, 16, 38)$, $H = 60.604$, $p = 0.000$).

Hypothesis 1 is therefore confirmed. Differences in routine logic deviation correlate significantly with the ToH total index and differences are significant. Means of high expertise participants and low/medium expertise participants vary significantly in terms of logic proportion "ToH_total".

Correlations

			expertise	ToH_tot
Spearman's rho	expertise	Correlation Coefficient	1,000	,839**
		Sig. (2-tailed)	.	,000
		N	87	87
	ToH_tot	Correlation Coefficient	,839**	1,000
		Sig. (2-tailed)	,000	.
		N	87	87

**. Correlation is significant at the 0.01 level (2-tailed).

Figure 6.2 Correlation results of expertise and ideal routine strategy in "well-defined" stages. *Source* own source

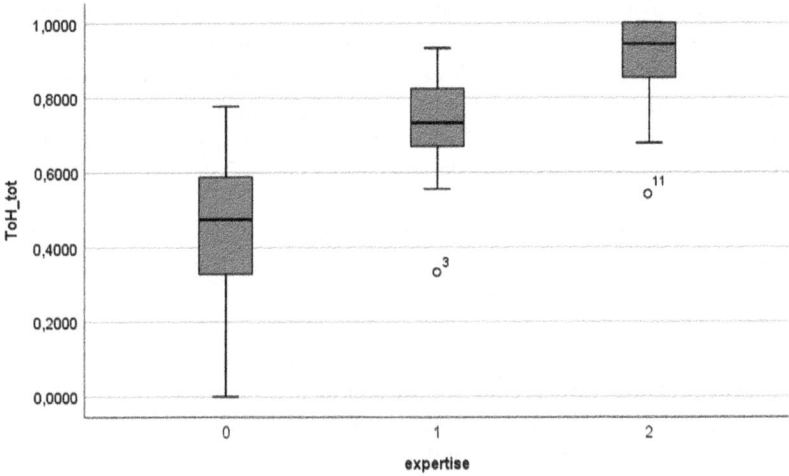

Figure 6.3 Boxplot results of expertise levels and logic proportion during „well-defined" stages. *Source* own source

6.3   Environmental Change and Human Error

Hypothesis 2: Change of goal rod during ToH and ToE games in the 4th level leads to the first actions in the same level deviating from the ideal path.

In order to confirm or not confirm this hypothesis, all first actions of all six ToH games were analyzed, whether or not this first move was an "ideal" move by F-L. This analysis excludes NB-L, as not a single ToE game was started by any of the 87 participants via an ideal NB-L move. The hypothesis was not analyzed for ToE games as too many factors influenced individual behavior aside from the goal rod change, making a statistical analysis questionable. The hypothesis was then modified to:

Hypothesis 2: Change of goal rod during ToH games in the 4th level leads to the first actions in the same level deviating from the ideal path.

As shown in table 6.1 (own source), not ideal first moves from ToH games one to three sunk from 45,98 % (n = 87) to 30,59 % (n = 85). With the introduction of goal rod change in ToH game 4, the not ideal first move proportion had risen to 51,16 % (n = 86), even being higher than the initial "mistake" proportion.

Mean average proportion of not ideal first moves of 0.4180 (std. deviation 0.0685, std. error 0.0278) differs significantly from 0.5116 (51.16 %) with p = 0.020. Mean average proportion of not ideal first moves do not significantly differ from the second highest value 0.4598 (45.98 %) with p = 0.195.

Modified Hypothesis 2 is therefore confirmed. Mistake rates on the first action in game 4, where the goal rod was changed, differed significantly from mean average mistake proportion.

Table 6.1 Impact of "macrostructure shift" on decision-making performance. *Source* own source

	ToH game 1	ToH game 2	ToH game 3	ToH game 4 (goal rod change)	ToH game 5	ToH game 6
not ideal	40	36	26	44	35	34
ideal	47	50	59	42	50	51
total	87	86	85	86	85	85
rel. not ideal	0,459770115	0,418604651	0,305882	**0,511628**	0,411765	0,4
rel. ideal	0,540229885	0,581395349	0,694118	0,488372	0,588235	0,6

6.4   Information Conditions and Logic Deviation

Hypothesis 3: Participants in the N-IC condition show the highest logic proportions in ToE levels one to three, expressed by "ToE parts 1", followed by proportions of D-IC participants, then C-IC, G-IC and R-IC.

Logic proportion is an index representing the proportion of actions being routine logic actions. The lower the index is, the higher the agent deviated from its routine strategy. The index „ToE parts 1" refers to the first three ToE games, which could be solved in 7 steps by sticking to the framed logic. The anticipated order by hypothesis 3 was: N-IC>D-IC>C-IC>G-IC>R-IC.

18 agents were part of the N-IC condition (6 groups), 24 agents were part of the G-IC condition (8 groups), 15 agents were part of the D-IC condition, 15 agents were part of the R-IC condition (5 groups) and 15 agents were part of the C-IC condition (5 groups). This was true for all hypotheses.

Mean average ToE parts 1 index of the N-IC was 0.7113 (std. error 0.6772, std. deviation 0.2873), with a range of 0.8. Mean average ToE parts 1 index of the G-IC was 0.7596 (std. error 0.0580, std. deviation 0.2841), with a range of 0.75. Mean average ToE parts 1 index of the D-IC was 0.6429 (std. error 0.0689, std. deviation 0.2666), with a range of 0.8. Mean average ToE parts 1 index of the R-IC was 0.9179 (std. error 0.0508, std. deviation 0.1966), with a range of 0.36. Mean average ToE parts 1 index of the C-IC was 0.7685 (std. error 0.0508, std. deviation 0.1966), with a range of 0.3636. Figure 6.4 shows the box-plot data.

Kruskal-Wallis H shows significant differences between conditions regarding the ToE parts 1 index, with (H(18, 24, 15, 15, 15), H = 10.119, p = 0.038).

Hypothesis 3 cannot be confirmed. The observed order of ToE parts 1 by information condition is R-IC>C-IC>G-IC>N-IC>D-IC, while the conditions' differences by this index were measured to be significant. The „routine information condition" shows the lowest routine logic deviation, while the „dissolution information condition" shows the highest routine logic deviation during the first three ToE games.

6.5   Complete Logic Proportions Over Information Conditions

Hypothesis 4: Participants in the N-IC condition show the highest total ToE logic proportion values, followed by proportions of D-IC participants, then C-IC, G-IC and R-IC.

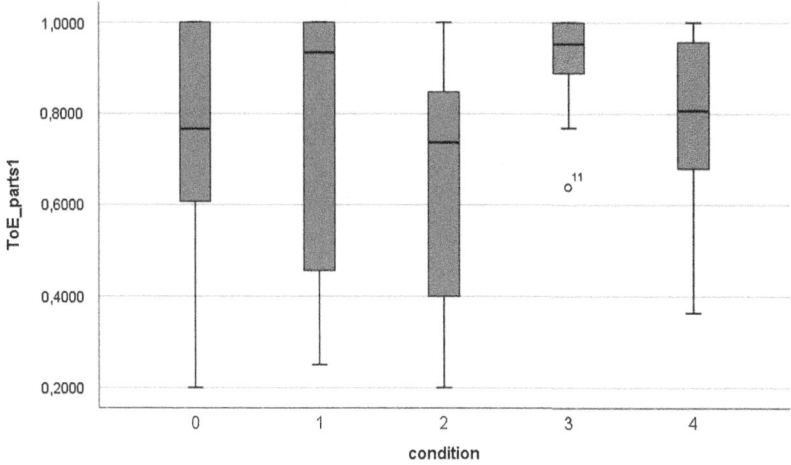

Figure 6.4   Boxplot results of logic proportion during "metastable" conditions over all information conditions: 0 = N-IC, 1 = G-IC, 2 = D-IC, 3 = R-IC, 4 = C-IC. *Source* own source

The index „ToE parts total" refers to the all six ToE games. The anticipated order by hypothesis 4 was: N-IC > D-IC > C-IC > G-IC > R-IC.

Mean average ToE total index of the N-IC was 0.7000 (std. error 0.0551, std. deviation 0.2339), with a range of 0.7218. Mean average ToE total index of the G-IC was 0.7409 (std. error 0.0580, std. deviation 0.2841), with a range of 0.6923. Mean average ToE total index of the D-IC was 0.7148 (std. error 0.0611, std. deviation 0.2366), with a range of 0.6768. Mean average ToE total index of the R-IC was 0.7970 (std. error 0.0475, std. deviation 0.1839), with a range of 0.5584 Mean average ToE total index of the C-IC was 0.7609 (std. error 0.0546, std. deviation 0.2114), with a range of 0.6205. Figure 6.5 shows the box-plot data.

Kruskal-Wallis H shows no significant differences between conditions regarding the ToE total index, with (H(18, 24, 15, 15, 15), H = 2,408, p = 0.661).

Hypothesis 4 cannot be confirmed. The observed order of ToE total by information condition is R-IC > C-IC > G-IC > N-IC > D-IC, while the conditions' differences by this index were not significant. The „routine information condition" shows the lowest routine logic deviation, while the „dissolution information condition" shows the highest routine logic deviation during the first three ToE games. However, the differences by this index were not significant.

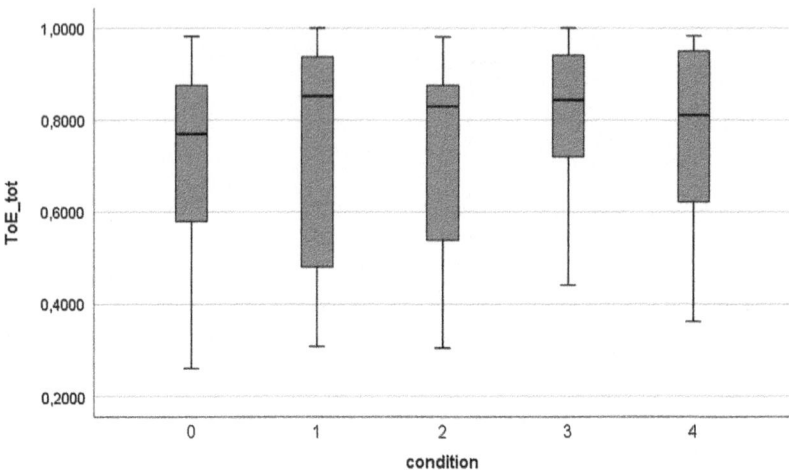

Figure 6.5 Boxplot results of logic proportion during "ill-defined" conditions over all information conditions: 0 = N-IC, 1 = G-IC, 2 = D-IC, 3 = R-IC, 4 = C-IC. *Source* own source

6.6   Expected States and Logic Proportion

Hypothesis 5: The higher expected states proportion values with respect to routine strategy during all ToE conditions, the higher logic proportion values are.

Expected states proportion is an index referring to the proportion of actions that were followed by the expected outcome, with respect to the actions' routine logic. The higher the expected state proportion the lower the expected state deviation. The lower the expected state proportion the higher the expected state deviation. Hypothesis 5 therefore assumed low expected states proportion to correlate with low logic proportion values, and high expected state proportion to correlate with high logic proportion values.

Just like logic proportion indexes there exist three expected states proportion indexes: "ToE_X_tot" refers to the expected states in all six ToE games. "ToE_X_parts1" refers to the expected states in the first three ToE games. "ToE_X_parts2" refers to the last three ToE games. All three expected states indexes were compared to all three logic proportion indexes, being ToE total, ToE parts 1 and ToE parts 2.

Spearman's rho correlation was significant at the 0.001 level (2-tailed) between all expected states and logic proportion indexes. Figure 6.6 sums up all mentioned data.

Hypothesis 5 was confirmed; expected states correlations with logic proportion were found to be highly significant.

6.7   Expected States and Logic Marker Proportion

Hypothesis 6: The higher expected states proportion values with respect to routine strategy during all ToE conditions, the lower the logic marker proportion values are.

Logic marker is an index representing the proportion of ToE actions of an agent which were not "captured" by any logic index. From the perspective of this thesis' model, such actions can be regarded as "random". It was expected that the agents who experience many actions to be followed by their expected outcome, would stick to some logic being framed by the model. In other words, it was expected that agents who experience seemingly "random" outcomes would also behave randomly. The higher the logic marker index is, the more "random" the agents behaved. The lower the logic marker index, the more this thesis' model can make sense of its behavior. Therefore, high expected states proportion was anticipated to lead to low logic marker values and therefore "less random behavior from the model's perspective" (Figure 6.7).

ToE_X_tot correlation with logic marker values was significant at the 0.01 level (2-tailed). ToE_X_parts1 correlation with the logic marker values was significant at the 0.05 level (2-tailed). ToE_X_parts2 correlation with the logic marker values was significant at the 0.01 level (2-tailed). Figure 6.7 sums up the results.

Hypothesis 6 was confirmed. All expected states indexes correlations with the logic marker index were either significant (p = 0.024) or highly significant (p = 0.000).

6.8   Complete Expected States Over Information Conditions

Hypothesis 7: Expected states proportion values during ToE parts 1, ToE parts 2 and ToE total in R-IC are the highest, followed by G-IC, C-IC, D-IC and lastly N-IC.

Correlations

		ToE_X_tot	ToE_X_parts1	ToE_X_parts2	ToE_tot	ToE_parts1	ToE_parts2
Spearman's rho	ToE_X_tot	Correlation Coefficient	1,000	,851**	,953**	,805**	,641**	,776**
		Sig. (2-tailed)	.	,000	,000	,000	,000	,000
		N	87	87	87	87	87	87
	ToE_X_parts1	Correlation Coefficient	,851**	1,000	,702**	,675**	,701**	,572**
		Sig. (2-tailed)	,000	.	,000	,000	,000	,000
		N	87	87	87	87	87	87
	ToE_X_parts2	Correlation Coefficient	,953**	,702**	1,000	,750**	,526**	,781**
		Sig. (2-tailed)	,000	,000	.	,000	,000	,000
		N	87	87	87	87	87	87
	ToE_tot	Correlation Coefficient	,805**	,675**	,750**	1,000	,811**	,937**
		Sig. (2-tailed)	,000	,000	,000	.	,000	,000
		N	87	87	87	87	87	87
	ToE_parts1	Correlation Coefficient	,641**	,701**	,526**	,811**	1,000	,601**
		Sig. (2-tailed)	,000	,000	,000	,000	.	,000
		N	87	87	87	87	87	87
	ToE_parts2	Correlation Coefficient	,776**	,572**	,781**	,937**	,601**	1,000
		Sig. (2-tailed)	,000	,000	,000	,000	,000	.
		N	87	87	87	87	87	87

**. Correlation is significant at the 0.01 level (2-tailed).

Figure 6.6 Correlation results between expected states and logic proportion. *Source* own source

Correlations

			ToE_X_tot	ToE_X_parts 1	ToE_X_parts 2	logic_marker
Spearman's rho	ToE_X_tot	Correlation Coefficient	1,000	,851**	,953**	-,448**
		Sig. (2-tailed)	.	,000	,000	,000
		N	87	87	87	87
	ToE_X_parts1	Correlation Coefficient	,851**	1,000	,702**	-,241*
		Sig. (2-tailed)	,000	.	,000	,024
		N	87	87	87	87
	ToE_X_parts2	Correlation Coefficient	,953**	,702**	1,000	-,440**
		Sig. (2-tailed)	,000	,000	.	,000
		N	87	87	87	87
	logic_marker	Correlation Coefficient	-,448**	-,241*	-,440**	1,000
		Sig. (2-tailed)	,000	,024	,000	.
		N	87	87	87	87

**. Correlation is significant at the 0.01 level (2-tailed).
*. Correlation is significant at the 0.05 level (2-tailed).

Figure 6.7 Correlation results between expected states and logic marker. *Source* own source

The anticipated order of expected states proportion values was: R-IC<G-IC<C-IC<D-IC<N-IC.

Mean average ToE_X_total index of the N-IC was 0.4435 (std. error 0.0573, std. deviation 0.2431), with a range of 0.7358. Mean average ToE_X_total index of the G-IC was 0.5322 (std. error 0.0490, std. deviation 0.2401), with a range of 0.7407. Mean average ToE_X_total index of the D-IC was 0.5322 (std. error 0.0490, std. deviation 0.2401), with a range of 0.7407. Mean average ToE_X_total index of the R-IC was 0.5171 (std. error 0.0486, std. deviation 0.1882), with a range of 0.68 Mean average ToE_X_total index of the C-IC was 0.4076 (std. error 0.0620, std. deviation 0.2401), with a range of 0.6552. Figure 6.8 shows the box-plot data.

Differences by ToE_X_total in all five conditions were not significant according to Kruskal-Wallis-H: (H(18, 24, 15, 15, 15) = 4.766, p = 0.312). Nevertheless, the observed order by this index was G-IC>R-IC>D-IC>N-IC>C-IC.

Mean average ToE_X_parts1 index of the N-IC was 0.5374 (std. error 0.0672, std. deviation 0.2853), with a range of 0.8571. Mean average ToE_X_parts1 index of the G-IC was 0.6620 (std. error 0.0537, std. deviation 0.2633), with a range of 0.8667. Mean average ToE_X_parts1 index of the D-IC was 0.5730 (std. error 0.0536, std. deviation 0.2075), with a range of 0.5826. Mean average ToE_X_parts1 index of the R-IC was 0.6983 (std. error 0.0464, std. deviation

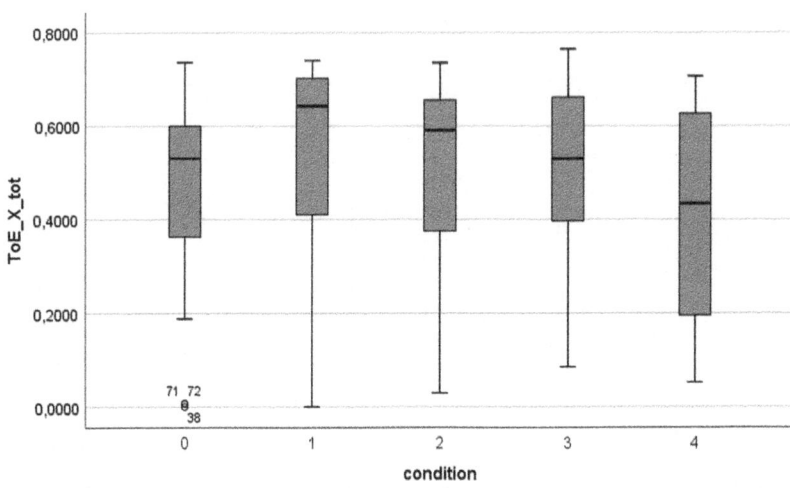

Figure 6.8 Boxplot results of expected states during "ill-defined" stages over information conditions: 0 = N-IC, 1 = G-IC, 2 = D-IC, 3 = R-IC, 4 = C-IC. *Source* own source

0.1797), with a range of 0.6750 Mean average ToE_X_parts1 index of the C-IC was 0.5119 (std. error 0.0666, std. deviation 0.2579), with a range of 0.6971.

Differences by ToE_X_parts1 in all five conditions were found to be significant at the 0.1 level according to Kruskal-Wallis-H: (H(18, 24, 15, 15, 15) = 8.944, p = 0.063). The observed order by this index was R-IC > G-IC > D-IC > N-IC > C-IC.

Mean average ToE_X_parts2 index of the N-IC was 0.3920 (std. error 0.0525, std. deviation 0.2227), with a range of 0.6774. Mean average ToE_X_parts2 index of the G-IC was 0.4667 (std. error 0.0455, std. deviation 0.2228), with a range of 0.7. Mean average ToE_X_parts2 index of the D-IC was 0.4655 (std. error 0.0537, std. deviation 0.2078), with a range of 0.7. Mean average ToE_X_parts2 index of the R-IC was 0.4210 (std. error 0.0566, std. deviation 0.2192), with a range of 0.7 Mean average ToE_X_parts2 index of the C-IC was 0.3585 (std. error 0.0653, std. deviation 0.2528), with a range of 0.6389.

Differences by ToE_X_parts2 in all five conditions were found to be not significant according to Kruskal-Wallis-H: (H(18, 24, 15, 15, 15) = 3,874, p = 0.423). The observed order by this index was G-IC > D-IC > R-IC > N-IC > C-IC.

Hypothesis 7 was not confirmed. Observed order by expected state proportion differed between ToE_X_total, ToE_X_parts1 and ToE_X_parts 2, while only ToE_X_parts1 differed between conditions with low significance (p = 0.063).

6.9   Routine Consistency

Hypothesis 8: Routine consistency index is the lowest in R-IC, followed by G-IC, C-IC, D-IC and N-IC.

The routine consistency is the proportion of all actions during the ill-defined stages falling into the routine logic category (either F-L or NB-L), where dir/nodir/ideal or not distinguished. Actions that do not fall into any category are added to the total amount of actions. The higher the routine consistency, the more actions by an agent fall into the routine strategy category. The lower the routine consistency the higher an agent's routine volatility. Since it was anticipated that agents would switch their strategy in the R-IC the most, this condition was anticipated to show the lowest routine consistency. The anticipated routine consistency order was N-IC > D-IC > C-IC > G-IC > R-IC.

Mean average routine consistency of the N-IC was 0.6511 (std. error 0.0491, std. deviation 0.2081), with a range of 0.72. Mean average routine consistency of the G-IC was 0.7250 (std. error 0.0490, std. deviation 0.2400), with a range of 0.69. Mean average routine consistency of the D-IC was 0.7140 (std. error 0.0615, std. deviation 0.2382), with a range of 0.68. Mean average routine consistency of the R-IC was 0.7853 (std. error 0.0533, std. deviation 0.2066), with a range of 0.63 Mean average routine consistency of the C-IC was 0.7607 (std. error 0.0544, std. deviation 0.2108), with a range of 0.62.

Differences by routine consistency in all five conditions were found to be not significant according to Kruskal-Wallis-H: ($H(18, 24, 15, 15, 15) = 5.018$, $p = 0.285$). The observed order by this index was R-IC > C-IC > G-IC > D-IC > N-IC.

Hypothesis 8 was not confirmed. The routine consistency did not differ significantly over all information conditions, and the observed order by routine consistency differed from what was anticipated.

6.10   Fundamental Strategy and Group Performance

Hypothesis 9: The lower the fundamental index the lower game group performance.

The fundamental index shows the proportion of group decisions, where all agents agreed upon, which disk to move. The lower the proportion, the higher the number of steps were expected to, represented by the variable "performance_toe". Again, "performance_toe" is the number of steps saved by a group solving all ToE games. However, if a game group failed to solve a ToE stage in time (3 minutes), the number of steps saved does not represent the number of steps required to solve a ToE stage.

If this was ignored, Spearman's rho showed the correlation between the fundamental index and the number of steps saved for a group *attempting* to solve all ToE games to be significant at the 0.01 level (2-tailed), with p = 0.002. Therefore, the lower the fundamental index was, the higher the variable "performance_toe".

However, the number of steps required to solve all ToE games is not represented by "performance_toe". For this reason, the "solved" variable was included, which marks group games, which were solved. However, the variable "solved" was unreliable, marking game group games which were not solved by action, but by failing to solve them in time.

Therefore, hypothesis 9 was not confirmed. The lower the proportion of group actions, where all agents agreed upon which disk to move, the more steps it took to solve all ToE games, however, the number of steps required did not represent group performance.

6.11   Group Expertise and Logic Proportions

Hypothesis 10: Lower inter-condition group expertise rankings lead to lower logic deviations proportions.

Group expertise is calculated by individual expertise levels of one game group (see table 5.4). It was assumed that group expertise correlates with group behavior and therefore impacts logic deviation. When information conditions are disregarded, group expertise seems to highly correlate positively with the proportion of routine strategy actions over all information conditions (N-IC, G-IC, D-IC, R-IC, C-IC) and all ill-defined system states (metastable, instable). The higher the deviation proportion index, the less an agent deviated from its routine from the well-defined stages. Group expertise correlated significantly and positively at the 0.01 level with the deviation proportion index of all ill-defined stages (ToE tot, p = 0.001), with metastable ill-defined stages (ToE 1, p = 0.000) and correlated significantly and positively at the 0.05 level with the deviation proportion index of instable ill-defined stages (ToE 2, p = 0.028). To avoid confusion it should be noted again that this means that this analysis, on first sight, can be interpreted as: the higher the group expertise, the less the group deviates from its routine strategy, which was learned during the well-defined stages.

However, these results were considering 87 individuals that are surrounded by the according group expertise. It is debatable whether or not these results are valid, as group expertise has to be considered to be the result of an entire group, which is facing different information conditions. Therefore, the following analysis is more precise, considering groups as a whole and the according information conditions.

In the N-IC condition, which held 18 participants amongst 6 game-groups, 9 agents were part of a game-group with a group expertise of "3". Three agents were part of a game-group with a group expertise of 5, of 7 and of 9 respectively. Kruskal-Wallis H (7.066) showed the difference of ToE total indexes amongst the game group expertise in N-IC to be of low significance, with $p = 0.070$. Spearman's rho measured the correlation between N-IC group expertise surrounding an agent, and the agent's ToE total index to be significant at the 0.05 level (2-tailed), with $p = 0.015$.

In the G-IC condition, which held 24 participants amongst 8 game-groups, 6 agents were part of a game-group with group expertise of "1" and "9". Three agents were part of a game-group of group expertise "2", of "3", of "8" and of "10" respectively. Kruskal-Wallis H (12.951) showed the difference of ToE total indexes amongst the game group expertise in G-IC to be significant, with $p = 0.024$. Spearman's rho measured the correlation between G-IC group expertise surrounding an agent, and the agent's ToE total index to be significant at the 0.01 level (2-tailed), with $p = 0.009$.

In the D-IC condition, which held 15 participants amongst 5 game-groups, three agents were part of a game-group with group expertise of "1", of "2", of "5", of "7" and of "8" respectively. Kruskal-Wallis H (11.387) showed the difference of ToE total indexes amongst the game group expertise in D-IC to be significant, with $p = 0.023$. Spearman's rho measured the correlation between D-IC group expertise surrounding an agent, and the agent's ToE total index to be not significant, with $p = 0.113$.

In the R-IC condition, which held 15 participants amongst 5 game-groups, three agents were part of a game-group with group expertise of "2", of "5", and of "9", respectively. 6 agents were part of a game-group with group expertise of "10" Kruskal-Wallis H (8.221) showed the difference of ToE total indexes amongst the game group expertise in R-IC to be significant, with $p = 0.042$. Spearman's rho measured the correlation between R-IC group expertise surrounding an agent, and the agent's ToE total index to be not significant, with $p = 0.209$.

In the C-IC, which held 15 participants amongst 5 game-groups, three agents were part of a game-group with group expertise of "8". 6 agents were part of a game-group with group expertise of "3" and "9" respectively. Kruskal-Wallis H (2.663) showed the difference of ToE total indexes amongst the game group expertise in C-IC to not be significant, with $p = 0.264$. Spearman's rho measured the correlation between C-IC group expertise surrounding an agent, and the agent's ToE total index to be not significant, with $p = 0.758$.

Results for hypothesis were mixed, as N-IC and G-IC showed very significant relations between group expertise and logic deviation proportions, as well as solid differences regarding overall logic deviations. D-IC barely touched significance at the 0.1 level for correlation between group expertise and logic deviations, but has shown highly significant difference regarding overall logic deviation. R-IC and C-IC results showed no significant correlation between group expertise and logic deviation, but groups in R-IC differed significantly regarding overall logic deviation. The latter supports the hypothesis and shows the high context dependency, which is regarded as natural, due to the high complexity of this analysis.

Hypothesis 10 cannot be clearly confirmed considering all details and can only be confirmed partially. However, results are regarded as promising enough that the correlation between group expertise and logic deviation can be drawn. After thorough consideration hypothesis 10 is therefore confirmed, and will be discussed in more detail in chapter 7.

6.12   Gender Effects

While no significant differences regarding performance between female and male agents in NPS was measured (Chlupsa & Strunz, 2019; Strunz & Chlupsa, 2019), which even held true for all country-origins (Strunz, 2019), adaption efficiency to more effective strategies had shown gender effects in behavioral experiments (Casal et al., 2017).

Hypotheses that potentially relate to strategy adaption efficiency are analyzed for gender effects. It is hypothesized that no significant gender effects will be found at all, as NPS performance, free of gender effects, is regarded as most fundamental for all forms of strategy adaption.

All 87 participants consisted of self-reported 29 female and 58 male participants.

Boxplot figure 6.9 shows that no significant gender effect testing hypothesis 1 seems to be visible.

Strategy adaption efficiency during well-defined stages is implicitly expressed by ToH expertise. As agents who fail to adapt their strategy during the well-defined stages to the new goal rod position will have a lower chance of falling into the high or medium expertise category.

Spearman's rho shows significant correlation at the 0.01 level between expertise and well-defined logic proportion (ToH total) for all 29 female participants.

Spearman's rho shows significant correlation at the 0.01 level between expertise and well-defined logic proportion for all 58 male participants. Therefore, no
gender effect was found for hypothesis 1.

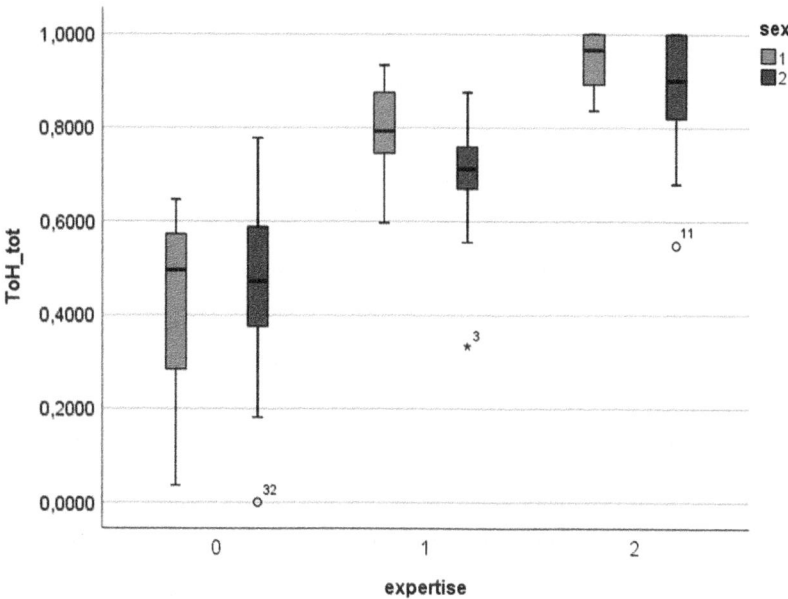

Figure 6.9 Boxplot graph showing no gender effect between expertise and well-defined
logic proportion: 1 = female, 2 = male. *Source* own source

Analyzing hypothesis 2 for gender effects, not ideal first moves proportion by
female participants during stage 1 was identical with not ideal first moves during
the stage 4 (44,83 %), where this performance does not significantly differ from
the mean (sum of rel. not ideal divided by 6) of overall not ideal first moves
(41.38 %), with p = 0.174. The results are summarized in table 6.2.

Not ideal first moves by male participants during stage 4 reached their maximum (54,39 %), which differed from the mean from not ideal first moves
(42.00 %) at the 0.05 level with p = 0.013. The results are summarized in
table 6.3. Female participants outperformed male participants regarding strategy
adaption with goal rod changes during well-defined stages. Not ideal first move

proportions are marked bold at game stage 4, where the goal rod change takes place and the former strategy has to be adapted efficiently.

Table 6.2 Impact of "macrostructure shift" on female decision-making performance. *Source* own source

female	ToH game 1	ToH game 2	ToH game 3	ToH game 4 (goal rod change)	ToH game 5	ToH game 6
not ideal	13	13	9	13	12	12
ideal	16	16	20	16	17	17
total	29	29	29	29	29	29
rel. not ideal	0,448276	0,448276	0,310345	**0,448276**	0,413793	0,413793
rel. ideal	0,551724	0,551724	0,689655	0,551724	0,586207	0,586207

Whether or not a gender effect was found for hypothesis 2 is debatable, as sample sizes differ greatly and are limited in their statistical validity. For both sexes, a global or local maximum of not ideal first moves was reached during stage 4. However, numbers have shown that female participants outperformed male participants regarding adaption to a "sudden" goal rod change, which required immediate, effective and efficient change of strategy.

This results suggest that, contrary to the findings of Casal et al. (2017), there can be particular cases where female participants are more likely to adapt their strategy efficiently although this result must be considered cautiously since the small sample size of the female group in this experiment. Whether or not this observation was enough to be regarded as a gender effect required further analysis, perhaps by inclusion of reflection times and greater sample sizes.

Analyzing for gender effects in hypothesis 3, logic deviation proportion results for the metastable ill-defined stages are shown in boxplot figure 6.10.

While deviation does not directly translate to a more efficient strategy, metastable stages benefit from sticking with well-defined strategies, as the metastable stages can be experienced as "well-defined" levels. For female participants, Kruskal-Wallis H showed weak significant differences at the 0.1 level ($p = 0.091$) amongst information conditions.

Differences amongst the information conditions regarding logic deviation in the metastable stages were less significant amongst male participants ($p = 0.156$).

Table 6.3 Impact of "macrostructure shift" on male decision-making performance. *Source* own source

male	ToH game 1	ToH game 2	ToH game 3	ToH game 4 (goal rod change)	ToH game 5	ToH game 6
not ideal	27	23	17	31	23	22
ideal	31	34	39	26	33	34
total	58	57	56	57	56	56
rel. not ideal	0,465517	0,403509	0,303571	**0,54386**	0,410714	0,392857
rel. ideal	0,534483	0,596491	0,696429	0,45614	0,589286	0,607143

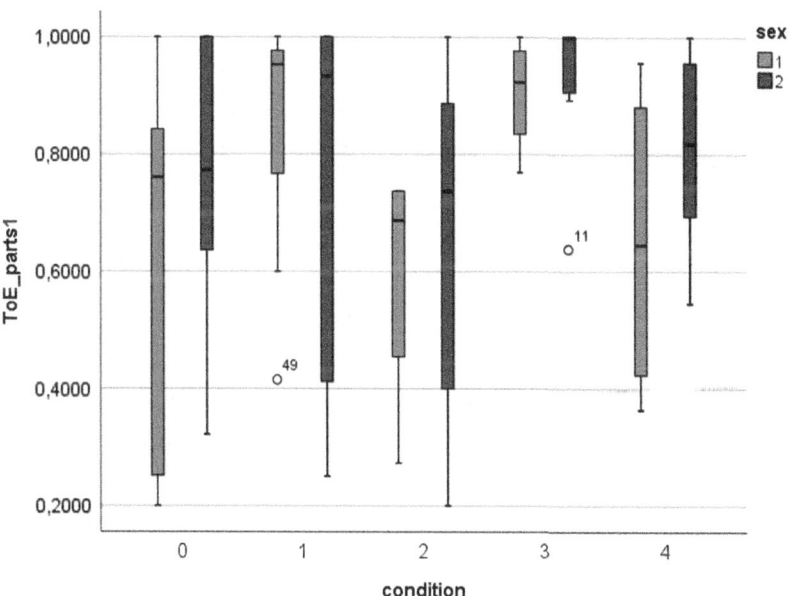

Figure 6.10   Logic deviation during metastable ill-defined stages: 0 = N-IC, 1 = G-IC, 2 = D-IC, 3 = R-IC, 4 = C-IC, and regarding sex: 1 = female, 2 = male. *Source* own source

Mann-Whitney U shows no significant differences between female and male deviation distances in metastable stages (p = 0.401).

As Mann-Whitney U shows no significant differences between female and male deviation distances amongst all ill-defined stages (p = 0.543), hypothesis 4 is not analyzed in further detail.

Regarding hypothesis 5, expecting a positive relationship between expected states proportions and logic deviation proportions, for both female and male participants, all expected states indices and all logic deviations indices correlated at the 0.01 significance level without exception. Figure 6.11 shows boxplot results of expected states proportion for all ill-defined stages.

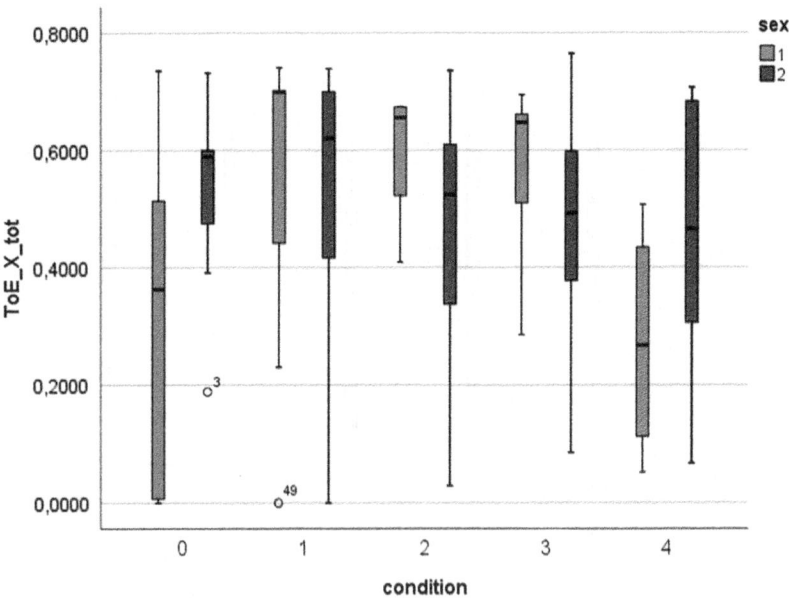

Figure 6.11 Expected states proportion during ill-defined stages: 0 = N-IC, 1 = G-IC, 2 = D-IC, 3 = R-IC, 4 = C-IC, and regarding sex: 1 = female, 2 = male. *Source* own source

Mann-Whitney U does not show significant differences regarding any expected state proportion (ToE X tot: p = 0.746, ToE X 1: p = 0,438, ToE X 2: p = 0,759).

Therefore, no significant gender effects were found for hypothesis 5. Regarding the logic marker analysis for hypothesis 6, Mann-Whitney U shows no significant difference regarding "strategy randomness" between sexes (p = 0.389). Boxplot figure 6.12 shows logic marker results for all information conditions.

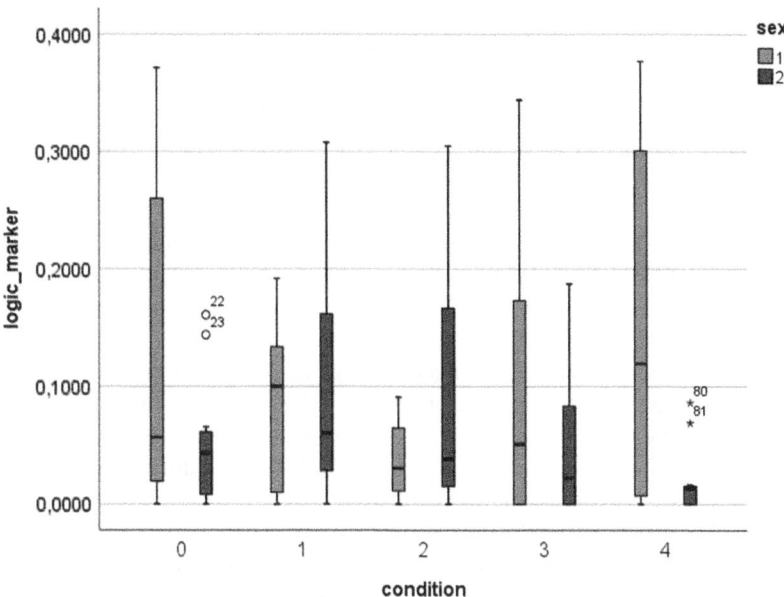

Figure 6.12 Logic marker results during ill-defined stages: 0 = N-IC, 1 = G-IC, 2 = D-IC, 3 = R-IC, 4 = C-IC, and regarding sex: 1 = female, 2 = male. *Source* own source

To avoid confusion, it should be noted that the higher the logic marker index results, the more random a participant behaved. Spearman's rho results are as follows: For female participants, expected states index results of all ill-defined stages (ToE X tot) correlated at the 0.01 level with logic marker results; expected states index results of metastable ill-defined stages (ToE X 1) correlated at the 0.05 level (p = 0.023) with logic marker results; expected states index results of instable ill-defined stages (ToE X 2) correlated at the 0.01 level with logic marker results. Results for male participants were slightly different. For male participants, correlation between expected states indices and logic marker results were significant at the 0.05 level for all ill-defined stages (ToE X tot, p = 0.017) and for instable ill-defined stages (ToE X 2, p = 0.024), but failed to show significant correlation for metastable ill-defined stages in isolation (ToE X 1, p = 0.397).

Therefore, small differences between female and male participants regarding "randomness" in their behavior was found during the metastable ill-defined stages. It seems that random behavior during metastable ill-defined stages are less explainable by (supposedly) personal expectation amongst male than amongst female participants. However, since all "random" logic forms are not framed by the experiment's model, influences stemming from other sources cannot be excluded and are, in fact, unknown. Thus, whether this was a true gender effect remains, at least, uncertain for hypothesis 6.

As described above, no significant differences between sexes regarding expected state proportion was found. Gender effects for hypothesis 7 are therefore disregarded.

As for hypothesis 8, routine consistency does not differ significantly between sexes according to Mann-Whitney U (p = 0.732). Boxplot figure 6.13 shows routine consistency (strategy volatility marker 1) of both female and male agents over all conditions.

Minor differences can be seen in the C-IC, however, whether or not this difference is related to gender cannot be clearly derived, especially as this information condition is the most complex with regards to public information content. In addition, the boxplot graphic does not differentiate between different ill-defined system states, being metastable and instable.

Thus, no significant gender effects were assumed for hypothesis 8.

For hypothesis 9, both fundamental index and game group performance were considered. However, game group performance cannot be analyzed, as raw data does not offer a reliable way to filter successfully solved stages. However, the fundamental index implicitly relates to the proportion of some group having used an effective strategy. From 29 game groups, 2 game groups were female only, 10 game groups were male only and 17 game groups were mixed with female and male participants. Female-only game group with game group ID 65 was part of the N-IC and female-only game group with ID 68 was part of the R-IC condition. While no correlation between information condition and results of fundamental index was found (Spearman's rho of p = 0.429), female and male only groups are sorted by conditions first.

Results for female-only game group with ID 65 (N-IC) showed that 32 % of all game group actions collectively agreed upon, which disk to move.

Results for female-only game group with ID 68 (R-IC) showed that 95 % of all game group actions collectively agreed upon, which disk to move.

From the 10 male-only game groups, game group 15 and game group 35 were part of the N-IC conditions. Male-only game group 43 was part of the R-IC condition.

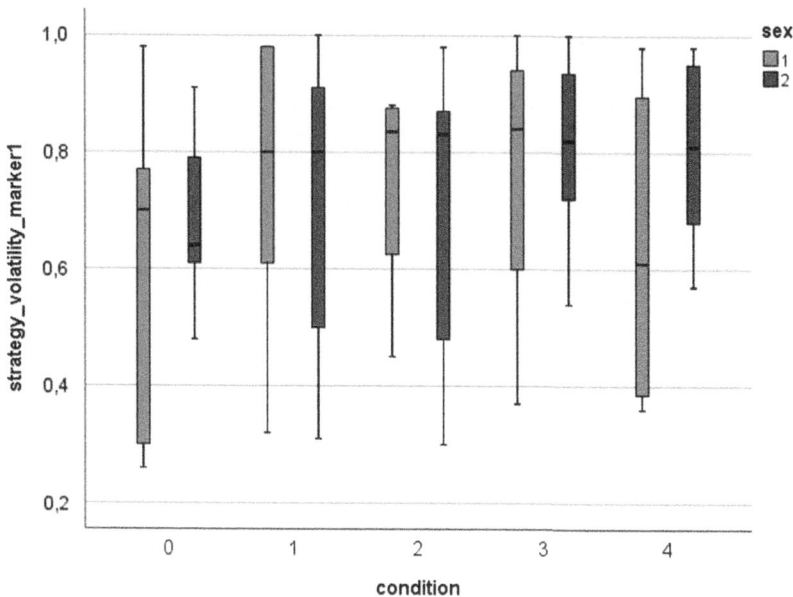

Figure 6.13 Routine consistency results during ill-defined stages: 0 = N-IC, 1 = G-IC, 2 = D-IC, 3 = R-IC, 4 = C-IC, and regarding sex: 1 = female, 2 = male. *Source* own source

Results for male-only game groups (in N-IC) showed that 59 % (game group 15) and 85 % (game group 35) of all game group actions collectively agreed upon, which disk to move.

Results for male-only game group 43 (R-IC) showed that 92 % of all game group actions collectively agreed upon, which disk to move.

Kruskal-Wallis H showed no significant difference between mixed, female-only and male-only results regarding fundamental index (p = 0.602). Fundamental index average of mixed groups was 0.7506 (SD = 0.1950), average of female-only groups was 0.6350 (SD = 0.3451), average of male-only groups was 0.7810 (SD = 0.2048). Figure 6.14 shows boxplot results of fundamental indices.

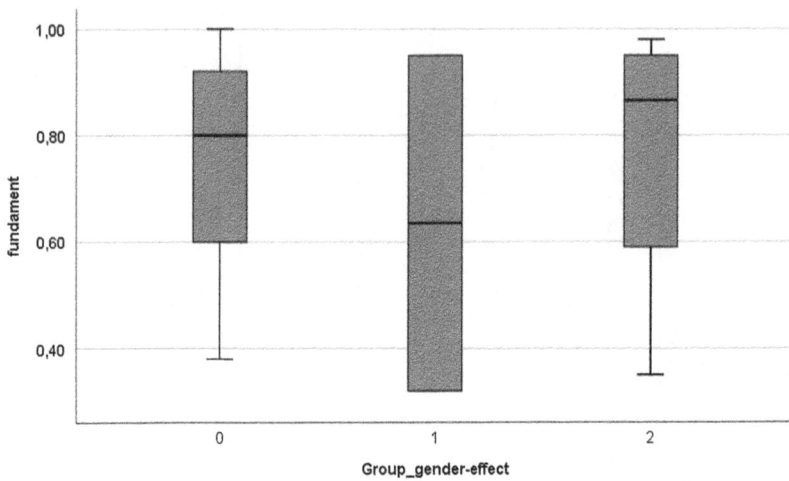

Figure 6.14 Fundamental index results for mixed sexes (0), female-only (1) and male-only (2) game groups. *Source* own source

Therefore, no significant gender effect regarding hypothesis 9 was found. The final hypothesis 10 considers group expertise. Kruskal-Wallis H shows no significant differences between mixed, female-only and male-only groups regarding group expertise ($p = 0.720$). Figure 6.15 shows boxplot results for group expertise in mixed, female-only and male-only game groups.

Gender effects for hypothesis 10 regarding correlation between group expertise and logic deviations were tested for mixed-gender, female-only and male-only game groups. This analysis was done without considering different information conditions, as this was not considered to be relevant for gender effects analysis.

For mixed-gender groups Spearman's rho correlation between group expertise and all ill-defined logic proportions (ToE tot) was significant at the 0.05 level ($p = 0.011$). For the two female-only groups Spearman's rho showed significance at the 0.05 level ($p = 0.017$). For the ten male-only groups Spearman's rho showed significance at the 0.05 level ($p = 0.014$). Therefore, gender effects are disregarded for hypothesis 10. A detailed discussion follows in chapter 7.

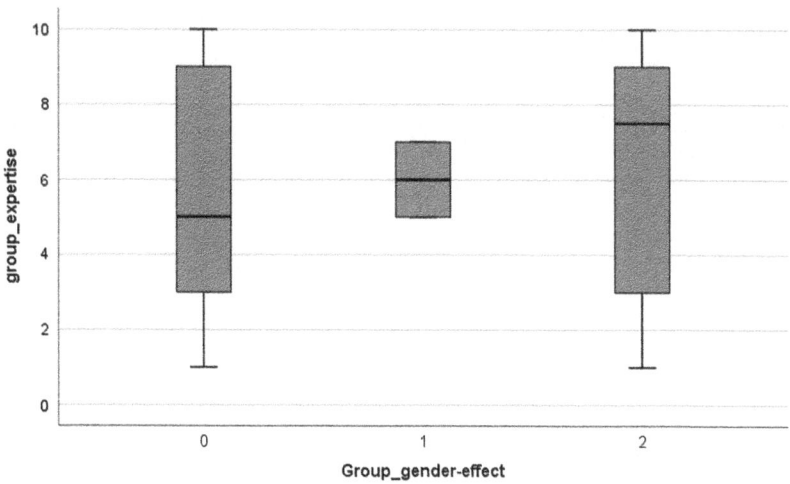

Figure 6.15 Group expertise results for mixed sexes (0), female-only (1) and male-only (2) game groups. *Source* own source

Discussion

7

This chapter discusses the empirical results, adds additional results, and compares derived insights to other scientific conclusions from the domain of behavioral economics. The first subchapter sums up understandings of agent behavior by the results of the various hypotheses, and includes further results from statistical analyses. The second subchapter discusses strengths, weaknesses, opportunities and threats of the scientific methods used. The third subchapter provides an overview of all limitations, and the fourth subchapter suggests potential methodological variations and recommendations for future research.

7.1 Discussion of Experimental Results

Evaluating individual expertise of the well-defined problem "Tower of Hanoi" by the number of "perfectly solved" games, and filtering by "failing not more than one game" has proven to categorize participants very reliably by their logic deviation. This is not only true for the well-defined problem-solving stage. For the ill-defined problem solving stages, where ToE has to be played, Kruskal-Wallis-H shows significant differences by individual expertise regarding ToE total, $(H(33, 16, 38) = 7,775, p = 0.021)$ and regarding ToE parts1, $(H(33, 16, 38) = 10.692, p = 0.005)$. The individual expertise difference only fails to show clear significant differences in the "chaotic" ill-defined stages, $(H(33, 16, 38) = 4.526, p = 0.104)$. Still, overall the expertise categorizes show significant difference in the ill-defined stages. Correlation of expertise with all ill-defined logic proportions shows significance at the 0.01 level for ToE total, with Spearman-Rho $p = 0.005$, shows significance at the 0.01 level for the "metastable" ill-defined stages ToE

© The Author(s) 2021
U. G. Strunz, *The Impact of Individual Expertise and Public Information on Group Decision-Making*, FOM-Edition Research,
https://doi.org/10.1007/978-3-658-33139-9_7

parts1, with Spearman-Rho p = 0.001, and shows significance at the 0.05 level for the "chaotic" ill-defined stages ToE parts2, with Spearman-Rho p = 0.038.

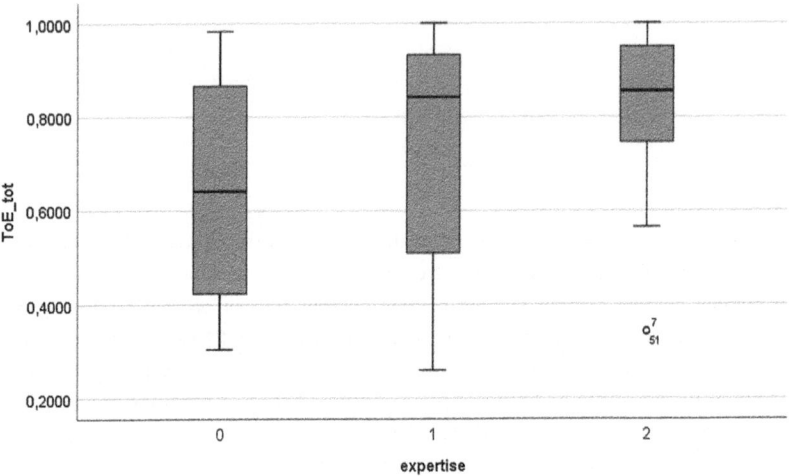

Figure 7.1 Boxplot results of logic proportion during „ill-defined" stages over expertise levels. *Source* own source

Agents with higher expertise in the well-defined problem-solving stages also behaved less "random" in the ill-defined stages, at least from the perspective of the methodological model. Kruskal-Wallis-H shows highly significant differences regarding logic marker proportions amongst the expertise levels, with (H(33, 16, 38) = 18.835, p = 0.000), and Spearman-Rho correlation between well-defined problem solving expertise and logic marker proportions proves to be significant at the 0.01 level, with p = 0.000. The logic marker is an index representing the proportion of ToE actions of an agent, which do not fall inside a known logic category. In addition, as shown in figure 7.1, the higher the expertise levels, the more actions during the ill-defined stages conform to the routine logic. Expertise levels are measured by skillful puzzle-solving of well-defined ToH stages, where the routine strategy is defined. The ToE tot variable represents the proportion of actions, which are part of the routine strategy. In other words, the higher individual expertise in the well-defined stages, the less participants seem to leave their routine strategy path during ill-defined stages.

Therefore, problem solving expertise, as is measured in this thesis, not only relates to well-defined problem-solving performance, but also to ill-defined problem-solving behavior. Agents with high well-defined problem-solving expertise deviated less from their routine strategy and also behaved less random during the ill-defined problem-solving stages.

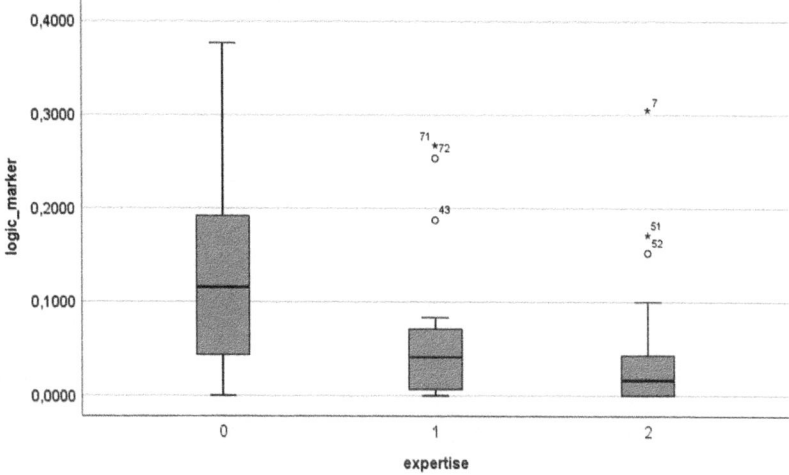

Figure 7.2 Boxplot results of logic marker proportions over expertise levels. *Source* own source

This is shown in figure 7.2, as higher individual expertise levels led to less actions by participants, which were not part of any category and are thus considered "random" actions. This correlation is shown by the logic marker variable, which represents the proportion of actions, which do not fall inside known logic categories, and expertise, which represents skill-full puzzle-solving of well-defined ToH stages. In other words, the higher individual expertise in the well-defined stages, the less random individuals behaved during ill-defined stages. As expected, the environmental change of the goal rod position influenced well-defined problem-solving performance significantly. Individual expertise can be linked to these agents, who did not fall for the goal rod change, and immediately shifted their routine strategy. From 33 low expertise agents, only 8 managed to start ToH level 4 with an ideal action. From 16 medium expertise agents, only 4 managed to start ToH level 4 with an ideal action. From 36 high expertise agents, 30 managed to start ToH level 4 with an ideal action. Those who do a mistake at the first move at ToH level 4, where the goal rod was changed, are more likely to be found in the "low" or "medium" expertise categories. Individual expertise significantly correlates with agents avoiding this mistake at the first action at level 4. Spearman-Rho shows the 2-sided correlation between expertise and this mistake to be significant at the 0.01 level, with p = 0.000, and Mann-Whitney-U shows the differences in expertise between agents who did the mistake and agents who did not to be highly significant, with (U(45, 42) = 436.000, z = −4.673, p = 0.000).

During metastable stages, Kruskal-Wallis H showed expected states deviation to differ significantly at the 0.1 level (p = 0.063) amongst the 5 information conditions during metastable conditions (ToE X parts 1), as shown in figure 7.3. This shows that agent experience regarding feedback was different, depending on the information conditions—yet, expertise remained a reliable predictor of consistent behavior.

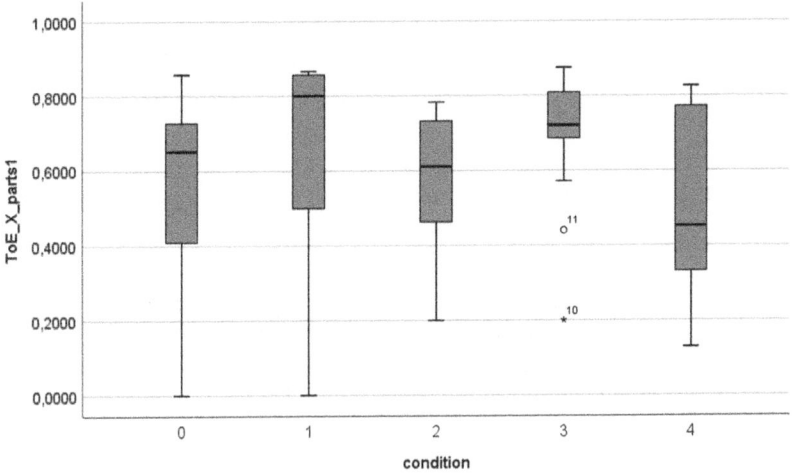

Figure 7.3 Boxplot results of expected states proportion during „metastable" stages over information conditions: 0 = N-IC, 1 = G-IC, 2 = D-IC, 3 = R-IC, 4 = C-IC. *Source* own source

This insight adds another important property to the significance of the expertise categories. Agents with high expertise were significantly more likely to adapt to visual environmental change, which influences their strategy performance, than agents with medium or low expertise.

Regarding all logic proportion analyses, behavior in the routine logic deviation was most surprising. Agents did not, as anticipated, deviate strongly from their routine strategy, and did, in fact, more or less stick to their routine strategy. It was rather the behavior in the no information condition and dissolution information condition that fulfilled the behavior that was thought to be measured in the routine information condition. Therefore, all anticipated orders of logic proportions were roughly observed to be turned "upside down".

Significant difference in routine logic proportion was found during the metastable ill-defined stages, where behavior in the routine information condition has proven to deviate least from its routine logic, while behavior in the dissolution information condition deviated the most. When logic proportions were analyzed over all ill-defined stages, including the "chaotic" stages, this statistical significance vanished. Differences in routine proportions were especially insignificant, when only the "chaotic" ill-defined stages are observed, with Kruskal-Wallis H (H(18, 24, 15, 15, 15) = 1,440, p = 0.837).

The proportion of individual experienced expected outcome was shown to correlate with individual logic proportions at the 0.01 level. Also differences in experienced expected outcome proportions only differed amongst the information conditions in the metastable ill-defined stages (figure 7.3) with weak significance (p = 0.063). Overall differences between the information condition regarding experienced logical feedback were not significant (p = 0.312), especially during the "chaotic" stages (p = 0.423). In other words, all agents experienced comparable level of "chaotic feedback" and did not differ too much in their behavior. Only during the metastable ill-defined stages, meaningful statements can be made regarding behavior and experience. Here, behavior in the routine information condition deviated least from its routine strategy, and feedback was the least "chaotic". During ill-defined and instable ToE stages, no significant difference in deviation from routine strategy (ToE parts 2) amongst information conditions was found, as shown in figure 7.4. In other words, agent behavior regarding logic deviation was comparable during stages that provided more chaotic feedback.

Random agent behavior, expressed by a high logic marker, did not differ amongst conditions significantly, with Kruskal-Wallis H being (H(18, 24, 15, 15, 15,) = 5.714, p = 0.222), but was shown to correlate with experiencing "chaotic" feedback amongst all ill-defined stages. As chaotic feedback was comparable amongst all conditions, this result was no surprise. In addition, routine consistency did not differ significantly amongst the information conditions as well. Routine consistency described how many actions performed were following the

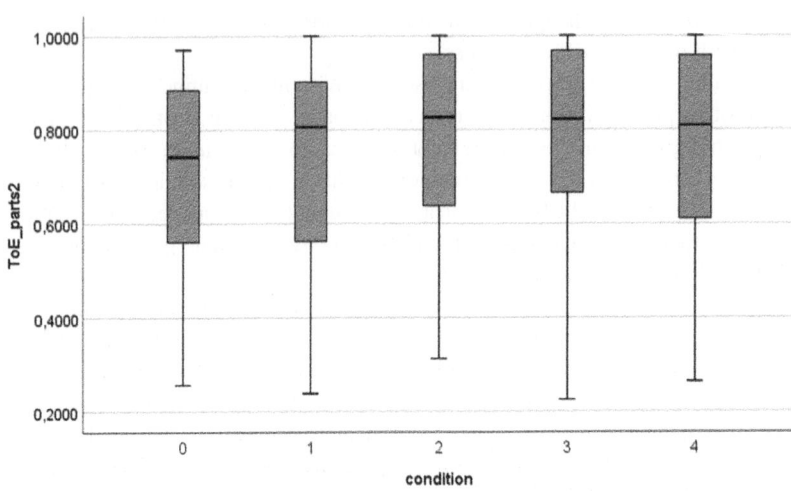

Figure 7.4 Boxplot results of logic proportion during „instable" stages over information conditions: 0 = N-IC, 1 = G-IC, 2 = D-IC, 3 = R-IC, 4 = C-IC. *Source* own source

routine strategy category. High individual expertise was found to significantly correlate with low random behavior, and is also found to correlate at the 0.01 level with high routine consistency, with Spearman-Rho of 0.002. Difference in routine consistency proportions amongst individual expertise was found to be highly significant, with Kruskal-Wallis-H (H(33, 16, 38) = 9.844, p = 0.007).

The higher individual expertise in well-defined problem solving, the more routine strategy actions were performed or in other words, the higher individual expertise the higher the routine consistency, as can be seen in figure 7.5.

Game-group performance was found to rely heavily on agents agreeing which disk to move, which enhances the chances to beat randomness significantly. In order to know how many moves were required to solve ToE when actions are being chosen randomly, five bot groups played 6 ill-defined ToE settings, with the goal rod changing at the fourth level, just as in the main experiment. The bot groups required more than 166 steps on average to solve a ToE game with the goal rod positioned at the center, and more than 113 steps on average to solve a ToE game with the goal rod positioned right. The minimum number of steps solving any ToE stage randomly was 25, the maximum number of steps solving any ToE stage randomly was 727. The bots required more than 139 steps on average to solve any ToE stage. At the time of measurement, the bot game group was

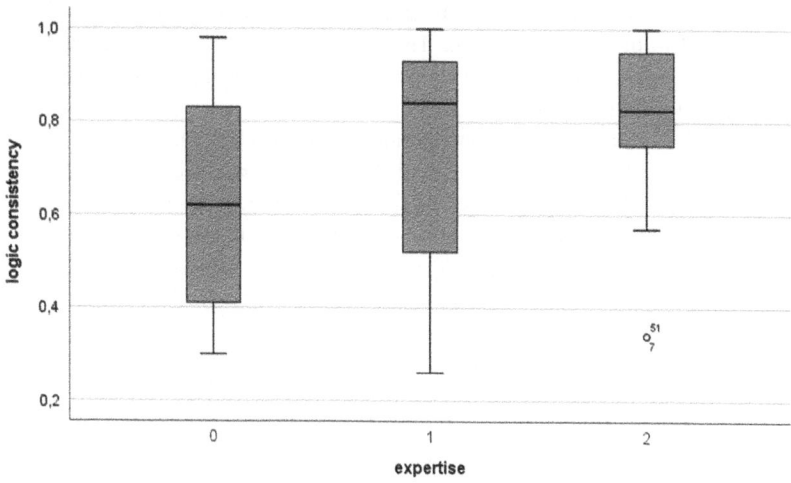

Figure 7.5   Boxplot results of routine consistency over expertise levels. *Source* own source

implemented in such a way that all three bots would have the identical random input, therefore always having a fundamental index of "1". For this reason, the bot groups did not behave perfectly random, as all bots agreed on disk and distance. From all 29 groups observed, only two groups did not outperform randomness, requiring more than 139 steps to solve all ToE stages. Due to unreliable variables it was unclear which game group managed to finish a ToE stage due to solving it properly in time or failing to solve it in time. Time in seconds required per game was saved, but also deemed unreliable. For this reason no statement about group performance can be made.

Correlation between group expertise and ToE logic proportions was significant at the 0.05 level for the N-IC and significant at the 0.01 level for the G-IC. Analysis with Kruskal-Wallis H was significant in all but the C-IC condition. Statistical analysis has shown enough potential correlations between group expertise and logic deviations to confirm hypothesis 10.

Gender effects were tested in detail and while some small deviations between female and male behavior were found, but in general, the existence of convincing gender effects was disregarded. Some small differences between goal rod change strategy adaption performances were found, where female participants outperformed. Random behavior by female participants was more framed by the experiment's model than was male behavior. Aside from these two minor differences, gender effects are not visible. This is in line with research regarding NPS performance, where no gender effects were visible for any age or country-origin (Strunz, 2019; Strunz & Chlupsa, 2019).

After thorough analyses the most promising independent variable was individual expertise. Agents with high expertise not only performed well during the well-defined problem-solving stages, adapting their strategy instantly to environmental change, but showed less routine logic deviation in the ill-defined stages, and behaved less random and volatile solving ill-defined games.

7.2   Methodological Analysis

The transfer from offline to online experimental analysis was a success, as interpersonal communication between agents was avoided. In addition, the online functionality enabled experiments to be done in a matter of minutes. Experiments running on CuriosityIO can be modified quickly if required. CuriosityIO enables live-observation of each agent. By implementing bots and time limitations, and kicking inactive players automatically, ethical payment was preserved, as agents played 31 minutes on average for a 6.10 USD pay. It took dozens of iterations to structure the multi-agent experiment in such a way that average completion time could be anticipated. As a safe-line, Amazon Mechanical Turks should be informed that submitting incomplete data would not lead to a rejection if a certain threshold of time was exceeded, in this case, 50 minutes. Otherwise MTurks tend to rather cancel the experiment without submitting the data, in order to avoid rejection. For MTurks the rejection rate is more important than financial loss, as the HIT rejection rate is the most common filter for experiments on Amazon Mechanical Turk, and usually lies between 95 and 99 %. When a large experiment fails due to a server crash for example, it is better to have MTurks to submit incomplete data quickly, as compensation of MTurks who did not submit their data comes along with problems. In such cases, individual "fake" experiments or "compensation HITs" have to be started for each agent. This can lead to huge organizational work. MTurks who failed to submit due to the server crash with 330 MTurks participating were partially compensated via paypal, however, paying MTurks via paypal is a violation of Amazon Mechanical Turk's terms of services. Also, live support via email during large online multi-agent experiments is mandatory. Participants need to be answered with a response time less than 2 minutes in order to make them feel guided. Many questions arise during all online experiments, leading to dozens and hundreds of emails to be answered in very short timeframes. The experimenter should prepare experiments accordingly to avoid being overwhelmed by organizational work due to compensation or support requirements. As experimenters are being rated online and MTurks are well connected, experimenter should take ethical payment and sound experiment structure seriously.

All in all, the way Amazon Mechanical Turks works deems to be not ideal for conducting multi-agent experiments under uncertainty. In order to avoid bots or low-quality data, the HIT rejection rate should be greater than or equal to 99 %. However, with such a high HIT rejection rate not enough participants will join in a short time span. Many agents had to join in a short amount of time, so that a game group was not automatically filled with a bot, in order to gain enough meaningful data. A bot had to be implemented, so that MTurks would not have to wait longer than a couple of minutes until the experiment started. This was mandatory for ethical payment, as for any HIT the time limit for a participant has to be pre-set. If a participant fails to finish a HIT (paid task like this experiment) in that pre-set amount of time, the MTurks will not be able to submit and the experimenter has a hard time to compensate. However, pre-setting the number of minutes is mandatory in order for the MTurks to calculate and anticipate their earnings. When the HIT rejection rate is lower than 99 %, the experimenter risks lower individual quality data, but enables more participants to join in a short time span. When the HIT rejection rate is lower, paradoxically data quality rises for this particular experiment, as more data becomes meaningful, but with a too low HIT rejection rate, individual data quality becomes less valuable. For the main experiment, a HIT rejection rate of "greater than 95 %" was chosen, and it is recommended that the experimenter takes into consideration the perspectives of the MTurks, via online communication channels such as "Reddit". Here the author gained enough insight by MTurks to find the ideal HIT rejection rate for the experiment.

Even though there exist many studies about the behavior and data quality gained by conducting experiments with MTurks, not much can be known about each participant in reality. More information about each individual MTurk had to be obtainable for the experimenter for higher quality experiments. An additional feature that enhanced data quality would be an online lobby, where MTurks could idle without losing time and money. Such features would have to be implemented for multi-agent experiments to be more effective, ethical and efficient. As most freelancers working with Amazon Mechanical Turk are mostly either from India or US-America, alternatives to Amazon Mechanical Turk should be regarded, if participants from e.g. Europe were required. The Amazon Mechanical Turk business model gains popularity, and many alternatives are currently being developed, which offer more information about the individual freelancers, and also enough European participants for more diverse country-origin experiments.

As response times are valuable predictors for behavior, online experiments should run on stable infrastructure, in order to ensure the saved response times to not be erroneous. Even after one year of optimizing both infrastructure and software performance, response times deemed not to be reliable enough to make statistically meaningful analyses. In addition, any server running multi-agent experiments should be equipped with way more memory capacity than anticipated to be required. While it was suggested that a server holding 1 GiB of working memory would certainly suffice for an experiment with 330 agents, in reality, the server with such a setup crashed. Even a 32 GiB working memory server showed a CPU load of 55 %, while calculating an experiment with only 180 agents. The author recommends at least 128 GiB working memory for experiments with a 4-digit number of participants. In addition, at least one stress test with a couple of hundred non-simulated participants should be conducted beforehand.

7.3   Limitation

Participants were confronted with the cognitive puzzle game "Tower of Hanoi", and its multiplayer version "Tower of Europe". As for some participants this puzzle game might be an undefined or well-defined task from the very beginning, ex-ante expertise can lead to a fast learning curve in the well-defined problem-solving stages. In addition, some participants self-reported having encountered the experiment before, and might have had some a-priori knowledge. However, none of the participants who self-reported having encountered the experiment before could have been playing the ill-defined stages, as the first experiment, with 1 GiB server memory, crashed right after the well-defined stages. Still, statistical analysis did not treat these participants differently during the second successful experiment, which was equipped with 32GiB of memory.

After the well-defined stages, the experiment makes the transition to an ill-defined problem, with the first three games being "metastable" and the last three games representing "chaotic" decision-making circumstances. The order of the experiment's problem-solving stages, being well-defined, ill-defined and metastable, ill-defined and chaotic, models real world experiences and challenges, but is also a limitation in itself, as in real world decision-making any order of problem categories or decision system states might occur.

Participants received information on the outcome of their individual action, but no further details about how the hidden ruleset works, i.e. how their decision influenced the outcome. Participants therefore received simple feedback and not rich feedback; therefore, learning was limited.

No analysis including response times was conducted, due to yet unreliable data. Group performance could not be evaluated due to yet missing variables that could clearly indicate, whether an ill-defined stage was solved via performing the right actions. Some statistical evaluations would clearly benefit from a larger pool of participant data; however, software efficiency and stability had to be tweaked further to enable experiments with more than one thousand participants. It is estimated that in order to derive insights with sound, statistical analyses about inter-group differences with five conditions, at least 2.700 participants would be required for nonparametric statistics. With a data dropout rate of about 50 %, participants should be in the thousands in order to ensure data quantity. This thesis relies on 87 data points derived from a pool of 180 participants; therefore, all insights are limited in their statistical validity.

7.4 Future Outlook

Tower of Hanoi experiments are both thoroughly researched and used for behavioral experiments. Flag Run and Tower of Europe are experimental novelties, which might benefit from scientific insights regarding insight problem solving, working memory capacity, cultural uncertainty avoidance, and from conducting the experiment with different models of learning environments. Multiple learning environments could be simulated via altering the content of the instruction or implementing rich feedback. Experiments which differ in their visual representation, yet still run on the identical logic of Flag Run or Tower of Europe, such as an interactive stock exchange game, could be designed. Interpersonal communication can be included via chat windows, holding a list of certain predefined text-passages, which can be chosen from. The algorithm ensures that in any case, a multi-agent group decision making domain is created, where each individual decision influences the outcome, while not necessarily having impact on the group decision output. The algorithm is fair, unbiased, and even if its rules are known, it can only be taken advantage of, when agents can agree on their order of action input; in other words, when agents were able to synchronize their actions. However, the algorithm can be set arbitrarily complex, so that even if communication between agents was enabled, and agents would communicate their order of inputs, they would not be able to take full control over the outcome. Therefore, stable, metastable and chaotic decision-making environments can be easily simulated. An arbitrary number of agents per group can be used, and the algorithm can also be used for games with multi-dimensional decisions.

Conclusion 8

The aim of this thesis was to create a decision-making domain, in which multiple agents would collectively engage a problem, without being able to communicate with each other. Furthermore, the group decision making was structured such that each agent would always have an influence over the outcome, but could not control the impact of their decisions. Different information conditions simulated information asymmetries, from which potential behavioral changes were to be analyzed. Agents were able to build up expertise in a well-defined learning environment, and later engaged in an ill-defined, metastable and instable decision-making domain, which was either dominated by seemingly deterministic or chaotic feedback. In order to create a problem under uncertainty, "Tower of Hanoi" was chosen as the problem for analysis, which lacks any numerical representations, and thus further avoids subjective or even objective probabilities being built up by human mental models. Different variations of logic, strategies, and feedback were examined in order to derive as much information as possible in this group decision making experiment. The core idea was that this experiment represents reality, where an agent would first gain experience and learn about the systematics of a market, (e.g. by visiting a business school), engaging in well-defined problems. Upon having gained some expertise, which varies amongst the agents, they could then explore the real world, and solve ill-defined problems with their expert knowledge. Real world problems were first simulated as metastable, changing to a more chaotic problem afterwards. Many economic decisions are taken without communicating directly with all shareholders- or stakeholders, and agents collectively solve ill-defined problems, with each agent having different sets of information, and different strategies and ideas about the "hidden rules" of some market or complex decision-making domain. From this idea, five different

© The Author(s) 2021
U. G. Strunz, *The Impact of Individual Expertise and Public Information on Group Decision-Making*, FOM-Edition Research, https://doi.org/10.1007/978-3-658-33139-9_8

research questions lead to 10 different hypotheses. The first research question probed, whether public information about environmental change would necessarily lead to a change of behavior, when the new environmental conditions would not have an impact on some strategy's performance. The routine information group has proven that this was not the case. Agents in the routine information group stuck to their routine strategy from the well-defined problem-solving stages during the metastable condition. The second research questions asked, whether change in behavior was the case if environmental change actually does have an impact on some strategy's performance; here, individual expertise has proven to be a strong predictor, of whether or not an agent was able to adapt or stick to an effective routine strategy. High expertise lead to less random and volatile behavior in the ill-defined problem-solving stages, and enabled agents to adapt quickly to environmental conditions in well-defined stages. The third research question regarded deviation from routine strategy when different types of information, their contents being truthful and deception-free, were provided. Here, results were not so clear, and individual expertise was certainly a stronger predictor than was public information. The fourth research question can also be answered by focusing on individual expertise, rather than on public information: the higher the individual expertise in the well-defined problem-solving domain, the higher the chances were that participants would maintain an effective routine strategy or adapt their routine if necessary. While public information did not significantly influence the overcoming of parts of a routine strategy, it seems that the dissolution information group deviated the most. Perhaps public information about the individuals being unable to obtain helpful information about the hidden rules discouraged agents, favoring random behavior or absorbed individual motivation to engage in problem-solving with smart heuristics. Further research on the influence of public information that favors a belief of lack of control could shed light on this assumption. The fifth and final research question was partially answered. Individual expertise in the well-defined problem-solving stage showed a strong significant correlation with behavior in the ill-defined stages. While the experiment failed to come to conclusions about group performance, the role and impact of individual expertise was surprising, truly holding more predictive power regarding group decision-making than public information.

All hypotheses were analyzed in detail for gender effects and no convincing differences in behavior between female and male participants led to the assumption that gender effects were found. Just as for NPS performance, where no gender effects were found for any age or country-origins, such as US America, India and Germany, solving ToE in a smart and intuitive way disregarded gender effects. If anything, female participants outperformed in strategy adaption during well-defined stages, which was a crucial part to rank high in individual expertise. Obviously, this result is very favorable for the idea of inclusion in modern workspaces, where NPS performance and smart decision-making under uncertainty will play an ever-growing role.

Expert knowledge could be the key factor for global and interconnected problems, where interpersonal communication is impossible or vastly limited. Identifying the ideal decision-making positions for experts through quick and effective online experiments could lead to less volatile, less chaotic system performance, from which all decision-makers can profit.

Bibliography

Adank, P., Hagoort, P., & Bekkering, H. (2010). Imitation improves language comprehension. *Psychological Science, 21*(12), 1903–1909. https://doi.org/10.1177/0956797610389192

Aimone, J. A., Ball, S., & King-Casa, B. (2016). 'Nudging' risky decision-making: The causal influence of information order. *Economic Letters, 149*, 161–163. https://doi.org/10.1016/j.econlet.2016.10.030

Alós-Ferrer, C., Garagnani, M., & Hügelschäfer, S. (2016). Cognitive reflection, decision biases, and response times. *Frontiers in Psychology, 7*, 1–21. https://doi.org/10.3389/fpsyg.2016.01402

Alós-Ferrer, C., Hügelschäfer, S., & Li, J. (2016). Inertia and Decision Making. *Frontiers in Psychology, 7*, 1–9. https://doi.org/10.3389/fpsyg.2016.00169

Andersen, S., Fountain, J., Harrison, G. W., & Rutström, E. E. (2014). Estimating Subjective Probabilities. *Journal of Risk and Uncertainty, 48*(3), 207–229. https://doi.org/10.1007/s11166-014-9194-z

Anderson, J. R. (1993). Problem solving and Learning American Psychologist. *American Psychologist, 48*(1), 35–44.

Arechar, A. A., Kraft-Todd, G. T., & Rand, D. G. (2017). Turking overtime: how participant characteristics and behavior vary over time and day on Amazon Mechanical Turk. *Journal of the Economic Science Association, 3*(1), 1–11. https://doi.org/10.1007/s40881-017-0035-0

Arthur, W. B. (1995). Complexity in Economic and Financial Markets. *Complexity, 1*(1), 20–25.

Arthur, W. B. (1999). Complexity and the Economy. *Science, 284*(5411), 107–109.

Artinger, F., Petersen, M., Gigerenzer, G., & Weibler, J. (2015). Heuristics as adaptive decision strategies in management. *Journal of Organizational Behavior, 36*(Suppl. 1), 33–52. https://doi.org/10.1002/job.1950

Baez, J. C., & Pollard, B. S. (2016). Relative entropy in biological systems. *Entropy, 18*(2), 1–18. https://doi.org/10.3390/e18020046

Baier, J. A., Bacchus, F., & McIlraith, S. A. (2007). A heuristic search approach to planning with temporally extended preferences. *IJCAI International Joint Conference on Artificial Intelligence, 173*(5–6), 1808–1815. https://doi.org/10.1016/j.artint.2008.11.011

© The Editor(s) (if applicable) and The Author(s) 2021
U. G. Strunz, *The Impact of Individual Expertise and Public Information on Group Decision-Making*, FOM-Edition Research,
https://doi.org/10.1007/978-3-658-33139-9

Baker, J., Lovell, K., & Harris, N. (2006). How expert are the experts? An exploration of the concept of "expert" within Delphi panel techniques. *Nurse Researcher, 14*(1), 59–70. Retrieved from http://www.embase.com/search/results?subaction=viewrecord& from=export&id=L44991752

Ballinger, T. P., Hudson, E., Karkoviata, L., & Wilcox, N. T. (2011). Saving behavior and cognitive abilities. *Experimental Economics, 14*(3), 349–374. https://doi.org/10.1007/s10 683-010-9271-3

Barca, E., Porcu, E., Bruno, D., & Passarella, G. (2017). An automated decision support system for aided assessment of variogram models. *Environmental Modelling and Software, 87,* 72–83. https://doi.org/10.1016/j.envsoft.2016.11.004

Baron, J. (1985). *Rationality and Intelligence.* https://doi.org/10.1017/CBO9780511571275

Baron, J. (2012). The point of normative models in judgment and decision making. *Frontiers in Psychology, 3,* 1–3. https://doi.org/10.3389/fpsyg.2012.00577

Barsade, S. G. (2002). The ripple effect: Emotional contagion and its influence on group behavior. *Administrative Science Quarterly, 47*(4), 644–675. https://doi.org/10.2307/309 4912

Baye, M. R., & Wright, J. D. (2011). Is Antitrust Too Complicated for Generalist Judges? The Impact of Economic Complexity and Judicial Training on Appeals. *The Journal of Law and Economics, 54*(1), 1–24. https://doi.org/10.1086/652305

Bayer, R. C., & Chan, M. (2007). *The Dirty Faces Game Revisited.* Retrieved from https:// www.researchgate.net/publication/46454722_The_Dirty_Faces_Game_Revisited

Bell, D. E., Raiffa, H., & Tversky, A. (Eds.). (1988). *Decision making: Descriptive, normative, and prescriptive interactions.* New York: Cambridge University Press.

Benkert, J. M., & Netzer, N. (2018). Informational requirements of nudging. *Journal of Political Economy, 126*(6), 2323–2355. https://doi.org/10.1086/700072

Bennett, N., & Lemoine, G. J. (2014). What a difference a word makes: Understanding threats to performance in a VUCA world. *Business Horizons, 57*(3), 311–317. https://doi.org/10. 1016/j.bushor.2014.01.001

Betsch, T., Haberstroh, S., Glöckner, A., Haar, T., & Fiedler, K. (2001). The Effects of Routine Strength on Adaptation and Information Search in Recurrent Decision Making. *Organizational Behavior and Human Decision Processes, 84*(1), 23–53. https://doi.org/10.1006/ obhd.2000.2916

Blanton, H., & Gawronski, B. (2019). Implicit Measures Procedures, Use, and Interpretation. In H. Blanton, J. M. LaCroix, & G. D. Webster (Eds.), *Measurement in Social Psychology* (pp. 29–55). https://doi.org/10.4324/9780429452925-2

Bohren, J. A. (2014). *Informational Herding with Model Misspecification, Second Version* (No. 15–022). Retrieved from http://ssrn.com/abstract=2619757

Bolisani, E., & Bratianu, C. (2018). The Elusive Definition of Knowledge. Emergent knowledge strategies: Strategic thinking in knowledge management. In E. Bolisani & C. Bratianu (Eds.), *Springer International Publishing* (pp. 1–22). https://doi.org/10.1007/ 978-3-319-60656_1

Brawley, A. M., & Pury, C. L. S. (2016). Work experiences on MTurk: Job satisfaction, turnover, and information sharing. *Computers in Human Behavior, 54,* 531–546. https:// doi.org/10.1016/j.chb.2015.08.031

Brighton, H., & Gigerenzer, G. (2015). The bias bias. *Journal of Business Research, 68*(8), 1772–1784. https://doi.org/10.1016/j.jbusres.2015.01.061

Brillouin, L. (1959). Inevitable experimental errors, determinism, and information theory. *Information and Control*, 2(1), 45–63. https://doi.org/10.1016/S0019-9958(59)90074-9

Brukner, Č. (2018). A No-Go theorem for observer-independent facts. *Entropy*, 20(5), 1–10. https://doi.org/10.3390/e20050350

Buhrmester, M., Kwang, T., & Gosling, S. D. (2011). Amazon's mechanical Turk: A new source of inexpensive, yet high-quality, data? *Perspectives on Psychological Science*, 6(1), 3–5. https://doi.org/10.1177/1745691610393980

Calvert, S. C., Taale, H., Snelder, M., & Hoogendoorn, S. P. (2018). Improving traffic management through consideration of uncertainty and stochastics in traffic flow. *Case Studies on Transport Policy*, 6(1), 81–93. https://doi.org/10.1016/j.cstp.2018.01.003

Camerer, C. F., & Ho, T. (2001). Behavioral game theory: Thinking, learning, and teaching. In *Caltech Working Paper*. https://doi.org/10.2139/ssrn.295585

Camerer, C. F., Ho, T., & Chong, K. J. (2001). Behavioral game theory: Thinking, learning, and teaching. In *Caltech Working Paper*. https://doi.org/10.2139/ssrn.295585

Camerer, C. F., & Ho, T. H. (2015). Behavioral Game Theory Experiments and Modeling. *Handbook of Game Theory with Economic Applications*, 4(1), 517–573. https://doi.org/10.1016/B978-0-444-53766-9.00010-0

Camerer, C. F., & Loewenstein, G. (2004). Chapter 1: Behavioural Economics – Past, Present & Future. In C. F. Camerer, G. Loewenstein, & M. Rabin (Eds.), *Advances in Behavioral Economics* (pp. 3–51). Princeton, N.J.: Princeton University Press.

Campitelli, G., & Gobet, F. (2010). Herbert Simon's Decision-Making Approach: Investigation of Cognitive Processes in Experts. *Review of General Psychology*, 14(4), 354–364. https://doi.org/10.1037/a0021256

Cañas, J. J., Quesada, J. F., Antolí, A., & Fajardo, I. (2003). Cognitive flexibility and adaptability to environmental changes in dynamic complex problem-solving tasks. *Ergonomics*, 46(5), 482–501. https://doi.org/10.1080/0014013031000061640

Carbone, E., Georgalos, K., & Infante, G. (2019). Individual vs. group decision-making: An experiment on dynamic choice under risk and ambiguity. *Theory and Decision*, 87(1), 87–122. https://doi.org/10.1007/s11238-019-09694-8

Casal, S., DellaValle, N., Mittone, L., & Soraperra, I. (2017). Feedback and efficient behavior. *PLoS ONE*, 12(4), 1–21. https://doi.org/10.1371/journal.pone.0175738

Cason, T. N., & Plott, C. R. (2014). Misconceptions and game form recognition: Challenges to theories of revealed preference and framing. *Journal of Political Economy*, 122(6), 1235–1270. https://doi.org/10.1086/677254

Charness, G., Cooper, D., & Grossman, Z. (2015). *Silence is Golden: Communication Costs and Team Problem Solving*. Retrieved from https://pdfs.semanticscholar.org/9dfb/414022 8ea8c5aac16e523d0c962b25eb4945.pdf

Chattha, M. A., Siddiqui, S. A., Malik, M. I., Elst, L. Van, Dengel, A., & Ahmed, S. (2012). *KINN: Incorporating Expert Knowledge in Neural Networks*.

Chen, D. L., Schonger, M., & Wickens, C. (2016). oTree-An open-source platform for laboratory, online, and field experiments. *Journal of Behavioral and Experimental Finance*, 9(1), 88–97. https://doi.org/10.1016/j.jbef.2015.12.001

Chen, W.-R., & Miller, K. (2007). Situational and Institutional Determinants of Firms' R&D Search Intensity. *Strategic Management Journal*, 28(4), 369–381. https://doi.org/10.1002/smj.594

Chen, W. (2008). Determinants of Firms' Backward- and Forward-Looking R&D Search Behavior. *Organization Science, 19*(4), 609–622. Retrieved from http://www.jstor.org/sta ble/25146205

Cheung, J. H., Burns, D. K., Sinclair, R. R., & Sliter, M. (2017). Amazon Mechanical Turk in Organizational Psychology: An Evaluation and Practical Recommendations. *Journal of Business and Psychology, 32*(4), 347–361. https://doi.org/10.1007/s10869-016-9458-5

Chlupsa, C. (2014). *The impact of implicit motives on the business to business decision-making process.* Retrieved from https://pearl.plymouth.ac.uk/bitstream/handle/10026.1/2893/201 4chlupsa10286392phd.pdf?sequence=1

Chlupsa, C. (2017). *Der Einfluss unbewusster Motive auf den Entscheidungsprozess – Wie implizite Codes Managemententscheidungen steuern.* Berlin, Germany: Springer.

Chlupsa, C., & Strunz, U. G. (2019). Overcoming mental models in complex problem solving. *2019 NeuroPsychoEconomics Conference Proceedings,* 19. Washington, DC: Association for NeuroPsychoEconomics.

Choi, N. Y., & Skiba, H. (2015). Institutional Herding in International Markets. *Journal of Banking & Finance, 55,* 246–259. https://doi.org/10.1016/j.jbankfin.2015.02.002

Chong, M. S. F., Shahrill, M., Putri, R. I. I., & Zulkardi. (2018). *Teaching problem solving using non-routine tasks.* https://doi.org/10.1063/1.5031982

Christensen, L. (1988). Deception in psychological research: When is its use justified? *Personality and Social Psychology Bulletin, 14*(4), 664–675. https://doi.org/10.1177/014616 7288144002

Clampitt, P. G., & Williams, M. L. (2000). *Managing Organizational Uncertainty: Conceptualization and Measurement.* Retrieved from http://www.imetacomm.com/otherpubs/res earch/manoruncertain.pdf

Cohen, S., & Williamson, G. (1988). Perceived Stress in a Probability Sample of the United States. In S. Spacapan & S. Oskamp (Eds.), *The Social Psychology of Health.* Newbury Park: CA: Sage.

Colman, A. M. (2003). Cooperation, psychological game theory, and limitations of rationality in social interaction. *Behavioral and Brain Sciences, 26*(2), 139–153. https://doi.org/10. 1017/S0140525X03000050

Dalton, P. S., & Ghosal, S. (2018). Self-confidence, overconfidence and prenatal testosterone exposure: Evidence from the lab. *Frontiers in Behavioral Neuroscience, 12,* 1–9. https:// doi.org/10.3389/fnbeh.2018.00005

Davidson, J. E., & Sternberg, R. J. (2003). *The psychology of problem solving.* Cambridge, United Kingdom: Cambridge University Press.

De Houwer, J., Barnes-Holmes, D., & Moors, A. (2013). What is learning? On the nature and merits of a functional definition of learning. *Psychonomic Bulletin and Review, 20*(4), 631–642. https://doi.org/10.3758/s13423-013-0386-3

Difallah, D., Filatova, E., & Ipeirotis, P. (2018). Demographics and dynamics of Mechanical Turk workers. *Proceedings of the 11th ACM International Conference on Web Search and Data Mining,* 135–143. https://doi.org/10.1145/3159652.3159661

Division for Sustainable Development. United Nations Department of Economic and Social Affairs. (2016). *Partnerships for Sustainable Development Goals. Supporting the Sustainable Development Goals through multi-stakeholder partnerships. Ensuring that no one is left behind.* 36. Retrieved from https://sustainabledevelopment.un.org/content/ documents/2329PartnershipReport2016web.pdf

Donnarumma, F., Maisto, D., & Pezzulo, G. (2016). Problem Solving as Probabilistic Inference with Subgoaling: Explaining Human Successes and Pitfalls in the Tower of Hanoi. *PLoS Computational Biology, 12*(4), 1–30. https://doi.org/10.1371/journal.pcbi.1004864

Dörner, D., & Funke, J. (2017). Complex problem solving: What it is and what it is not. *Frontiers in Psychology, 8*, 1–11. https://doi.org/10.3389/fpsyg.2017.01153

Doshi-velez, F., & Kortz, M. (2017). *Accountability of AI Under the Law: The Role of Explanation.* Retrieved from https://arxiv.org/abs/1711.01134

Doyle, E. E. H., McClure, J., Paton, D., & Johnston, D. M. (2014). Uncertainty and decision making: Volcanic crisis scenarios. *International Journal of Disaster Risk Reduction, 10*, 75–101. https://doi.org/10.1016/j.ijdrr.2014.07.006

Durlauf, S. N. (1998). What should policymakers know about economic complexity? *Washington Quarterly, 21*(1), 155–165. https://doi.org/10.1080/01636609809550300

Efatmaneshnik, M., & Ryan, M. J. (2016). A general framework for measuring system complexity. *Complexity, 21*(Suppl. 1), 533–546. https://doi.org/10.1002/cplx.21767

Eisenberger, R., & Cameron, J. (1996). Detrimental Effects of Reward: Reality or Myth? *American Psychologist, 51*(11), 1153–1166. https://doi.org/10.1037/0003-066X.51.11.1153

Erev, I., & Roth, A. E. (2014). Maximization, learning, and economic behavior. *Proceedings of the National Academy of Sciences of the United States of America, 111*(Suppl. 3), 10818–10825. https://doi.org/10.1073/pnas.1402846111

Ericsson, K. A., & Charness, N. (1994). Expert performance: Its structure and acquisition. *American Psychologist, 49*(8), 725–747. https://doi.org/10.1037/0003-066X.49.8.725

European Commission. (2018). *Communication from the Commission to the European Parliament, the Council, the European Economic and Social Committee and the Committee of the Regions.* Retrieved from https://ec.europa.eu/info/sites/info/files/economy-finance/com_2018_335_en.pdf

European Food and Safety Authority. (2014). Guidance on Expert Knowledge Elicitation in Food and Feed Safety Risk Assessment. *EFSA Journal, 12*(6), 1–278. https://doi.org/10.2903/j.efsa.2014.3734

Fazio, R. H., Eiser, J. R., & Shook, N. J. (2004). Attitude formation through exploration: Valence asymmetries. *Journal of Personality and Social Psychology, 87*(3), 293–311. https://doi.org/10.1037/0022-3514.87.3.293

Fazio, R. H., Pietri, E. S., Rocklage, M. D., & Shook, N. J. (2015). Positive versus negative valence: Asymmetries in attitude formation and generalization as fundamental individual differences. In *Advances in Experimental Social Psychology* (Vol. 51, pp. 97–146). https://doi.org/10.1016/bs.aesp.2014.09.002

Felipe, J., Kumar, U., Abdon, A., & Bacate, M. (2012). Product complexity and economic development. *Structural Change and Economic Dynamics, 23*(1), 36–68. https://doi.org/10.1016/j.strueco.2011.08.003

Fischbacher, U. (2007). Z-Tree: Zurich toolbox for ready-made economic experiments. *Experimental Economics, 10*(2), 171–178. https://doi.org/10.1007/s10683-006-9159-4

Freeling, A. N. S. (1984). A philosophical basis for decision aiding. *Theory Decision, 16*(2), 179–206. https://doi.org/10.1007/BF00125877

Fudenberg, D., & Levine, D. K. (2016). Whither game theory? Towards a theory of learning in games. *Journal of Economic Perspectives, 30*(4), 151–170. https://doi.org/10.1257/jep.30.4.151

Fudenberg, D., & Tirole, J. (1991). *Game Theory.* Cambrdige, MA: Massachusetts Institute of Technology.

Fuller, C. M., Biros, D. P., & Delen, D. (2011). An investigation of data and text mining methods for real world deception detection. *Expert Systems with Applications, 38*(7), 8392–8398. https://doi.org/10.1016/j.eswa.2011.01.032

Funke, J. (2014). Analysis of minimal complex systems and complex problem solving require different forms of causal cognition. *Frontiers in Psychology, 5,* 1–3. https://doi.org/10. 3389/fpsyg.2014.00739

Furley, P., & Dörr, J. (2016). "Eddie would(n't) go!" perceptual-cognitive expertise in surfing. *Psychology of Sport and Exercise, 22,* 66–71. https://doi.org/10.1016/J.PSYCHSPORT. 2015.06.008

Garcia-Retamero, R., Takezawa, M., & Gigerenzer, G. (2009). Does imitation benefit cue order learning? *Experimental Psychology, 56*(5), 307–320. https://doi.org/10.1027/1618-3169.56.5.307

Gavetti, G. (2012). Comment on "toward a behavioral theory of strategy." *Organization Science, 23*(1), 285–286. https://doi.org/10.1287/orsc.1110.0699

Gigerenzer, G. (1996). *On Narrow Norms and Vague Heuristics: A Reply to Kahneman and Tversky (1996). 103*(3), 592–596.

Gigerenzer, G., & Gaissmaier, W. (2011). Heuristic Decision Making. *Annual Review of Psychology, 62*(1), 451–482. https://doi.org/10.1146/annurev-psych-120709-145346

Gilovich, T., Griffin, D., & Kahneman, D. (Eds.). (2002). *Heuristics and Biases: The Psychology of Intuitive Judgment.* Cambridge, United Kingdom: Cambridge University Press.

Giones, F., Brem, A., & Berger, A. (2019). Strategic decisions in turbulent times: Lessons from the energy industry. *Business Horizons, 62*(2), 215–225. https://doi.org/10.1016/J. BUSHOR.2018.11.003

Gosselin, P., Ladouceur, R., Evers, A., Laverdière, A., Routhier, S., & Tremblay-Picard, M. (2008). Evaluation of intolerance of uncertainty: Development and validation of a new self-report measure. *Journal of Anxiety Disorders, 22*(8), 1427–1439. https://doi.org/10. 1016/j.janxdis.2008.02.005

Green, S., Page, F., De'ath, P., Pei, E., & Lam, B. (2019). Vuca Challenges oOn tThe Design-Engineering Student Spectrum. *Proceedings of the 21st International Conference on Engineering and Product Design Education (E&PDE 2019),* 1–6. https://doi.org/https://doi. org/10.35199/epde2019

Grünig, R., & Kühn, R. (2013). *Successful Decision-Making* (3rd ed.). Berlin, Germany: Springer.

Guerrien, B. (2018). On the Current State of Game Theory. *Real-World Economics Review, 83,* 35–44. Retrieved from http://www.paecon.net/PAEReview/issue83/Guerrien83.pdf

Güss, C. D. (2011). Fire and ice: Testing a model on culture and complex problem solving. *Journal of Cross-Cultural Psychology, 42*(7), 1279–1298. https://doi.org/10.1177/002202 2110383320

Güss, C. D., Devore Edelstein, H., Badibanga, A., & Bartow, S. (2017). Comparing Business Experts and Novices in Complex Problem Solving. *Journal of Intelligence, 5*(2), 1–18. https://doi.org/10.3390/jintelligence5020020

Güss, C. D., Fadil, P., & Strohschneider, S. (2012). The influence of uncertainty avoidance on dynamic business decision making across cultures: A growth mixture modeling approach.

International Business: Research, Teaching and Practice, 6(2), 12–30. Retrieved from https://www.researchgate.net/publication/258832973_The_influence_of_uncertainty_ avoidance_on_dynamic_business_decision_making_across_cultures_A_growth_mix ture_modeling_approach/stats

Hadfi, R., & Ito, T. (2013). Uncertainty of Cognitive Processes with High-information Load. *Procedia – Social and Behavioral Sciences*, 97, 612–619. https://doi.org/10.1016/j.sbs pro.2013.10.280

Harrison, G. W. (2008). Neuroeconomics: A critical reconsideration. *Economics and Philosophy*, 24(3), 303–344. https://doi.org/10.1017/S0266267108002009

Hausmann, R., & Hidalgo, C. A. (2010). *Country Diversification, Product Ubiquity, and Economic Divergence*. (No. 201). Retrieved from https://dash.harvard.edu/bitstream/han dle/1/4554740/RWP10-045_Hausmann_Hidalgo.pdf

Hausmann, R., Hidalgo, C., Bustos, S., Coscia, M., Chung, S., Jimenez, J., … Yıldırım, M. A. (2014). *Atlas of Economic Complexity Part II*. Retrieved from http://atlas.media.mit. edu/static/atlas/pdf/AtlasOfEconomicComplexity_Part_II.pdf

Hernán, D. M., Córdova, F. M., Cañete, L., Palominos, F., Cifuentes, F., Sánchez, C., & Herrera, M. (2015). Order and chaos in the brain: Fractal time series analysis of the EEG activity during a cognitive problem solving task. *Procedia Computer Science*, 55, 1410–1419. https://doi.org/10.1016/j.procs.2015.07.135

Hernandez, I., & Preston, J. L. (2013). Disfluency disrupts the confirmation bias. *Journal of Experimental Social Psychology*, 49(1), 178–182. https://doi.org/10.1016/j.jesp.2012. 08.010

Hidalgo, C. A., & Hausmann, R. (2009). The Building Blocks of Economic Complexity. *Proceedings of the National Academy of Sciences*, 106(26), 10570–10575. https://doi. org/10.1073/pnas.0900943106

Hilpinen, R. (1970). Knowing That One Knows and the Classical Definition of Knowledge. *Synthese*, 21(2), 109–132. Retrieved from https://www.jstor.org/stable/20114716?origin= JSTOR-pdf&seq=1

Hinz, A. M., Kostov, A., Kneißl, F., Sürer, F., & Danek, A. (2009). A mathematical model and a computer tool for the Tower of Hanoi and Tower of London puzzles. *Information Sciences*, 179(17), 2934–2947. https://doi.org/10.1016/j.ins.2009.04.010

Hofstede, G. (2001). *Culture's consequences: Comparing values, behaviors, institutions and organizations across nations*. (2nd ed.). Thousand Oaks, CA: Sage.

Holland, J. H., Holyoak, K. J., Nisbett, R. E., Thagard, P. R., & Smoliar, S. W. (2008). Induction: Processes of Inference, Learning, and Discovery. *IEEE Expert*, 2(3), 92–93. https://doi.org/10.1109/mex.1987.4307100

Holmes-Rovner, M., Valade, D., Orlowski, C., Draus, C., Nabozny-Valerio, B., & Keiser, S. (2000). Implementing shared decision-making in routine practice: Barriers and opportu-nities. *Health Expectations*, 3(3), 182–191. https://doi.org/10.1046/j.1369-6513.2000.000 93.x

Houser, D., & McCabe, K. (2013). Experimental Economics and Experimental Game Theory. In P. W. Glimcher & E. Fehr (Eds.), *Neuroeconomics: Decision Making and the Brain (2nd ed.)* (pp. 19–34). https://doi.org/10.1016/B978-0-12-416008-8.00002-4

Hsu, M., Bhatt, M., Adolphs, R., Tranel, D., & Camerer, C. F. (2005). Neuroscience: Neural systems responding to degrees of uncertainty in human decision-making. *Science*, 310(5754), 1680–1683. https://doi.org/10.1126/science.1115327

Hutchinson, J. B., & Barrett, L. F. (2019). The Power of Predictions: An Emerging Paradigm for Psychological Research. *Current Directions in Psychological Science, 28*(3), 280–291. https://doi.org/10.1177/0963721419831992

Hwang, S., & Salmon, M. (2004). Market stress and herding. *Journal of Empirical Finance, 11*(4), 585–616. https://doi.org/10.1016/j.jempfin.2004.04.003

Irani, Z., Sharif, A., Kamal, M. M., & Love, P. E. D. (2014). Visualising a knowledge mapping of information systems investment evaluation. *Expert Systems with Applications, 41*(1), 105–125. https://doi.org/10.1016/j.eswa.2013.07.015

Jang, S., Shen, W., Allen, T. D., & Zhang, H. (2018). Societal individualism–collectivism and uncertainty avoidance as cultural moderators of relationships between job resources and strain. *Journal of Organizational Behavior, 39*(4), 507–524. https://doi.org/10.1002/job.2253

Janssen, G. T. L., De Mey, H. R. A., Egger, J. I. M., & Witteman, C. L. M. (2010). Celeration of executive functioning while solving the Tower of Hanoi: Two single case studies using protocol analysis. *International Journal of Psychology and Psychological Therapy, 10*(1), 19–40.

Jeschke, B. G. (2017). *Entscheidungsorientiertes Management.* Berlin, Germany: Walter de Gruyter.

Jeschke, B. G., & Mahnke, N. (2013). Sudest – sustainable decision support tool. Ein entscheidungsorientierter Ansatz zur Unterstützung nachhaltigen Managements. In L. O'Riordan & S. Heinemann (Eds.), *KCC Schriftenreihe der FOM (Band 1).* Berlin, Germany: Akademie Verlag.

Jeschke, B. G., & Mahnke, N. (2016). Systematizing Corporate Decision-Making in a Complex World. *International Journal of Managerial Studies and Research, 4*(8), 73–88. https://doi.org/10.20431/2349-0349.0408006

Kahneman, D. (2003). Maps of Bounded Rationality: Psychology for Behavioral Economics. *The American Economic Review, 93*(5), 1449–1475. Retrieved from https://scholar.princeton.edu/sites/default/files/kahneman/files/maps_bounded_rationality_dk_2003.pdf

Kameramans, M., & Schmits, T. (2004). *The History of the Frame Problem.* Retrieved from https://www.semanticscholar.org/paper/The-History-of-the-Frame-Problem-Kamermans-Schmits/fadbdfb1fe17be0916ab1e64b655336dca72022a

Kannengiesser, U., & Gero, J. S. (2017). Can Pahl and Beitz' systematic approach be a predictive model of designing? *Design Science, 3,* 1–20. https://doi.org/10.1017/dsj.2017.24

Kashdan, T. B., Stiksma, M. C., Disabato, D. D., McKnight, P. E., Bekier, J., Kaji, J., & Lazarus, R. (2018). The five-dimensional curiosity scale: Capturing the bandwidth of curiosity and identifying four unique subgroups of curious people. *Journal of Research in Personality, 73,* 130–149. https://doi.org/10.1016/j.jrp.2017.11.011

Keil, T., Kostopoulos, K., Syrigos, E., & Meissner, F. (2016). *Learning From Performance Feedback in Complex Environments.* Retrieved from https://www.researchgate.net/publication/307639857

Kido, M., Ha, P., & Kinzie, R. (1993). *Insect Introductions and Diet Changes in an Endemic Hawaiian Amphidromous Goby, Awaous stamineus (Pisces: Gobiidae). 47*(1), 43–50.

Kiss, H. J., Rodriguez-Lara, I., & Rosa-Garcia, A. (2018). Panic bank runs. *Economics Letters, 162,* 146–149. https://doi.org/10.1016/j.econlet.2017.11.014

Knight, F. H. (1957). *Risk, uncertainty and profit.* New York, NY: Sentry.

Knoblock, C. A. (2000). Abstracting the Tower of Hanoi. In *Working Notes of AAAI-90 Workshop on Automatic Generation of Approximations and Abstractions*. Retrieved from http://citeseerx.ist.psu.edu/viewdoc/download?doi=10.1.1.32.9149&rep=rep1&type=pdf%5Cnpapers2://publication/uuid/555E1006-F271-4395-A6AE-D2773B7A665B

Kohavi, R., Longbotham, R., Sommerfield, D., & Henne, R. M. (2009). Controlled experiments on the web: Survey and practical guide. *Data Mining and Knowledge Discovery, 18*(1), 140–181. https://doi.org/10.1007/s10618-008-0114-1

Krajbich, I., Oud, B., & Fehr, E. (2014). Benefits of neuroeconomic modeling: New policy interventions and predictors of preference. *American Economic Review, 104*(5), 501–506. https://doi.org/10.1257/aer.104.5.501

Krawczyk, M. (2019). What should be regarded as deception in experimental economics? Evidence from a survey of researchers and subjects. *Journal of Behavioral and Experimental Economics, 79*, 110–118. https://doi.org/10.1016/j.socec.2019.01.008

Kreimeyer, M., Lauer, W., Lindemann, U., & Heyman, M. (2006). *Die Konstruktionsmethodik im Wandel der Zeit – Ein Überblick zum 100sten Geburtstag von Prof. Wolf Rodenacker*. Retrieved from https://www.researchgate.net/profile/Matthias_Kreimeyer/publication/258211575_Die_Konstruktionsmethodik_im_Wandel_der_Zeit_-_ein_Uberblick_zum_100sten_Geburtstag_von_Prof_Wolf_Rodenacker/links/00463527428f73f2b4000000/Die-Konstruktionsmethodik-im-Wandel-d

Kunreuther, H., Gupta, S., Bosetti, V., Cooke, R., Dutt, V., Held, H., ... Kingdom, U. (2014). Integrated Risk and Uncertainty Assessment of Climate Change Response Policies. In O. Edenhofer, R. Pichs-Madruga, Y. Sokona, E. Farahani, S. Kadner, K. Seyboth, ... J. C. Minx (Eds.), *Climate Change 2014: Mitigation of Climate Change. Contribution of Working Group III to the Fifth Assessment Report of the Intergovernmental Panel on Climate Change* (pp. 151–206). Cambridge, United Kingdom: Cambridge University Press.

Larkin, J., McDermott, J., Simon, D. P., & Simon, H. A. (1980). Expert and novice performance in solving physics problems. *Science, 208*(4450), 1335–1342. https://doi.org/10.1126/science.208.4450.1335

Le, N. T., Loll, F., & Pinkwart, N. (2013). Operationalizing the continuum between well-defined and ill-defined problems for educational technology. *IEEE Transactions on Learning Technologies, 6*(3), 258–270. https://doi.org/10.1109/TLT.2013.16

Legare, C. H., & Nielsen, M. (2015). Imitation and Innovation: The Dual Engines of Cultural Learning. *Trends in Cognitive Sciences, 19*(11), 688–699. https://doi.org/10.1016/j.tics.2015.08.005

Levinthal, D., & March, J. G. (1981). A model of adaptive organizational search. *Journal of Economic Behavior and Organization, 2*(4), 307–333. https://doi.org/10.1016/0167-2681(81)90012-3

Li, C., Turmunkh, U., & Wakker, P. P. (2019). Trust as a decision under ambiguity. *Experimental Economics, 22*(1), 51–75. https://doi.org/10.1007/s10683-018-9582-3

Li, G., Kou, G., & Peng, Y. (2018). A Group Decision Making Model for Integrating Heterogeneous Information. *IEEE Transactions on Systems, Man, and Cybernetics: Systems, 48*(6), 982–992. https://doi.org/10.1109/TSMC.2016.2627050

Liebherr, M., Schiebener, J., Averbeck, H., & Brand, M. (2017, December 6). Decision making under ambiguity and objective risk in higher age – A review on cognitive and emotional contributions. *Frontiers in Psychology*, Vol. 8, pp. 1–12. https://doi.org/10.3389/fpsyg. 2017.02128

Liu, B. (2018). *Uncertainty Theory*. Berlin, Germany: Springer.

Losee, R. M. (1998). A Discipline Independent Definition of Information. *The British Journal of Psychiatry*, *48*(3), 254–269.

Louçã, F. (2007). Erring to be right: the paradox of error in the foundation of probability in economics. In J. S. Metcalfe & J. Foster (Eds.), *Evolution and Economic Complexity* (pp. 151–171). Cheltenham, United Kingdom: Edward Elgar.

Lovett, M., Bajaba, S., Lovett, M., & Simmering, M. J. (2018). Data Quality from Crowdsourced Surveys: A Mixed Method Inquiry into Perceptions of Amazon's Mechanical Turk Masters. *Applied Psychology*, *67*(2), 339–366. https://doi.org/10.1111/apps.12124

Lucas, R. E. (1972). Expectations and the neutrality of money. *Journal of Economic Theory*, *4*(2), 103–124. https://doi.org/10.1016/0022-0531(72)90142-1

Luhmann, N. (2012). *Soziale Systeme* (15th ed.). Berlin, Germany: Suhrkamp.

Madden, A. D. (2004). Universities of Leeds, Sheffield and York Paper: *Journal of Documentation*, *60*(1), 9–23. https://doi.org/10.1108/00220410410516626

Maier, H. R., Guillaume, J. H. A., Van Delden, H., Riddell, G. A., Haasnoot, M., & Kwakkel, J. H. (2016). An uncertain future, deep uncertainty, scenarios, robustness and adaptation: How do they fit together? *Environmental Modelling and Software*, *81*, 154–164. https://doi.org/10.1016/j.envsoft.2016.03.014

Mandel, D. R., Navarrete, G., Dieckmann, N., & Nelson, J. (2019). Editorial: Judgment and Decision Making Under Uncertainty: Descriptive, Normative, and Prescriptive Perspectives. *Frontiers in Psychology*, *10*, 10–12. https://doi.org/10.3389/fpsyg.2019. 01506

Mäs, M., & Nax, H. H. (2016). A behavioral study of "noise" in coordination games. *Journal of Economic Theory*, *162*, 195–208. https://doi.org/10.1016/j.jet.2015.12.010

McBride, M. F., & Burgman, M. A. (2012). What Is Expert Knowledge, How Is Such Knowledge Gathered, and How Do We Use It to Address Questions in Landscape Ecology? In A. Perera, C. Drew, & C. Johnson (Eds.), *Expert knowledge and its application in landscape ecology* (pp. 11–38). https://doi.org/10.1007/978-1-4614-1034-8_2

McDaniel, T. M., & Rutström, E. E. (2001). Decision making costs and problem solving performance. *Experimental Economics*, *4*(2), 145–161. https://doi.org/10.1007/bf0167 0010

McKelvey, R. D., & Page, T. (1990). Public and private information: An experimental study of information pooling. *Econometrica: Journal of the Econometric Society*, *58*(6), 1321–1339. https://doi.org/10.2307/0012-9682(199011)58:6<1321:PAPIAE>2.0.CO;2-P

Messick, D. M., Allison, S. T., & Samuelson, C. D. (1988). Framing and Communication Effectson Group Members' Responses to Environmental and Social Uncertainty. In S. Maital (Ed.), *Applied Behavioral Economics* (pp. 677–700). New York, NY: New York University press.

Mousavi, S., & Gigerenzer, G. (2014). Risk, uncertainty, and heuristics. *Journal of Business Research*, *67*(8), 1671–1678. https://doi.org/10.1016/j.jbusres.2014.02.013

Moynihan, D. P. (2008). Learning Under Uncertainty: Networks in Crisis Management. *Public Administration Review*, *68*(2), 1–32. https://doi.org/10.1111/j.1540-6210.2007.00867.x

Müller-Christ, G. (2014). *Nachhaltiges Management: Einführung in Ressourcenorientierung und widersprüchliche Managementrationalitäten* (2nd ed.). Stuttgart, Germany: UTB.

Neubert, J. C., Mainert, J., Kretzschmar, A., & Greiff, S. (2015). The assessment of 21st century skills in industrial and organizational psychology: Complex and collaborative problem solving. *Industrial and Organizational Psychology, 8*(2), 238–268. https://doi.org/10.1017/iop.2015.14

Newell, A. (1980). Physical symbol systems. *Cognitive Science, 4*(2), 135–183. https://doi.org/10.1016/S0364-0213(80)80015-2

Newell, A. (1990). *Unified Theories of Cognition.* Cambridge, MA: Harvard University Press.

Nindl, B. C., Billing, D. C., Drain, J. R., Beckner, M. E., Greeves, J., Groeller, H., … Friedl, K. E. (2018). Perspectives on resilience for military readiness and preparedness: Report of an international military physiology roundtable. *Journal of Science and Medicine in Sport, 21*(11), 1116–1124. https://doi.org/10.1016/j.jsams.2018.05.005

Nota, G., & Aiello, R. (2014). Managing Uncertainty in Complex Projects. In M. Faggini & A. Parziale (Eds.), *Complexity in Economics: Cutting Edge Research* (pp. 81–97). https://doi.org/10.1007/978-3-319-05185-7_5

Ntounis, N., & Parker, C. (2017). Engaged scholarship on the High Street: the case of HSUK2020. *Journal of Place Management and Development, 10*(4), 349–363. https://doi.org/10.1108/JPMD-02-2017-0024

Numminen, H., Lehto, J. E., & Ruoppila, I. (2001). Tower of Hanoi and working memory in adult persons with intellectual disability. *Research in Developmental Disabilities, 22*(5), 373–387. https://doi.org/10.1016/S0891-4222(01)00078-6

Nye, B. D., Boyce, M. W., & Sottilare, R. A. (2016). Defining the Ill-Defined: From Abstract Principles to Applied Pedagogy. In R. A. Sottilare, A. C. Graesser, X. Hu, A. M. Olney, B. D. Nye, & A. M. Sinatra (Eds.), *Design Recommendations for Intelligent Tutoring Systems* (pp. 19–38). Orlando, FL: United States Army Research Laboratory.

Ohlsson, S. (2012). The Problems with Problem Solving: Reflections on the Rise, Current Status, and Possible Future of a Cognitive Research Paradigm. *The Journal of Problem Solving, 5*(1), 101–128. https://doi.org/10.7771/1932-6246.1144

Onnis, L., Christiansen, M. H., Chater, N., & Gómez, R. L. (2002). Reduction of uncertainty in human sequential learning: Evidence from artificial grammar learning. *Proceedings of the 25th Annual Conference of the Cognitive Science Society*, (January), 886–891. Retrieved from https://escholarship.org/content/qt7r51f2n0/qt7r51f2n0.pdf

Ortmann, A., & Hertwig, R. (2005). The Costs of Deception: Evidence from Psychology. *SSRN Electronic Journal, 5*(2), 111–131. https://doi.org/10.2139/ssrn.317861

Osman, M. (2017). Problem solving: Understanding complexity as uncertainty. In B. Csapó & J. Funke (Eds.), *The Nature of Problem Solving: Using Research to Inspire 21st Century Learning* (pp. 29–42). https://doi.org/10.1787/9789264273955-5-en

Padalkar, M., & Gopinath, S. (2016). Are complexity and uncertainty distinct concepts in project management? A taxonomical examination from literature. *International Journal of Project Management, 34*(4), 688–700. https://doi.org/10.1016/j.ijproman.2016.02.009

Page, S. E. (2008). Uncertainty, Difficulty, and Complexity. *Journal of Theoretical Politics, 2*(20), 115–149. https://doi.org/10.1177/0951629807085815

Palmer, T. (2017). The primacy of doubt: Evolution of numerical weather prediction from determinism to probability. *Journal of Advances in Modeling Earth Systems, 9*(2), 730–734. https://doi.org/10.1002/2017MS000999.Received

Paolacci, G., Chandler, J., & Ipeirotis, P. G. (2010). Running experiments on Amazon mechanical turk. *Judgment and Decision Making, 5*(5), 411–419.

Payne, J. W. (1976). HEURISTIC SEARCH PROCESSES IN DECISION MAKING. *Advances in Consumer Research Volume, 3*(1), 321–327. Retrieved from http://acrwebsite.org/volumes/9285/volumes/v03/NA-03

Peer, E., Vosgerau, J., & Acquisti, A. (2013). Reputation as a sufficient condition for data quality on Amazon Mechanical Turk. *Behavior Research Methods, 46*(4), 1023–1031. https://doi.org/10.3758/s13428-013-0434-y

Ravid, D., Roesler, A.-K., & Szentes, B. (2019). *Learning Before Trading: On the Inefficiency of Ignoring Free Information.* https://doi.org/10.2139/ssrn.3317917

Reisch, L. A., & Zhao, M. (2017). Behavioural economics, consumer behaviour and consumer policy: state of the art. *Behavioural Public Policy, 1*(2), 190–206. https://doi.org/10.1017/bpp.2017.1

Robinson, S. J., & Brewer, G. (2016). Performance on the traditional and the touch screen, tablet versions of the Corsi Block and the Tower of Hanoi tasks. *Computers in Human Behavior, 60*, 29–34. https://doi.org/10.1016/j.chb.2016.02.047

Rocklage, M. D., & Fazio, R. H. (2014). Individual differences in valence weighting: When, how, and why they matter. *Journal of Experimental Social Psychology, 50*(1), 144–157. https://doi.org/10.1016/j.jesp.2013.09.013

Rubin, D. B. (2008). Comment : The Design and Analysis of Go Standard Randomized Experimen. *Journal of the American Statistical Association, 103*(484), 1350–1356. Retrieved from https://www.jstor.org/stable/27640187

Rubinstein, A. (2007). Instinctive and cognitive reasoning: A study of response times. *Economic Journal, 117*(523), 1243–1259. https://doi.org/10.1111/j.1468-0297.2007.02081.x

Ruiz-Díaz, M., Hernández-González, M., Guevara, M. A., Amezcua, C., & Ågmo, A. (2012). Prefrontal EEG Correlation During Tower of Hanoi and WCST Performance: Effect of Emotional Visual Stimuli. *Journal of Sexual Medicine, 9*(10), 2631–2640. https://doi.org/10.1111/j.1743-6109.2012.02782.x

Saini, M., Arif, M., & Kulonda, D. J. (2017). Critical factors for transferring and sharing tacit knowledge within lean and agile construction processes. *Construction Innovation, 18*(1), 64–89. https://doi.org/10.1108/CI-06-2016-0036

Samson, A., & Gigerenzer, G. (Eds.). (2016). *The Behavioral Economics Guide 2016.* Retrieved from http://www.behavioraleconomics.com

Schilke, O., Wiedenfels, G., Brettel, M., & Zucker, L. G. (2017). Interorganizational trust production contingent on product and performance uncertainty. *Socio-Economic Review, 15*(2), 307–330. https://doi.org/10.1093/ser/mww003

Schmitz, L., & Weber, W. (2014). Are Hofstede's dimensions valid? A test for measurement invariance of uncertainty avoidance. *Interculture Journal: Online-Zeitschrift Für Interkulturelle Studien, 13*(22), 11–26.

Scholten, K., Sharkey Scott, P., & Fynes, B. (2019). Building routines for non-routine events: supply chain resilience learning mechanisms and their antecedents. *Supply Chain Management, 24*(3), 430–442. https://doi.org/10.1108/SCM-05-2018-0186

Schraw, G., Dunkle, M. E., & Bendixen, L. D. (1995). Cognitive processes in well-defined and ill-defined problem solving. *Applied Cognitive Psychology, 9*(6), 523–538. https://doi.org/10.1002/acp.2350090605

Schul, Y., Mayo, R., Burnstein, E., & Yahalom, N. (2007). How people cope with uncertainty due to chance or deception. *Journal of Experimental Social Psychology*, *43*(1), 91–103. https://doi.org/10.1016/j.jesp.2006.02.015

Schwaber, K. (1997). Scrum development process. In *Business object design and implementation*. https://doi.org/10.1007/978-1-4471-0947-1_11

Schwardmann, P., & Van der Weele, J. J. (2017). *Deception and Self-Deception*. https://doi.org/10.2139/ssrn.2734736

Seow, P.-S., Pan, G., & Koh, G. (2019). Examining an experiential learning approach to prepare students for the volatile, uncertain, complex and ambiguous (VUCA) work environment. *The International Journal of Management Education*, *17*(1), 62–76. https://doi.org/10.1016/J.IJME.2018.12.001

Shamay-Tsoory, S. G., Saporta, N., Marton-Alper, I. Z., & Gvirts, H. Z. (2019). Herding Brains: A Core Neural Mechanism for Social Alignment. *Trends in Cognitive Sciences*, *23*(3), 174–186. https://doi.org/10.1016/j.tics.2019.01.002

Sidenvall, J., Jäder, J., & Sumpter, L. (2015). Mathematical reasoning and beliefs in non-routine task solving. In L. Sumpter (Ed.), *Current State of Research on Mathematical Beliefs XX : Proceedings of the MAVI-20 Conference*. Retrieved from http://urn.kb.se/resolve?urn=urn:nbn:se:du-19138

Silva, A., & Gombolay, M. (2019). *ProLoNets: Neural-encoding Human Experts' Domain Knowledge to Warm Start Reinforcement Learning*. Retrieved from http://arxiv.org/abs/1902.06007

Simoes, A., & Hidalgo, C. A. (2011). The Economic Complexity Observatory: An Analytical Tool for Understanding the Dynamics of Economic Development. *Workshops at the Twenty-Fifth AAAI Conference on Artificial Intelligence*, 39–42. Retrieved from https://pdfs.semanticscholar.org/7733/68ce1faa36d9ac833b3c3412d136033b91c1.pdf http://atlas.media.mit.edu/

Simon, H. A. (1955). A Behavioral Model of Rational Choice. *The MIT Press*, *69*(1), 99–118. Retrieved from https://www.jstor.org/stable/1884852?origin=JSTOR-pdf&seq=1

Simon, H. A., & Newell, A. (1971). Human problem solving: The state of the theory in 1970. *American Psychologist*, *26*(2), 145–159. https://doi.org/10.1037/h0030806

Sitzia, S., & Zheng, J. (2019). Group behaviour in tacit coordination games with focal points – an experimental investigation. *Games and Economic Behavior*, *117*, 461–478. https://doi.org/10.1016/j.geb.2019.08.001

Sniezek, J. A. (1992). Groups under uncertainty: An examination of confidence in group decision making. *Organizational Behavior and Human Decision Processes*, *52*(1), 124–155. https://doi.org/10.1016/0749-5978(92)90048-C

Solway, A., Diuk, C., Córdova, N., Yee, D., Barto, A. G., Niv, Y., & Botvinick, M. M. (2014). Optimal Behavioral Hierarchy. *PLoS Computational Biology*, *10*(8), 1–10. https://doi.org/10.1371/journal.pcbi.1003779

Sterman, J. D. (1989). Misperceptions of feedback in dynamic decision making. *Organizational Behavior and Human Decision Processes*, *43*(3), 301–335. https://doi.org/10.1016/0749-5978(89)90041-1

Sterman, J. D. (2002). All models are wrong: Reflections on becoming a systems scientist. *System Dynamics Review*, *18*(4), 501–531. https://doi.org/10.1002/sdr.261

Sterman, J. D. (2006). Learning from evidence in a complex world. *American Journal of Public Health*, *96*(3), 505–514. https://doi.org/10.2105/AJPH.2005.066043

Stewart, N., Ungemach, C., Harris, A. J. L., Bartels, D. M., Newell, B. R., Paolacci, G., & Chandler, J. (2015). The average laboratory samples a population of 7,300 amazon mechanical turk workers. *Judgment and Decision Making*, *10*(5), 479–491.

Strunz, U. G. (2019). Non-Routine Problem Solving Performance by Country Origin. In P. Suresh (Ed.), *Proceedings of 270th The IIER International Conference* (pp. 58–65). Florence, Italy: Institute for Technology and Research.

Strunz, U. G., & Chlupsa, C. (2019). Overcoming Routine: A 21st Century Skill for a 21st Century Economy. *International Journal of Economic Sciences*, *8*(2), 109–126. https://doi.org/10.20472/ES.2019.8.2.008

Syll, L. P. (2018). Why Game Theory Never will be Anything but a Footnote in the History of Social Science. *Real-World Economics Review*, *83*, 45–64. Retrieved from http://www.paecon.net/PAEReview/issue83/Syll83.pdf

Teng, J. (2018). Shelling Point as a Refinement of Nash Equilibrium. *Contributions to Game Theory and Management*, *11*, 249–259.

Theocharis, G., Kuhrmann, M., Münch, J., & Diebold, P. (2015). Is water-scrum-fall reality? On the use of agile and traditional development practices. In P. Abrahamsson, L. Corral, M. Oivo, & B. Russo (Eds.), *Lecture Notes in Computer Science* (pp. 149–166). https://doi.org/10.1007/978-3-319-26844-6_11

Tindale, S., & Winget, J. R. (2019). *Group Decision-Making*. https://doi.org/10.31234/osf.io/kq2ft

Traub, J. F., Wasilkowski, G. W., Wozniakowski, H., Bartholdi, J. J., & Ford, J. (1985). Information, Uncertainty, Complexity. *Physics Today*, *38*(6), 75–76. https://doi.org/10.1063/1.2814598

Trevelyan, J. (2014). The Making of an Expert Engineer. In *The Making of an Expert Engineer*. https://doi.org/10.1201/b17434

Tripp, J., Saltz, J., & Turk, D. (2018). Thoughts on Current and Future Research on Agile and Lean: Ensuring Relevance and Rigor. *Proceedings of the 51st Hawaii International Conference on System Sciences*, *9*, 5465–5472. https://doi.org/10.24251/hicss.2018.681

Trueblood, J. S., & Busemeyer, J. R. (2011). A quantum probability account of order effects in inference. *Cognitive Science*, *35*(8), 1518–1552. https://doi.org/10.1111/j.1551-6709.2011.01197.x

Tversky, A., & Kahneman, D. (1974). Judgment under uncertainty: Heuristics and biases. *Science*, *185*(4157), 1124–1131.

Tversky, A., & Kahneman, D. (1981). The framing of decisions and the evaluation of prospects. *Studies in Logic and the Foundations of Mathematics*, *211*(4481), 453–458. https://doi.org/10.1126/science.7455683

United Nations Economic and Social Council. (2019). *Annual overview report of the United Nations System Chief Executives Board for Coordination for 2018*. Retrieved from https://www.un.org/ga/search/view_doc.asp?symbol=E/2019/10

Van de Ven, A. H. (2007). *Engaged scholarship : A guide for organizational and social research*. New York, NY: Oxford University Press.

Van der Kleij, F. M., Feskens, R. C. W., & Eggen, T. J. H. M. (2015). Effects of Feedback in a Computer-Based Learning Environment on Students' Learning Outcomes: A Meta-Analysis. *Review of Educational Research*, *85*(4), 475–511. https://doi.org/10.3102/0034654314564881

Walker, W. E., Harremoës, P., Rotmans, J., Van der Sluijs, J. P., Van Asselt, M. B. A., Janssen, P., & Krayer von Krauss, M. P. (2003). Defining Uncertainty: A Conceptual Basis for Uncertainty Management in Model-Based Decision Support. *Integrated Assessment, 4*(1), 5–17. https://doi.org/10.1076/iaij.4.1.5.16466

West, D. (2011). *Water-Scrum-Fall Is the Reality of Agile for Most Organizations Today*. Retrieved from http://www.storycology.com/uploads/1/1/4/9/11495720/water-scrum-fall.pdf

Wisdom, T. N., & Goldstone, R. L. (2011). Innovation, imitation, and problem-solving in a networked group. *Nonlinear Dynamics, Psychology, and Life Sciences, 15*(2), 229–252.

Wüstenberg, S., Greiff, S., & Funke, J. (2012). Complex problem solving – More than reasoning? *Intelligence, 40*(1), 1–14. https://doi.org/10.1016/j.intell.2011.11.003

Yan, T., & Tourangeau, R. (2008). Fast Times and Easy Questions: The Effects of Age, Experience and Question Complexity on Web Survey Response Times. *Applied Cognitive Psychology, 22*(1), 51–68. https://doi.org/10.1002/acp.1331

Yoshida, W., & Ishii, S. (2006). Resolution of uncertainty in prefrontal cortex. *Neuron, 50*(5), 781–789. https://doi.org/10.1016/j.neuron.2006.05.006

Zagzebski, L. (2017). What is Knowledge? In J. Greco & E. Sosa (Eds.), *The Blackwell Guide To Epistemology* (pp. 92–116). https://doi.org/10.1002/9781405164863.ch3

Zeleny, M. (2005). Knowledge of Enterprise: Knowledge Management or Knowledge Technology? In T. Menkhoff, H. D. Evers, & Y. W. Chay (Eds.), *Governing and Managing Knowledge in Asia* (pp. 23–60). Singapore, Singapore: World Scientific.

Zhu, S., & Li, R. (2017). Economic complexity, human capital and economic growth: empirical research based on cross-country panel data. *Applied Economics, 49*(38), 3815–3828. https://doi.org/10.1080/00036846.2016.1270413

Zook, N. A., Davalos, D. B., DeLosh, E. L., & Davis, H. P. (2004). Working memory, inhibition, and fluid intelligence as predictors of performance on Tower of Hanoi and London tasks. *Brain and Cognition, 56*(3), 286–292. https://doi.org/10.1016/j.bandc.2004.07.003

Zuckerman, I., Kraus, S., & Rosenschein, J. S. (2011). Using focal point learning to improve human-machine tacit coordination. *Autonomous Agents and Multi-Agent Systems, 22*(2), 289–316. https://doi.org/10.1007/s10458-010-9126-5

The manufacturer's authorised representative in the EU is Springer
Nature Customer Service Centre GmbH, Europaplatz 3, 69115 Heidelberg,
Germany. If you have any concerns regarding our products, please
contact ProductSafety@springernature.com

Printed and bound by CPI Group (UK) Ltd, Croydon, CR0 4YY
28/04/2026
02098489-0002